D. U. W. (B)

D.U.W. (B)

DICTIONARY

OF

UNUSUAL WORDS

PART "B"

1948

THE THAMES BANK PUBLISHING COMPANY LIMITED
1773 LONDON ROAD : LEIGH-ON-SEA : ESSEX

First published in 1948 by
The Thames Bank Publishing Company Limited
1773 London Road, Leigh-on-Sea, Essex

Printed in Great Britain
by W. H. Houldershaw, Ltd.,
49 London Road, Southend-on-Sea, Essex.

This order is, to use a word which can be found in the Oxford Dictionary, a subject for " Flocci-nauci-nihili-pilification," which means that it is useless, stupid and superfluous.—*Col. Dower* (Penrith and Cockermouth), in the House of Commons. See *Hansard,* 27th November, 1947, column 2256.

PURPOSE

SINCE PREFACES are widely unread we have designated this foreword, without any logical or grammatical justification, as a Purpose. The purpose of this book, and of this series, is to facilitate freedom of expression. The teacher of language should attempt, by all possible means, to release the student of language from the inhibitions created by the powerful precedent of modern speech. The common person of this century, as of others, trudges ceaselessly over the same trampled, muddy ground of familiar language, and is bored and disappointed with its lack of grace and meaning. The London streets would be drab without the bright red of London Transport. Imagine a slow-moving mass of grey buses, passing like a weed-clogged wave between surrounding areas of bomb-struck desolation. That, we think, is a visual approximation to the normal habit of speech, and that is why slang is used so avidly. There is an appetite for new language. Here we offer, not slang, not toy words, but genuine articles of speech; a satisfying diet of etymological vitamins.

This leads to the reflection that any luxury which enters into our present austere and restricted way of life is more likely to be a result of intellectual endeavour than a consequence of increased physical prosperity. What may be described as our long-term policy therefore is the breeding of intellectualism. For the intellectual is (as is well known) a creature with a poor physical appetite. The creature requires a relatively low intake of calories. Education thus plays its part in the reduction of imports. It is both a substitute for, and a solvent of, gross material needs.

Much must be left, in a book of this sort, to the imagination and the intelligence of the reader. The parts of speech, for example, are not distinguished. The system of pronunciation is pragmatical, that is, designed for utility. It does not sacrifice the claims of utility to the claims of perfect accuracy. The meanings are indicative and not definitive.

The Forms which were included in Part " A " are omitted from this Part, as forms are anathema to many who live in this quasi-totalitarian epoch. We welcome suggestions, corrections, praise and blame, indiscriminately. We are open-minded to a fault.

ACKNOWLEDGMENTS

Our sincere thanks are due to our correspondents. Miss Grace E. Ball of Westcliff-on-Sea has generously supplied a total of some forty quotations from authors both ancient and modern, and has materially assisted in the work of producing this book. Mr. L. G. Rhind of Liverpool; Mr. M. F. Yorke of Longniddry, East Lothian; Mr. A. C. White of Duncan, British Columbia; Mr. Edvard Giese of Copenhagen; Mr. W. H. C. Moreton of Potters Bar; and Mr. S. Russell Gurney of Aberdeen have sent quotations which have been incorporated in Part " B." A number of quotations have been taken or adapted from the edition of Johnson's Dictionary published in 1871 under the editorship of Professor R. G. Latham.

The following authors, publishers, agents and others have kindly granted permission to quote from copyright works: George Allen & Unwin and Professor Lancelot Hogben; Chapman & Hall and Mr. Evelyn Waugh; Chatto & Windus (numerous extracts from the works of Mr. Aldous Huxley); William Collins; Constable & Co. and Mr. Michael Sadleir; Mr. Harold Nicolson; Mr. Geoffrey Cumberlege (Oxford University Press); Curtis Brown; Gerald Duckworth & Co.; Faber & Faber; Victor Gollancz Ltd.; Heinemann Ltd., and Mr. Evan John; Hodder & Stoughton; Mr. Adrian Conan Doyle (on behalf of the Executors of the estate of the late Sir Arthur Conan Doyle); Jarrolds Publishers (London) Ltd.; Herbert Jenkins Ltd.; John Lane, The Bodley Head Ltd.; Macmillan & Co. Ltd.; Methuen & Co. Ltd.; John Murray; Pearn, Pollinger & Higham; Mr. A. D. Peters; Sampson, Low, Marston & Co.; A. P. Watt & Son.

The name of the author and publisher is appended to every modern quotation used in this book, except in the few cases in which we have not been able to discover the publisher. We will gladly rectify any error or make good any omission which may be pointed out.

NOTES

(1) The phonetic spellings are intended merely as a guide to pronunciation. The oblique stroke indicates the syllable which is to be accented.

(2) Entries which are included for pronunciation only are printed in *ITALIC CAPITALS*.

(3) A * indicates that the entry has alternative meanings, and that only one of several possible meanings has been given.

(4) A † indicates that the entry has appeared in Part " A." The pronunciation and meaning has therefore been omitted in Part " B."

ABACUS

ABBÉ

ABDOMINOUS

ABDUCE

ABEAM

ABERCROMBIE

ABERRANT

ABJURE

ABNORMOUS

ABSTERSIVE

ACCABLÉ

ACCIACATURA

ACCIDENCE

ACCLIVITY

ACHERON

ACHROMATIC

ACUITY

ACULEATE

ACUMINATE

ADAGIO

ADIAPHORISM

ADOBE

AERATE

AERIAL

AESCHYLUS

AGAR

AGIO

AGNAIL

AGNUS CASTUS

AGNUS DEI

AIGRETTE

AIGUILLE

AIT

ALBEIT

ALCAIC

ALCHYMY

ALEXANDRINE

ALEXIPHARMIC

ALHAMBRA

ALLEYN

ALL OVERISH

ALL SAINTS' DAY

ALL SOULS' DAY

ALMA TADEMA

ALTO-RELIEVO

AMARACUS

AMARANTH

AMARANTHINE

AMARI ALIQUID

AMARYLLIS

AMBERGRIS

AMBIENT

AMBIVALENT

AMETHYST

AMPHIBOLOGY

AMPHITHEATRE

AMUSIVE

ANACREONTIC

ANADEM

ANALOGUE

ANAPEST

ANASTROPHE

ANATHEMA

ANFRACTUOUS

ANIMALCULE

ANIMISM

ANNUNCIATE

ANNUNZIO

ANODYNE

ANTELUCAN

ANTEMUNDANE

ANTHROPOMORPHOUS

ANTHROPOPHAGI

APHASIAC

APLOMB

APOCALYPSE

APPETENCE

APPLAUSIVE

APPOSITE

À PRIORI

APSE

AQUILON

ARBUTUS

ARCHANGEL

ARCH-FLAMEN

ARCHIDIACONAL

ARCHITECTONIC

ARCHIVES

ARCUATE

AREA

ARGAL

ARGENTINE

ARIETTA

ARMAGEDDON

ARMOZEEN

ARRAS

ASCETIC

ASHLAR

ASSEMBLY ROOM

ASSEVERATE

ASYNDETON

ATOLL

ATRAMENTAL

ATROPOS

ATTIC

AUREOLE

AUTONOMY

AVATAR

ABACUS (ab/a-kus) *(1) the summit of a column;*   **A**
     (2) a frame containing wires and beads

In Architecture, an abacus is a slab resting upon the summit of a column and giving immediate support to the structure which the column upholds. Below the abacus lies the capital. Above the abacus lies the entablature, which comprises—in an ascending order, from the lowest to the highest—the architrave, the frieze and the cornice.

The word has a second meaning—a primitive device formerly used for the purpose of counting; now manufactured as a toy. The usual form consists of a frame within which four parallel wires are stretched, with ten beads on each wire. The first wire is used for counting units, the next for tens, the third for hundreds and the fourth for thousands.

Civilized mankind developed written symbols for numbers long before the need for rapid and simple means of calculation arose. In fashioning their number script men had no prevision of the requirements of a script with which simple arithmetical performances could be carried out. As men were forced to deal with larger numbers they came to rely upon a piece of physical apparatus which circumscribed their whole horizon of number and measurement . . . . So came the counting frame . . . . The counting frame or *abacus* was a very early achievement of mankind. It follows the megalithic culture routes all round the world. The Mexicans and Peruvians were using the abacus when the Spaniards got to America. The Chinese and the Egyptians already possessed the abacus several millennia before the Christian era. The Romans took it from the Etruscans. Till about the beginning of the Christian era this fixed frame remained the only instrument for calculation that mankind possessed.— *Lancelot Hogben.* Mathematics for the Million, pp. 45-6. (Allen & Unwin).

ABBÉ (ab/ay) *a priest*   **A2**

A prefix of indefinite meaning to the name of a French ecclesiastic. It is no indication of entitlement to a specific right or a specific office.

He [Lord Mahon] is so bigoted a purist that he transforms the *Abbé* d'Estrées into an Abbot. We do not like to see French words introduced into English composition; but, after all, the first law of writing, that law to which all other laws are subordinate, is this, that the words employed shall be such as to convey to the reader the meaning of the writer. Now an Abbot is the head of a religious house; an *Abbé* is quite a different sort of person. It is better undoubtedly to use an English word than a French word; but it is better to use a French word than to misuse an English word.—*Macaulay.* Essays. (Lord Mahon's War of the Spanish Succession).

ABDOMINOUS (ab-dom/in-us) *heavy-bellied; corpulent* A3

May be used used e.g. of cheeses, cupids, sows or any class or sect of persons which has incurred one's dislike.

> Like a fat squab upon a Chinese fan.
> Gorgonius sits abdominous and wan,
> —*Cowper*. Progress of Error.

ABDUCE (ab-duce/) *to draw from or to* A4

If we abduce the eye unto either corner, the object will not duplicate; for in that position, the axes of the cones remain in the same plain, as is demonstrated in the optics delivered by Galen.—*Sir Thomas Browne*. Vulgar Errors, Book III, Ch. 20.

ABEAM (a-beam/) *on one side* A5

Normally, on one side or the other of a ship. Thus, " on the port beam " or " on the starboard beam "; or " the *Wild Rose* came abeam of the lightship."

ABERCROMBIE (ab/er-krum-bi) A6

ABERRANT (ab-er/ant) *ambient; restless; eccentric* A7

Derived from the obsolete verb *aberr*. Related words are *aberrance, aberrancy* and *aberration*. The latter is most often used in relation to mental disorder.

The more aberrant any form is, the greater must have been the number of connecting forms, which, on my theory, have been exterminated or utterly lost. And we have some evidence of abberrant forms having suffered severely from extinction, for they are generally represented by extremely few species. The genera Ornithorhynchus and Lepidosiren, for instance, would not have been less aberrant had they been represented by a dozen species instead of a single one.—*Darwin*. The Origin of Species. Ch. 13.

" . . . I am not really Mrs. Richard Phillotson, but a woman tossed about, all alone, with aberrant passions, and unaccountable antipathies . . . ."—*Thomas Hardy*. Jude the Obscure. Part IV (i). (Macmillan).

ABJURE (ab-joor/) *to renounce* A8

The introduction of barbarians into the Roman armies became every day more universal, more necessary, and more fatal. The most daring of the Sythians, of the Goths, and of the Germans, who delighted in war, and who found it more profitable to defend than to ravage the provinces, were enrolled not only as auxiliaries of their respective nations, but in the legions themselves, and among the most distinguished of the Palatine troops. As they freely mingled with the subjects of the empire, they gradually learned to despise their manners and to imitate their arts. They abjured the implicit reverence which the pride of Rome had exacted from their ignorance, while they acquired the knowledge and possession of those advantages by which alone she supported her declining greatness. The barbarian soldiers who displayed any military talents were advanced, without exception, to the most important commands; and the names of the tribunes, of the counts and dukes, and of the generals themselves, betray a foreign origin, which they no longer condescended to disguise.— *Gibbon.* The Decline and Fall of the Roman Empire. Ch. 17.

ABNORMOUS (ab-nor/mous) *extraordinary* A9

The eccentric appearance of this adjective is derived from its proximity to *enormous.* Thus while its meaning is practically synonymous with *abnormal* it should be used only for the abnormal and fearful or the abnormal and magnificent. The devils in James Branch Cabell's *Jurgen* are abnormous: Dithican, with the head of a tiger but otherwise the appearance of a large bird, with shining feathers and four feet. Amaimon, a thick suet-coloured worm going upright upon its tail which shines like the tail of a glowworm, without feet but with two short hands under the chops and with the bristles of a hedgehog. Cannagosta, something like an ox but rather more like a cat, with curly hair. Satan himself " like a man of sixty or it might be sixty-two in all things save that he was covered with grey fur and had horns like those of a stag " sitting in a chair of black marble on a daïs.

ABSTERSIVE (ab-ster/siv) *cleansing* A10

" The natural human constitution," said the blond-haired man, " is perfectly simple, with one simple condition—you must leave it to Nature. But if you mix up things so distinctly and essentially separated as the animal and vegetable kingdoms for example, and ram *that* in for it to digest, what can you expect?"

" Ill health! There isn't such a thing—in the course of Nature. But you shelter from Nature in houses, you protect yourselves by clothes that are useful instead of being ornamental, you wash—with such abstersive chemicals as soap for example—and above all you consult doctors." He approved himself with a chuckle.—*H. G. Wells.* A Modern Utopia. Ch. 4. (Collins).

Related to the adjective *abstersive* is the word ABSTERGENT, which may be used either as a noun (a cleansing substance) or as an adjective (the possession of cleansing qualities) e.g.: " The repulsively abstergent miasma of a public library." ABSTERSION (noun) means the act of cleansing.

. . . accomodable into the office of abstersion.—*Sir Thomas Browne.* Garden of Cyrus. Ch. III.

" The abstersion of slaughter-yards in Toronto " is vivid; " the abstersion of politics " strikes a more solemn, an intellectually more pregnant note.

ACCABLÉ (a-kab/lay) *overwhelmed; crushed*   A11

Normally to be used, out of politeness, in a hyperbolical sense. Thus, following some witty retort, the Count declares: " Madam, I am accablé " at the same time making an appropriate gesture. See the works of E. Phillips Oppenheim *passim.*

ACCIACATURA (a-che/a-ka-too/ra)   A12

A very short note—a grace note—which is to be played as rapidly as possible.

ACCIDENCE (ak/si-dens) (1) *study of inflexions;* (2) *an elementary treatise on any subject*   A13

ACCLIVITY (a-kliv/i-ti) *an inclined surface; an ascent*   A14

The scene . . . was a gradual series of ascents from the level of the road backward into the heart of the heath. It embraced hillocks, pits, ridges, acclivities, one behind the other, till all was finished by a high hill . . .—*Thomas Hardy.* The Return of the Native. Bk. I (2). (Macmillan).

Rainborrow had again become blended with night when Wildeve ascended the long acclivity at its base.—*Thomas Hardy.* The Return of the Native. Bk. ii (7). (Macmillan).

ACHERON (ak/er-on) *the river of Hell*   A15

. . . kings and rich men coming down to the shore of Acheron, in lamenting and lamentable crowds, casting their crowns into the dark waters, and searching, sometimes in vain, for the last coin out of all their treasures that could ever be of use to them.—*John Ruskin.* The Political Economy of Art (I). Lecture delivered at Manchester, July 10th, 1857.

ACHROMATIC†   A16

The vivacious Miss Poppy was not swarthy, but pale with a strange ichthyoid pallor, a slimy, deep-sea achromatism, the complement of her father's darkness.—*Osbert Sitwell.* Miracle on Sinai. Bk. I, Ch. iii. (Duckworth).

ACUITY† A17

THE EIGHTEENTH CENTURY

In art and architecture the achievement of the century as a whole is not so conspicuous, and we should remind ourselves that all the smaller Georgian houses, which are now so greatly admired, were the result of standardisation. Painting in the earlier half of the century was not at a high level; indeed, it hardly existed at all. The fashionable portrait painter of this period, Vanloo, was a Dutchman who came to London in 1737. Yet this period was distinguished by the appearance of an extraordinary and entirely original genius, William Hogarth, a social satirist of unsurpassed acuity and invention (pretending to be concerned with pointing morals), the master of a flexible and energetic style on canvas, and an engraver of no mean ability.—*C. E. Vulliamy.* Ursa Major. Ch. 1. (Michael Joseph).

ACULEATE (a-ku/le-ate) *prickly; pointed* A18

. . . the aculeous prickly plantation upon the heads of several common thistles, remarkably in the notable palisades about the flower of the milk Thistle.—*Sir Thomas Browne.* Garden of Cyrus. Ch. III.

To contain anger from mischief, though it take hold of a man, there be two things whereof you must have special caution; the one, of extreme bitterness of words; especially, if they be aculeate; for *communia maledicta* are nothing so much. And again, that in anger a man reveal no secrets.— *Bacon.* Essays. lvii.

Cf. ACUMINATE (A 19).

ACUMINATE (a-ku/min-ate) *to rise to a point* A19

They [the prelates] according to their heirarchies accuminating still higher and higher in a cone of prelaty, instead of healing up the gashes of the church, as it happens in such pointed bodies meeting, fall to gore one another with their sharp spires, for upper places and precedence.— *Milton.* Reason of Church Government, Bk. i.

Cf. ACULEATE (A 18).

ADAGIO (a-dar/ji-o) *slow; graceful* A20

Scientifically I could never be made to understand (yet have I taken some pains) what a note in music is; or how one note should differ from another. Much less in voices can I distinguish a soprano from a tenor. Only sometimes the thorough bass I contrive to guess at, from its being supereminently harsh and disagreeable. I tremble, however, for my misapplication of the simplest terms of *tha*t which I disclaim. While I profess my ignorance, I scare know what to *say* I am ignorant of. I hate, perhaps, by misnomers. *Sostenuto* and *adagio* stand in the like relation of obscurity to me; and *Sol, Fa, Mi, Re,* is as conjuring as *Baralipton.*—*Charles Lamb.* Essays of Elia. " A Chapter on Ears."

ADIAPHORISM (ad-i-af/or-ism) *indifference*   A21

One of the excuses suggested in these Memoirs for his [Lord Burleigh] conforming, during the reign of Mary, to the Church of Rome, is that he may have been of the same mind with those German Protestants who were called Adiaphorists, and who considered the popish rites as matters indifferent.   Melancthon was one of these moderate persons.   We should have thought this not only an excuse, but a complete vindication, if Cecil had been an Adiaphorist for the benefit of others as well as for his own.—*Macaulay*.   Essays.   " Burleigh and his Times."

ADOBE (a-doe/be) *clay or brick*   A22
ANTIGUA

Formerly the capital of one whole quarter of the Indies, it was partly destroyed by a great earthquake in the 1760's and its ground space is in consequence too vast for the present population, and therefore no wave of modern American construction has ensued.   It remains to-day a partly ruined city of enormous, crumbling, seventeenth-and-eighteenth-century churches, made of golden stone, or of adobe of the same rich tone, the intricate sculptural and arabesque decoration fitted in between the twisting pillars and round the pompous coats of arms upon the façades being the work of Indian craftsmen trained by the Jesuits.—*Osbert Sitwell*.   Sing High!   Sing Low!   (Still Life (1)).   (Macmillan).

Of all building materials Lawrence liked adobe the best; its extreme plasticity and extreme impermanence endeared it to him.   There could be no everlasting pyramids in adobe, no mathematically accurate Parthenons. *Aldous Huxley*.   D. H. Lawrence.

AERATE (ay/er-ate) *to oxygenize*   A23

Not the quantity only, but also the condition of the blood passing through the nervous system, influences the mental manifestations.   The arterial currents must be duly aerated, to produce the normal amount of cerebration.   At the one extreme, we find that if the blood is not allowed to exchange its carbonic acid for oxygen, there results asphyxia, with its accompanying stoppage of ideas and feelings.   While, at the other extreme, we find that by the inspiration of nitrous oxide, there is produced an excessive, and indeed irrepressible, nervous activity.—*Herbert Spencer*. Principles of Psychology.

AERIAL (air/i-al) *of or in the sky or heavens*   A24

> Before the starry threashold of *Joves* Court
> My mansion is, where those immortal shapes
> Of bright aereal Spirits live insphear'd
> In Regions milde of calm and serene Air,
> Above the smoak and stirr of this dim spot,
> Which men call Earth.—*Milton*.   Comus, 2.

. . . the clouds of the central region have, as has been before observed, pure and aerial greys for their dark sides, owing to their necessary distance from the observer; and as this distance permits a multitude of local phenomena capable of influencing colour, such as accidental sunbeams, refractions, transparencies, or local mists and showers, to be collected into a space apparently small, the colours of these clouds are always changeful and palpitating.—*John Ruskin.* Modern Painters (1 (i)). The Region of the Rain-cloud.

AESCHYLUS (ess/ki-lus)   A25
(525—456 B.C.)

Greek dramatist who wrote seventy tragedies, only seven of which are extant. The seven plays include three, perhaps the greatest, dealing with the return of Agamemnon from Troy— Agamemnon, Choephoroe and Eumenides.

AGAR (ay/gar) *tidal wave in a river*   A26
See EAGRE in Part " A."

He [Neptune] sendeth a monster called the agar, against whose coming the waters roare, the fowles flie away and the cattle of the field, for terror, shun the banks.—*Lyly.* Galathea, i. 1.

AGIO (aj/i-o) *money-changer's discount*   A27

Foremost here are the Cordelier Trio; hot Merlin from Thionville, hot Bazire, Attorneys both; Chabot, disfrocked Capuchin, skilful in agio —*Carlyle.* The French Revolution. Pt. ii, Bk. v, Ch. ii.

AGNAIL (ag/nail)   A28

A tear in the skin round a finger-nail, resulting in soreness.

AGNUS CASTUS (ag/nus kas/tus) *an aromatic shrub*   A29

. . . a bosket of *Vitex agnus castu*s, that shrub whose sacred twigs the Vestal Virgins carried. The flowers are like small verbenas of every pastel shade of fawn and mauve and cloudy pink. Monk's Pepper it is sometimes called, for its fruits, spiced though they be, are a powerful opponent of Aphrodite as becomes a shrub beneath whose scanty shade Hera was born.—*Compton Mackenzie.* Gallipoli Memories, Ch. 9.

AGNUS DEI (ag/nus dee/i) *the lamb and flag*   A30

A representation of a lamb carrying a flag or cross, sometimes used as a sign for a public house.

AIGRETTE†   A31

Sitting beside the Queen [Victoria], Canrobert was able to study her more closely. She had changed into a white evening dress, cut very low, and, he says, " she wore geranium flowers placed here, there, and everywhere. She had plump hands with rings on every finger and even on her

thumbs; one of these contained a ruby of prodigious size and of a superb
blood-red. She found it difficult to use her knife and fork with her hands
thus laden like reliquaries, and even more difficult to take off and put on
her gloves. On her head was a diamond aigrette, pushed well back;
and she wore her hair in long loops which fell over her ears. Her eyes
were beautiful; they were straightforward and intelligent, and she had a
sweet expression which filled one with confidence. She had a good complexion; but her mouth rather spoilt her face which was otherwise pretty."
—*Edith Saunders.* A Distant Summer. Ch. vi. (Sampson Low, Marston
& Co.).

AIGUILLE (ay/gwil) *a sharp peak*   A32

It is, I believe, to those broad wooded steeps and swells of Yorkshire
downs that we in part owe the singular massiveness that prevails in
Turner's mountain drawing, and gives it one of its chief elements of
grandeur. Let the reader open the *Liber Studiorum,* and compare the
painter's enjoyment of the lines in the Ben Arthur, with his comparative
uncomfortableness among those of the aiguilles about the Mer de Glace.
Great as he is, those peaks would have been touched very differently by
a Savoyard as great as he.—*John Ruskin.* Modern Painters. Vol. 1 (5).
The Artist's Environment.

AIT (ate) *small island in a lake or river*   A33

About ten years ago I used to spend some weeks yearly at Sunbury,
which is one of those pleasant villages lying on the Thames, near Hampton
Court. In the autumn, I could not help being much amused with those
myriads of the swallow kind which assemble in those parts. But what
struck me most was, that, from the time they began to congregate, for-
saking the chimneys and houses, they roosted every night in the osier-beds
of the aits of that river. Now this resorting towards that element at that
season of the year, seems to give some countenance to the northern
opinion (strange as it is) of their retiring under water. A Swedish
naturalist is so much persuaded of that fact, that he talks, in his calendar
of Flora, as familiarly of the swallow's going under water in the beginning
of September, as he would of his poultry going to roost a little before
sunset.—*Gilbert White.* The Natural History of Selborne. Letter 12 to
Thomas Pennant.

ALBEIT†   A34

OTHELLO: . . . I pray you, in your letters,
              When you shall these unlucky deeds relate,
              Speak of me as I am; nothing extenuate,
              Nor set down aught in malice: then must you speak
              Of one that loved not wisely but too well;
              Of one not easily jealous, but, being wrought,
              Perplex'd in the extreme; of one whose hand,
              Like the base Indian, threw a pearl away
              Richer than all his tribe; of one whose subdued eyes,
              Albeit unused to the melting mood,
              Drop tears as fast as the Arabian trees
              Their medicinal gum.—*Shakespeare.* Othello, v. 2.

ALCAIC (al-kay/ik) A35

A verse-form invented by Alcæus (c. 600 B.C.).

There was no region of the globe, no walk of speculative or of active life, in which Jesuits were not to be found. They guided the counsels of Kings. They deciphered inscriptions. They observed the motions of Jupiter's satellites. They published whole libraries, controversy, casuistry, history, treatises on optics, Alcaic odes, editions of the fathers, madrigals, catechisms and lampoons.—*Macaulay.* History of England.

ALCHYMY (al/ke-mi) A36

A word now used to indicate some magical or wonderful process or transformation.

There is nothing more dangerous than this deluding art, which changeth the meaning of words, as alchymy doth, or would do, the substance of metals, maketh of anything what it listeth, and bringeth, in the end, all truth to nothing.—*Hooker.* Ecclesiastical Polity.

O, he sits high in all the people's hearts;
And that which would appear offence in us,
His countenance, like richest alchymy,
Will change to virtue and to worthiness.
—*Shakespeare.* Julius Cæsar, i. 3.

ALEXANDRINE (al-ex-arn/drine) (*adjective*) *of six* A37 *iambic beats;* (*noun*) *Alexandrine verse*

A needless Alexandrine ends the song,
That, like a wounded snake, drags its slow length along.
—*Pope.* Essay on Criticism.

ALEXIPHARMIC (al-eks-i-far/mik) *an antidote* A38

Some antidotal quality it may have, since not only the bone in the heart, but the horn of a deer is alexipharmick.—*Sir Thomas Browne.* Vulgar Errors.

ALHAMBRA (al-am/bra) A39

In Spanish, *alhambra* means " the red house." The name has been adopted from time to time by a number of music halls, theatres and cinemas. It is considered one of the few appropriate names for this purpose, just as Percy is considered a suitable name for a child. It is thought that, just as you cannot christen a child Odeon, you cannot name a cinema Violet. But why should this convention remain with us as a sort of necessity? Why not the Green Palace or the Red Palace cinema? Why not the Saracen's Head theatre, or the White Horse, or the Dog and Gridiron, or the Magpie, or the Black Prince, or the Cat and Fiddle? Why not

the Seven Pillars; the Doll's House? Why not the Herculaneum,
the Skager-Rack, the Thessolonica, the Osiris, the Cadillac, the
Andrea del Sarto, the Yangtze Kiang, the Ulysses, or the
Tschaikowsky?

ALLEYN (al/en)   A40

ALL OVERISH (awl o/ver-ish) *indisposed*   A41
    Now out of date, but an enterprising advertising agent might
do worse than attempt a revival. ALL OVERISH as a splash
head. Then—" eyes burn and smart, head and limbs ache. Helen
is always too tired to go out in the evening . . . " Her admirer,
arriving in full evening dress, is obviously shaken by this turn
of events. He looks naïvely worried, distressed. He is clearly
a man of changeable affections. He departs, for an unknown
destination, and is later discovered in a palais de dance with a
numerous body of his friends. He finds that, with a moderate
indulgence in alcohol, he has the capacity to enjoy himself in
these surroundings. Not in the deeper sense, whatever that means,
but with a superficial and somewhat feverish gaiety. There is a
sinister quality in this enjoyment, which may be due to the female
elements of the party. They gyrate. They pose in attitudes of
sophisticated attention. And unvaryingly, metallicly, inevitably
they laugh. Our thoughts, all the while, are fixed on the bilious
Helen, and now she comes back into the picture. She is receiving
advice. Her hand is pressed to her disordered brow. And so on.
It is the old story, and in the last picture she has become a happy,
smiling bride.

ALL SAINTS' DAY *the 1st November*   A42
    Known as All Hallows, or *jour des morts.*

ALL SOULS' DAY *the 2nd November*   A43
BUCKINGHAM: This is All-Souls' day, fellows, is it not?
SHERIFF: It is, my lord.
BUCKINGHAM: Why, then, All-Souls' day is my body's doomsday
This is the day that, in King Edward's time,
I wish'd might fall on me when I was found
False to his children or his wife's allies;
This is the day wherein I wish'd to fall
By the false faith of him I trusted most;
This, this All-Souls' day to my fearful soul
Is the determined respite of my wrongs.
—*Shakespeare.* Richard III, v. 1.

ALMA TADEMA (al/ma tad/e-ma) **A44**

ALTO-RELIEVO (al/to re-lee/vo) *deeply sculptured;* **A45**
    in high relief

FROM LADY BLESSINGTON'S JOURNAL

" The bed, which is silvered, instead of gilt, rests on the backs of two large silver swans, so exquisitely sculptured that every feather is in alto-relievo, and looks nearly as fleecy as those of the living bird."—*Michael Sadleir.* Blessington D'Orsay. Ch. iv. (Constable).

THE PALLAZZO BELVEDERE

" The windows of the principal salons open on a garden, formed on an elevated terrace, surrounded on three sides by a marble balustrade and inclosed on the fourth by a long gallery, filled with pictures, statues and alti and bassi relievi."—*Michael Sadleir.* Blessington D'Orsay, Ch. iii. (Constable).

AMARACUS (a-mar/a-kus) *a plant, also known as* **A46**
    marjoram

> And at their feet the crocus brake like fire,
> Violet, amaracus, and asphodel,
> Lotus and lilies.—*Tennyson.* Œnone.

AMARANTH (am/a-ranth) *an eternal flower* **A47**

That in strewing their Tombs the *Romans* affected the Rose, the Greeks *Amaranthus* and myrtle; that the Funerall pyre consisted of sweet fuell Cypresse, Firre, Larix, Yewe, and Trees perpetually verdant, lay silent expressing of their surviving hopes.—*Sir Thomas Browne.* Urn Burial, Ch. IV.

> Immortal Amarant, a Flour which once
> In Paradise, fast by the Tree of Life
> Began to bloom, but soon for man's offence
> To Heav'n remov'd where first it grew, there grows,
> And flours aloft shading the Fount of Life,
> And where the river of Bliss through midst of Heav'n
> Rowls o're *Elisian* Flours her Amber Stream.
>
> —*Milton.* Paradise Lost, iii, 353.

AMARANTHINE (am-a-ran/thin) *unfading* **A48**

> By the streams that ever flow,
> By the fragrant winds that blow
>   O'er the Elysian flowers,
> By those happy souls that dwell
> In yellow meads of Asphodel,
>   Or amaranthine bowers.
>
> —*Pope.* Ode on St. Cecilia's Day. (v).

But see! where Daphne wond'ring mounts on high
Above the clouds, above the starry sky
Eternal beauties grace the shining scene,
Fields ever fresh, and groves for ever green!
There while you rest in Amaranthine bowers,
Or from those meads select unfading flowers,
Behold us kindly, who your name implore,
Daphne, our Goddess, and our grief no more!

—*Pope*. The Fourth Pastoral.

AMARI ALIQUID (a-mar/i al/i-quid) *a dash of bitterness* A49

. . . *amari aliquid*, a tang of sadness.—*W. M. Thackeray*. The
Virginians. Ch. 34.

AMARYLLIS (am-a-ril/is) A50

Alass! What boots it with uncessant care
To tend the homely slighted Shepherds trade
And strictly meditate the thankless Muse,
Were it not better don as others use,
To sport with *Amaryllis* in the shade,
Or with the tangles of *Neæra's* hair?

—*Milton*. Lycidas.

AMBERGRIS (am/ber-grese) A51

" A light, fatty, inflammable substance, ashy in colour, found
floating in tropical seas, a morbid secretion from the intestines of
whales. Used in perfumery, formerly in cookery and medicine."
—*Cassell's Dictionary*.

Violet Strasburg, made in the city of that name, of powdered rappee
and bitter almonds mixed with ambergris and attarjul, was the favourite
snuff of Queen Charlotte and every morning she added to it a spoonful
of green tea.—*Sacheverell Sitwell*. Sacred and Profane Love. Bk. vi.
" The Geography of Snuff." (Faber & Faber).

Bermudas wall'd with rocks, who does not know
That happy island, where huge lemons grow,
Where shining pearl, coral, and many a pound,
On the rich shore, of ambergris is found.

—*Edmund Waller*.

AMBIENT (am/bi-ent) *surrounding* A52

Thus Common-sense, and hard on its heels came Conscience, reminding Stephen that he was a young man engaged to be married to a charming
girl and that it would look very Queer indeed for him to be Approaching
a strange young woman in Chelling High Street with no valid excuse beyond
the fact that she had once laughed at him in a restaurant.

Freely admitting the validity of all these criticisms, Stephen nevertheless continued his course towards the Gas Light & Coke Co.'s showrooms, all too aptly emulating the proverbial moth that circles closer and closer to the flame whilst perfectly aware that the ambient temperature is becoming dangerously high.—*Hugh McGraw.* The Boon Companions, Ch. 11. (Heinemann).

AMBIVALENT (am-biv/a-lent) *equivocal; undecided*　　A53

The analysis of dreams of normal individuals has shown that our own temptation to kill others is stronger and more frequent than we had suspected, and that it produces psychic effects even where it does not reveal itself to our consciousness. And when we have learnt that the obsessive rules of certain neurotics arc nothing but measures of self-reassurance and self-punishment erected against the reinforced impulse to commit murder, we can return with fresh appreciation to our previous hypothesis that every prohibition must conceal a desire. We can then assume that this desire to murder actually exists and that the taboo as well as the moral prohibition are psychologically by no means superfluous but are, on the contrary, explained and justified through our ambivalent attitude towards the impulse to slay.—*Sigmund Freud.* Totem and Taboo.

AMETHYST (am/e-thist) *a violet-blue precious stone*　　A54

. . . the olive-green chrysoberyl that turns red by lamp-light, the cymophane with its wire-like line of silver, the pistachio-coloured peridot, rose-pink and wine-yellow topazes, carbuncles of fiery scarlet with tremulous four-rayed stars, flame-red cinnamon stones, orange and violet spinels, and amethysts with their alternate layers of ruby and sapphire.—*Oscar Wilde.* The Picture of Dorian Gray.

AMPHIBOLOGY (am-fi-bol/o-gi) *an ambiguous statement*　　A55
THE END OF THE WORLD

How shall we interpret Elias six thousand years, or imagine the secret communicated to a Rabbi, which GOD hath denied unto His Angels? It had been an excellent quære to have posed the Devil of Delphos, and must needs have forced him to some strange amphibology. It has not only mocked the predictions of sundry Astrologers in Ages past, but the prophecies of many melancholy heads in these present, who, neither understanding reasonably things past or present, pretend a knowledge of things to come.—*Sir Thomas Browne.* Religio Medici. First Part.

> For goddis speke in ampibologies.
> And for one sothe they tellin twenty lie.
> 　　—*Chaucer.* Troylus and Cryseyde. iv. 1406.

Now the fallacies whereby men deceive others, and are deceived themselves, the ancients have divided into verbal and real; of the verbal, and such as conclude from mistakes of the word, there are but two worthy our notation; the fallacy of equivocation and amphibology.—*Sir Thomas Browne.* Vulgar Errors.

> Come leave your schemes,
> And fine amphibolies.
> 　　—*Ben Jonson.* Magnetick Lady. ii, 5.

AMPHITHEATRE (am/fi-the-a-tr) *an arena; an open-air*   A56
theatre, natural or artificial

The trades blew strong and squally; the surf roared loud on the shingle beach; and the fifty-ton schooner of war, that carries the flag and influence of France about the islands of the cannibal group, rolled at her moorings under Prison Hill. The clouds hung low and black on the surrounding amphitheatre of mountains; rain had fallen earlier in the day, real tropic rain, a waterspout for violence; and the green and gloomy brow of the mountain was still seamed with many silver threads of torrent.—*R. L. Stevenson and Lloyd Osbourne*. The Wrecker. (Prologue).

AMUSIVE (a-mu/siv) *amusing*   A57

When day declining sheds a milder gleam,
What time the May-fly haunts the pool or stream;
When the still owl skims round the grassy mead,
What time the timorous hare limps forth to feed;
Then be the time to steal adown the vale,
And listen to the vagrant cuckoo's tale;
To hear the clamorous curlew call his mate,
Or the soft quail his tender pain relate;
To see the swallow sweep the dark'ning plain
Belated, to support her infant train;
To mark the swift in rapid giddy ring
Dash round the steeple, unsubdued of wing;
Amusive birds! say where your hid retreat
When the frost rages and the tempests beat;
Whence your return, by such nice instinct led,
When spring, soft season, lifts her gloomy head?
Such baffled searches mock man's prying pride,
The GOD of NATURE is your secret guide!

> —*Gilbert White*. The Natural History of Selborne.
> (" The Naturalist's Summer-Evening Walk.")

ANACREONTIC (a-nak-re-on/tik) *a poem extolling*   A58
Love, and pleasure (especially drinking)

To the miscellanies [of Cowley] succeed the anacreontiques, or paraphrastical translations of some little poems, which pass, however justly, under the name of anacreon.—*Dr. Johnson*. The Lives of the Poets. (Cowley).

ANADEM (an/a-dem) *a crown of flowers*   A59

In anadems for whom they curiously dispose
The red, the dainty white, the goodly damask rose,
For the rich ruby, pearl, and amethyst men place
In kings' imperial crowns.

> —*Drayton*. Polyolbion.   xv.

The self-lov'd will
Of man or woman should not rule in them
But each with other wear the anademe.
                    —*Ben Jonson*. Masques at Court.

And Venus could not through the thick air pierce,
Till the day's king, god of undaunted verse,
Because she was so plentiful a theme
To such as wore his laurel anademe,
Like to a fiery bullet made descent,
And from her passage those fat vapours rent,
That, being not thoroughly rarefied to rain,
Melted like pitch, as blue as any vein.
                    Marlowe. Hero and Leander.

Of garlands, anademes, and wreaths,
This Nymphal nought but sweetness breathes.
                    Drayton. The Muses' Elysium. v.

Making sweet close of his delicious toils—
    Lit light in wreaths and anadems,
And pure quintessences of precious oils
    In hollow'd moons of gems.
                    Tennyson. The Palace of Art.

ANALOGUE (an/a-log) *analogy*   A60

I stood there on the extreme shore of the West and of to-day. Seventeen hundred years ago, and seven thousand miles to the east, a legionary stood, perhaps, upon the walls of Antoninus, and looked northward toward the mountains of the Picts. For all the interval of time and space I, when I looked from the cliff-house on the broad Pacific, was that man's heir and analogue: each of us standing on the verge of the Roman Empire (or, as we now call it, Western civilisation), each of us gazing onward into zones unromanised.—*R. L. Stevenson and Lloyd Osbourne*. The Wrecker. Ch. viii.

ANAPEST (an/a-pest) *two short syllables followed by*   A61
a long syllable; a metrical foot

The feet that principally enter into the composition of Greek and Latin verses are either of two or three syllables; those of two syllables are either both long, as the spondee, or both short as the pyrrhic; or one short and the other long as the iambic; or one long and the other short, as the trochee. Those of three syllables are the dactyl, of one long and two short syllables; the anapest of two short and one long; the tribachium of three short; and the molossus of three long. Thus, Spenser, Shakespeare, Milton, Dryden, Pope, and all our poets abound with dactyls, spondees, trochees, anapests, etc.—*Oliver Goldsmith*. Essay 19.

ANASTROPHE (a-nas/tro-fi) *inversion of the natural*   A62
order of words

Anastrophe [is] a preposterous order, or a backward setting of words, thus: " All Italy about I went," which is contrary to plain order, " I went about all Italy."—*Peacham.* Garden of Eloquence.

The opening lines of Milton's " Paradise Lost " may be given as an example of anastrophe:

> Of Mans First Disobedience, and the Fruit
> Of that Forbidden Tree, whose mortal tast
> Brought Death into the World, and all our woe,
> With loss of *Eden,* till one greater Man
> Restore us, and regain the blissful Seat,
> Sing Heav'nly Muse . . .

ANATHEMA (a-nath/e-ma) (1) *a curse* (2) *a thing to*   A63
be avoided

An anathema maranatha is an especially strong form of imprecation. See 1 *Corinthians* xvi, 22.

The principles of liberty were the scoff of every grinning courtier, and the Anathema Maranatha of every fawning dean.—*Macaulay.* " Milton." (Edinburgh Review, August, 1825).

Between them the two families got a great portion of her private savings out of her; and finally she fled to London followed by the anathemas of both, and determined to seek for servitude again as infinitely less onerous than liberty—*W. M. Thackeray.* Vanity Fair.

After his death, Shaw remarked that Ricketts lived " en grand seigneur." Like most of his comments, it was extremely acute. Ricketts himself said: " I live like a grandee." And when I did not see the point, he explained how grandees used to live. Their reception-rooms would be rich and luxurious, filled with noble and beautiful things, fit places in which to dispense hospitality and receive their peers; but the rooms in which they habitually passed their days would be almost poverty-stricken, puritan in their simplicity. The studio, in which Ricketts lived, was such a room. He had no sense of comfort. The easy-chair, with its deep feather cushions into which you " relax " was anathema to him. His " easy " chairs cost 35s. and were almost devoid of padding; his sofa was as uncomfortable as a waiting-room seat at a railway station. All were covered with blue cotton cloth at a shilling a yard, the stuff out of which butchers made their aprons. His ash-trays were saucers, his palate an old plate, his warmth a square black-leaded stove.—*Cecil Lewis.* Preface to *Self-Portrait.* Letters and Journals of Charles Ricketts, R.A. (Peter Davies).

ANFRACTUOUS (an-fract/u-us) *tortuous; winding*   A64

Arteries taking their rise from the left capsula of the heart, bringing through several circuits, ambages, and anfractuosities, the vital spirits.—*Rabelais.* Gargantua and Pantagruel. iii, 22.

ANIMALCULE (an-i-mal/kule) *microscopic creature*   A65

I remember well the thrill of delight and admiration that shot through me the first time I discovered the common wheel animalcule (*Rotifera vulgaris*) expanding and contracting its flexible spokes, and seemingly rotating through the water.—*Fitz-James O'Brien.* The Diamond Lens.

The ciliated spores of the algæ; the simplest of the ciliated animalcules; the most regular of the compound ciliated organisms, as the Volvox globator; together with the sponges and their allies; may be instanced as this order of life.—*Herbert Spencer.* Principles of Psychology.

ANIMISM (an/im-ism) *attribution of spiritual quality*   A66
or intelligence to inanimate objects

. . . if intuition, or instinct, were regarded as possessing absolute authority, its earliest expressions would have become permanent. We should still be in the stage of primitive animism, seeing spirits in the streams and the trees, phantom terrors in the jungle, gods in the sun and the moon.— *Viscount Samuel.* Belief and Action. Ch. v.

ANNUNCIATE (a-nun/ci-ate) *announce*   A67
See ANNUNCIATION in Part " A."

> Lo Sampson, which that was annunciat
> By the angel, long or his nativitee.
>
> —*Chaucer.* Monk's Tale.

ANNUNZIO (a-noond/zi-o)   A68

ANODYNE (an/o-dine) *relief; alleviation*   A69

> Yet durst she not too deeply probe the wound,
> As hoping still the nobler parts were sound :
> But strove with anodynes t'assuage the smart,
> And mildly thus her med'cine did impart.
>
> —*Dryden.*

The churchmen, at the time of the Revolution, justified their conduct by all those profligate sophisms which are called Jesuitical, and which are commonly reckoned among the peculiar sins of Popery, but which, in fact, are every where the anodynes employed by minds rather subtle than strong, to quiet those internal twinges which they cannot but feel and which they will not obey.—*Macaulay.* Essays.

ANTELUCAN (an-te-lu/kan) *before dawn*   A70

How serene does she now arise, a queen among the Pleiades, in the penultimate antelucan hour, shod in sandals of bright gold . . .—*James Joyce.* Ulysses (II). (John Lane).

ANTEMUNDANE (an-te-mun/dane) *before the creation*   A71
    of the world

> The Supreme,
> Great, antemundane Father!
> > —*Young*.   Night Thoughts, v.

ANTHROPOMORPHOUS (an-thro-po-mor/fus)   A72
    in human shape

. . . affliction makes opposing forces loom anthropomorphous.—
Thomas Hardy. Jude the Obscure. Pt. vi (iii). (Macmillan).

But we still look for meaning in life and above all for meaning in
beauty, meaning that we can somehow relate to ourselves. We still judge
the universe anthropomorphically and see in events portents of hope or
menace to humanity.—*C. E. M. Joad.* The Book of Joad. Ch. xiii, p. 219.
(Faber & Faber).

ANTHROPOPHAGI (an-thro-pof/a-ji) *cannibals*   A73

Nay further, we are what we all abhor, Anthropophagi and Cannibals,
devourers not only of men, but of our selves; and that not in an allegory,
but a positive truth; for all this mass of flesh we behold, came in at our
mouths; this frame we look upon, hath been upon our trenchers; in brief
we have devour'd our selves.—*Sir Thomas Browne.* **Religio Medici.** First
Part.

> The cannibals that each other eat,
> The anthropophagi, and men whose heads
> Do grow beneath their shoulders.
> > *Shakespeare.* Othello.   i, 3

> It would make our cannibal Christians
> Forbear the mutual eating one another,
> Which they do do, more cunningly than the wild
> Anthropophagi, that snatch only strangers!
> > —*Ben Jonson.* Staple of News.   iii, 2.

APHASIAC (a-fase/i-ak) *imperfect; broken*   A74

I stepped toward the window. It was the old familiar room, with
the tables set like a Greek P, and the sideboard, and the aphasiac piano,
and the panels on the wall. There were Romeo and Juliet, Antwerp from
the river, Enfield's ships among the ice, and the huge huntsman winding
a huge horn; mingled with them a few new ones, the thin crop of a
succeeding generation, not better and not worse. It was to one of these
I was directed—a thing coarsely and wittily handled, mostly with the
palette-knife, and the colour in some parts excellent, the canvas in others
loaded with mere clay. But it was the scene and not the art or want of
it that riveted my notice. The foreground was of sand and scrub and
wreckwood; in the middle distance the many-hued and smooth expanse of
a lagoon, enclosed by a wall of breakers; beyond, a blue strip of ocean.
The sky was cloudless, and I could hear the surf break. For the place was
Midway Island.—*R. L. Stevenson and Lloyd Osbourne.* The Wrecker.
Ch. xxi.

APLOMB (a-plon/) *self-possession* A75

TALLBOYS: And how do you come to be a private now?

MEEK: I prefer the ranks, sir. I have a freer hand. And the conversation in the officers' mess doesn't suit me. I always resign a commission and enlist again.

TALLBOYS: Always! How many commissions have you held?

MEEK: I don't quite remember, sir. Three, I think.

TALLBOYS: Well, I'm dashed!

THE PATIENT: Oh, Colonel! and you mistook this great military genius for a half wit!!!

TALLBOYS (*with aplomb*): Naturally. The symptoms are precisely the same. (*To Meek*): Dismiss.—*G. B. Shaw*. Too True to be Good. Act II. (Constable).

APOCALYPSE† A76

Not many hundred yards beyond Browndean, however, a sudden jarring of brakes set everybody's teeth on edge, and there was a brutal stoppage. Morris Finsbury was aware of a confused uproar of voices, and sprang to the window. Women were screaming, men were tumbling from the windows on the track, the guard was crying to them to stay where they were; at the same time the train began to gather way and move very slowly backward towards Browndean; the next moment, all these various sounds were blotted out in the apocalyptic whistle and the thundering onslaught of the down express.—*R. L. Stevenson and Lloyd Osbourne*. The Wrong Box. Ch. 2.

APPETENCE (ap/e-tens) *craving* A77

Bred onely and completed to the taste
Of lustful appetence, to sing, to dance,
To dress, and troule the Tongue, and roule the Eye.
—*Milton*. Paradise Lost. xi, 618.

APPLAUSIVE (a-plaw/siv) *approbative* A78

Euclia, or a fair glory, appears in the heavens, singing an applausive song, or pæan of the whole.—*Ben Jonson*. Masque of Love's Triumph.

Greet her with applausive breath,
Freedom, gaily doth she tread,
In her right a civic wreath,
In her left a human head.
Tennyson. Vision of Sin.

APPOSITE† A79

Natural talk, like ploughing, should turn up a large surface of life, rather than dig mines into geological strata. Masses of experience, anecdote, incident, cross-lights, quotation, historical instances, the whole flotsam and jetsam of two minds formed in and in upon the matter in hand from every point of the compass, and from every degree of mental elevation and abasement—these are the material with which talk is forti-fied, the food on which the talkers thrive. Such argument as is proper to the exercise should still be brief and seizing. Talk should proceed by instances; by the apposite, not the expository. It should keep close along the lines of humanity, near the bosoms and businesses of men, at the level where history, fiction and experience intersect and illuminate each other.—*R. L. Stevenson.* Talk and Talkers. 1.

À PRIORI (ay pri-ore/i) *known by intuition*   A80

This is not an accurate definition. More strictly, the expression implies an argument from cause to effect; an argument from anticipation rather than experience; which latter leads to the argument *à posteriori.*

This is the à priori necessity, and this the generalization à posteriori. —*Herbert Spencer.* Principles of Psychology. Pt. iv. Ch. iii.

APSE (aps) *arched or domed recess, usually in a church*   A81

In a corner a burning taper put a halo about the head of a priest, burnishing his shining, bald skull, his white surplice, and the open book before him. "Amen," he chanted: the book was closed with a snap, the light moved up the apse, some dark figures of women rose from their knees and passed quickly towards the door.—*Vernon Lee.* A Vernon Lee Anthology. (John Lane).

AQUILON (ak/wi-lon) *the north-east wind*   A82

AJAX: Thou, trumpet, there's my purse,
        Now crack thy lungs, and split thy brazen pipe;
        Blow, villian, till thy sphered bias cheek
        Outswell the colic of puff'd Aquilon:
        Come, stretch thy chest, and let thy eyes spout blood;
                    —*Shakespeare.* Troilus and Cressida. iv, 5.

ARBUTUS (ar/bu-tus) *an evergreen shrub*   A83
LA RICCIA

The noon-day sun came slanting down the rocky slopes of La Riccia, and its masses of entangled and tall foliage, whose autumnal tints were mixed with the wet verdure of a thousand evergreens, were penetrated with it as with rain. I cannot call it colour, it was conflagration. Purple, and crimson, and scarlet, like the curtains of God's tabernacle, the rejoicing trees sank into the valley in showers of light, every separate leaf quivering with buoyant and burning life; each, as it turned to reflect or to transmit the sunbeam, first a torch and then an emerald. Far up into the recesses of the valley, the green vistas arched like the hollows of mighty waves of some crystalline sea, with the arbutus flowers dashed

along their flanks for foam, and silver flakes of orange spray tossed into
the air around them, breaking over the grey walls of rock into a thousand
separate stars, fading and kindling alternately as the weak wind lifted and
let them fall. Every glade of grass burned like the golden floor of
heaven, opening in sudden gleams as the foliage broke and closed above
it, as sheet-lightning opens in a cloud at sunset; the motionless masses of
dark rock—dark though flushed with scarlet lichen—casting their quiet
shadows across its restless radiance, the fountain underneath them filling
its marble hollow with blue mist and fitful sound, and over all—the
multitudinous bars of amber and rose, the sacred clouds that have no
darkness, and only exist to illumine, were seen in fathomless intervals
between the solemn and orbed repose of the Stone pines, passing to lose
themselves in the last, white, blinding lustre of the measureless line where
the Campagna melted into the blaze of the sea.—*John Ruskin.* Modern
Painters. Vol. 1 (6). " Turner's Overcharged Brilliancy."

They emerged in the fine young grass before the grotto and exploring
to the left they came upon the inspiration of the scented air. A diminutive
glade in the brushwood hidden from the casual glance by a clump of
arbutus was completely white with violets.—*Compton Mackenzie.* West
to North. (Chatto & Windus).

ARCHANGEL (ark/ane-gel) *an angel of Ministerial rank*   A84

In the work of Orcagna, an intense solemnity and energy in the
sublimest groups of his figures, fading away as he touches inferior objects,
indicates that his home was among the archangels, and his rank among
the first sons of men; while Correggio, in the sidelong grace, artificial
smiles, and purple languors of his saints, indicates the inferior instinct
which would have guided his choice in quite other directions, had it not
been for the fashion of the age, and the need of the day.—*John Ruskin.*
Modern Painters. Vol. III.

. . . You are either an archangel or a very bourgeois gentleman indeed if
you admit to having spoken English prose all your life without knowing
it.—*Sir Arthur Quiller-Couch.* The Practice of Writing.

ARCH-FLAMEN (arch-flay/men) *archbishop*   A85

Hail to thy returning festival, old Bishop Valentine! Great is thy
name in the rubric, thou venerable Archflamen of Hymen! Immortal
Go-between! who and what manner of person art thou?—*Charles Lamb.*
Essays of Elia. " Valentine's Day."

ARCHIDIACONAL (arch-i-dee-ak/on-al) *like an*   A86
archdeacon; respectable; morose

THE Ph.D.

. . . Littlefield was old for a man of forty-two. He was tall, broad,
thick; his gold-rimmed spectacles were engulfed in the folds of his long
face; his hair was a tossed mass of greasy blackness; he puffed and
rumbled as he talked; his Phi Beta Kappa key shone against a spotted
black waistcoat; he smelled of old pipes: he was altogether funereal and
archidiaconal.—*Sinclair Lewis.* Babbitt. Ch. iii (1). (Jonathan Cape).

ARCHITECTONIC (ark-i-tek-ton/ik) *relating to*   A87
      architecture or building

      May be extended to any kind of structure, literary or material.

      This, indeed, is no small addition to Grecian poetical celebrity, as it
stood in the days of Solon, Alkæus, Sappho, and Stesichorus; but we
must remember that the epical structure of the Odyssey, so ancient and
long acquired to the Hellenic world, implies a reach of architectonic
talent quite equal to that exhibited in the most symmetrical drama of
Sophokles.—*Grote.* History of Greece, Ch. lxvii.

ARCHIVES (ar/kivz) *records*   A88

      The real criminal was not named; nor, till the archives of the House
of Stuart were explored, was it known to the public that Talmash had
perished by the basest of all the hundred villanies of Marlborough.—
Macaulay. History of England, Ch. XX.

ARCUATE (ar/ku-ate) *arched*   A89

      Sounds that move in oblique and arcuate lines, must needs encounter
and disturb the one the other.—*Bacon.* Natural History.

AREA (air/e-a) *forecourt below street level*   A90

ARGAL (ar/gal) *therefore*   A91

      "What writing!" he exclaimed; "*le style c'est l'homme.* Lypiatt
hasn't got a style. Argal—inexorable conclusion—Lypiatt doesn't exist!"
—*Aldous Huxley.* Antic Hay. Ch. vii. (Chatto & Windus).

ARGENTINE†   A92

            Now rose the moon, full and argentine,
            While round stood the maidens, as at a shrine.
                  —*Translation of a fragment from a poem of Sappho.*

ARIETTA (ar-i-et/a) *a brief, lively musical composition*   A93

      "It's like the Arietta, don't you think?" said Emily suddenly, "the
Arietta of Op. 111." And she hummed the first bars of the air. "Don't
you feel it's like that? "
      "What's like that?"
      "Everything," said Emily. "To-day, I mean. You and me. These
gardens—" And she went on humming.
      Gumbril shook his head. "Too simple for me," he said.
      Emily laughed, "Ah, but then think how impossible it gets a little
farther on." She agitated her fingers wildly, as though she were trying to
play the impossible passage.—*Aldous Huxley.* Antic Hay. Ch. xii.
(Chatto & Windus).

ARMAGEDDON (ar-ma-ged/on)   A94

A name, taken from the Bible, to indicate the final and decisive battle between the powers of Good and Evil. Hence it has come to denote any great conflict, real or imagined.

ARMOZEEN (ar-mo-zeen/) *a thick silk used for*   A95
        ecclesiastical vestments

The student cannot afford to neglect so strong, so well-flavoured, an expression of the ecclesiastical mode of life; a mode repulsive to some—to others reposeful, and a source of spiritual security.

Note that it is a *thick* silk—good stuff, although plain—hard-wearing, glossy, pontifical, reassuring. The Church is secure, and the dignitary clad in this black armozeen is a tower of strength, a pillar of society, and a guide to eternity and its everlasting rewards.

ARRAS (ar/as) *tapestry; wall hanging*   A96

I have of yore made many a scrambling meal
In corners, behind arrasses, on stairs.
      —Beaumont and Fletcher. The Woman Hater. iii, 4.

He's going to his mother's closet;
Behind the arras I'll convey myself,
To hear the process.
      —Shakespeare. Hamlet. iii, 3.

For some were hung with arras green and blue,
    Showing a gaudy summer-morn,
Where with puff'd cheek the belted hunter blew
    His wreathed bugle-horn.
      —Tennyson. The Palace of Art.

ASCETIC†   A97

Asceticism has not improved the form, or the physical well-being, or the heart of any human being. On the contrary, the hetaira is often the warmest hearted and the most generous. Casuistry and self-examination are perhaps the most injurious of all the virtues, utterly destroying independence of mind. Self-denial has had no result, and all the self-torture of centuries has been thrown away. Lives spent in doing good have been lives nobly wasted. Everything is in vain. The circle of ideas we possess is too limited to aid us. We need ideas as far outside our circle as ours are outside those that were pondered by Augustus Cæsar.— *Richard Jefferies.* The Story of My Heart. Ch. x.

ASHLAR (ash/lar) *square block of stone*   A98

THE NEW LONDON

. . . were these towered ashlar edifices; were these fair bounteous leas, with their bosky umbrages and yellow harvests; and the sunshine that lights them from above, and the granite rocks and fire-reservoirs that support them from below, made by *thee?*—*Carlyle.* The Diamond Necklace. Vol. III. " Critical & Miscellaneous Essays."

Was it wise to quit the bosky verdures of Brienne, and thy new ashlar chateau there, and what it held, for this? Soft were those shades and lawns; sweet the hymns of poetasters, the blandishments of high-rouged Graces.—*Carlyle.* The French Revolution, Pt. i, Bk. iii, Ch. vii.

In the middle . . . of that great elliptical Piazza at the eastern end of the new City, stands, four-square, the Royal Exchange. Pierced only with small dark windows, and built of rough ashlars of the silvery Portland stone, the ground floor serves as a massy foundation for the huge pilasters that slide up, between base and capital, past three tiers of pedimented windows. Upon them rest the cornice, the attic and the balustrade, and on every pier of the balustrade a statue holds up its symbol against the sky. Four great portals, rich with allegory, admit to the courtyard with its double tier of coupled columns, its cloister and its gallery. The statue of Charles the Martyr rides triumphantly in the midst, and within the windows one guesses the great rooms, rich with heavy garlands of plaster, panelled with carved wood.—*Aldous Huxley.* Antic Hay. Ch. xi. (Chatto & Windus).

ASSEMBLY ROOM *a public hall*   A99

No sooner did the reputation of the poem begin to spread, than she heard it repeated in all places of concourse; nor could she enter the assembly-rooms, or cross the walks, without being saluted with some lines from The Bastard.—*Dr. Johnson.* The Lives of the Poets. (Richard Savage).

ASSEVERATE (a-sev/er-ate) *to affirm*   A100

That which you are persuaded of, ye have it no otherwise than by your own probable collection; and therefore such bold asseverations as in him were admirable, should, in your mouths, but argue rashness.—*Hooker.* Ecclesiastical Polity.

While Wharton had been making his report to the Commons, Leeds had been haranguing the Lords. He denied with the most solemn asseverations that he had taken any money for himself. But he acknowledged, and indeed almost boasted, that he had abetted Bates in getting money from the company, and seemed to think that this was a service which any man in power might be reasonably expected to render to a friend.—*Macaulay.* History of England. Ch. xxi.

ASYNDETON (a-sin/de-ton) A101

The illustration given below explains the meaning.

Asyndeton is a figure, which keeps the parts of our speech together without help of any conjunctions—"Warn them that are unruly, comfort the feeble minded, support the weak, be patient toward all men." (I Thess. v. 14.) "Heal the sick, cleanse the lepers, raise the dead, cast out devils." (S. Matt. x, 8.) When matters require brevity, this figure is chiefly to be used, or when we signify the quick despatch of a deed.—*Peacham.* Garden of Eloquence, sign I, iv.

See also Winston Churchill's speech containing the asyndeton: "Plough the fields, build the ships," etc. A further example is Cæsar's "I came, I saw, I conquered."

ATOLL (a-tol/) *a circular island of coral surrounding* A102
a lagoon

It was just a common·atoll about four miles round, with a few trees growing and a spring in one place, and the lagoon full of parrot-fish. I took the egg ashore and put it in a good place, well above the tide lines and in the sun, to give it all the chance I could, and pulled the canoe up safe, and loafed about prospecting. It's rum how dull an atoll is.—*H. G. Wells.* Aepyornis Island, from "The Country of the Blind."

ATRAMENTAL (at-ra-men/tal) *black* A103

If we enquire in what part of vitriol this atramental and denigrating condition lodgeth, it will seem especially to lie in the more fixed salt thereof.—*Sir Thomas Browne.* Vulgar Errors.

ATRAPOS (at/ra-pos) *wasting; lack of nourishment* A104

Diffuse thy beneficence early, and while thy Treasures call thee Master; there may be an Atropos of thy Fortunes before that of thy life . . .— *Sir Thomas Browne.* Christian Morals. Pt. i, Sect. v.

> Daemoniac phrenzie, moaping Melancholie
> And Moon-struck madness, pining Atrophie,
> Marasmus, and wide-wasting Pestilence,
> Dropsies, and Asthma's and Joint-racking Rheums.
> Dire was the tossing, deep the groans, despair
> Tended the sick busiest from Couch to Couch;
> And over them triumphant Death his Dart
> Shook, but delaid to strike, though oft invok't
> With vows, as their chief good, and final hope.
>
> —*Milton.* Paradise Lost. xi.

ATTIC (at/ik) *classical; elegant*   A105

> What near repast shall feast us, light and choice,
> Of Attick taste.—*Milton.* Sonnets. xx, 10.

The choice histories, heroick poems, and attick tragedies of stateliest and most regal argument, with all the famous political orations, offer themselves.—*Milton.* Tractate on Education.

AUREOLE (or/e-ol) *halo*   A106

> Salute the sacred dead
> Who went and who return not.—Say not so! . . .
> We rather seem the dead, that stayed behind.
> Blow, trumpets, all your exultations blow!
> For never shall their aureoled presence lack . . .
> They came transfigured back,
> Secure from change in their high-hearted ways,
> Beautiful evermore, and with the rays
> Of morn on their white shields of Expectation.
>
>   —*J. R. Lowell.* From " Ode at the Harvard
>   Commemoration, 1865."

> When round his head the aureole clings
> And he is clothed in white,
> I'll take his hand and go with him
> To the deep wells of light;
> We will step down as to a stream,
> And bathe there in God's sight.
>
>   —*Dante Gabriel Rossetti.* The Blessed Damozel,
>   from " Poems and Translations."

AUTONOMY (aw-ton/o-mi) *self-government*   A107

The taboo then gradually became an autonomous power which has detached itself from demonism.—*Sigmund Freud.* Totem & Taboo. Ch. ii.

AVATAR (av/a-tar) *incarnation*   A108

The " Red Death " had long devastated the country. No pestilence had ever been so fatal or so hideous. Blood was its avatar and its seal— the redness and horror of blood.—*Edgar Allan Poe.* The Masque of the Red Death.

. . . old Feudal Europe has fallen a-dozing to die! Her next awakening will be with no tavern-brawl at the *King's Head* or *Prime Minister* Tavern; but with the stern Avatar of Democracy, hymning its world-thrilling birth-and-battle song in the distant west . . .—*Carlyle.* Count Cagliostro. Vol. iii, " Critical & Miscellaneous Essays."

BACCHANTE

BAEDEKER

BAGGAGE-SMASHER

BALCARRES

BALEFUL

BALLAD

BALSAMOUS

BARBECUE

BARBICAN

BARTON

BASHI-BAZOUK

BASILISK

BAVIN

BEACONSFIELD

BEAD-ROLL

BEATIFY

BEAUCHAMP

BEAULIEU

BEAUNE

BÉCASSE

BEDEL

BEDIZEN

BED-PRESSER

BEEROCRACY

BELAMOUR

BELLEROPHON

BENTHAM

BERKELEY

BERKSHIRE

BERSERK

BERYL

BESTEAD

BHAGAVAD-GITA

BIBLIOPHILE

BIBLIOPOLE

BICAMERAL

BICESTER

BISTRE

BLACKAMOOR

BLACK MASS

BLACK MONDAY

BLAZE

BLOWZE

BODEGA

BŒOTIAN

BOHEA

BOSCAGE

BOSKY

BOTRYOIDAL

BOUGAINVILLÆA

BOUILLABAISSE

BOUILLON

BOURBON

BOURDON

BOURG

BOURGEON

BOVARY

BRAGGADOCIO

BRASSARD

BRASSERIE

BRAVURA

BREAKDOWN

BROCADE

BUCKRAM

BUGLOSS

BUHL

BULIMY

BY-END

BACCHANTE (bak/ant) *intoxicated or disorderly woman* **B**
> May also be pronounced *ba-kan/ti.*

Men peer from windows—not women, lest they be pressed. Sight of sights; Bacchantes, in these ultimate Formalised Ages! Bronze Henri looks on, from his Pont-Neuf; the Monarchic Louvre, Medicean Tuileries see a day like none heretofore seen.—*Carlyle.* The French Revolution. Pt. i, Bk. vii, Ch. v.

BAEDEKER (bay/de-ker) **B2**

BAGGAGE-SMASHER (bag/aj smash/er) *a railway porter* **B3**

An early, and comparatively unknown, example of American verbal felicity, which deserves wider recognition.

BALCARRES (bal-kar/is) **B4**

BALEFUL (bale/ful) *sad; miserable* **B5**
> Ah! luckless babe, born under cruel star
> And in dead parents' baleful ashes bread.
>> —*Spenser.* The Faerie Queene.

> . . . for now the thought
> Both of lost happiness and lasting pain
> Torments him; round he throws his baleful eyes,
> That witness'd huge affliction and dismay,
> Mixt with obdurate pride and stedfast hate.
>> *Milton.* Paradise Lost. i.

The "morbid melancholy," which was lurking in his constitution, and to which we may ascribe those particularities, and that aversion to regular life which, at a very early period, marked his character, gathered such strength in his twentieth year as to afflict him in a dreadful manner. While he was at Lichfield, in the college vacation of the year 1729, he felt himself overwhelmed with an horrible hypochrondria, with perpetual irritation, fretfulness, and impatience; and with a dejection, gloom and despair, which made existence misery. From this dismal malady he never afterwards was perfectly relieved; and all his labours, and all his enjoyments, were but temporary interruptions of its baleful influence.—*James Boswell.* Life of Johnson. A.D. 1729, Ætat. 20.

BALLAD (bal/ad) *poem in short stanzas* **B6**
> FALSTAFF: An I have not ballads made on you all, and sung to filthy tunes, let a cup of sack be my poison.
>> —*Shakespeare.* Henry IV. Pt. i, ii, 2.

BALSAMOUS (bal/sam-us) *soothing*   B7

Now the radical moisture is not the tallow or fat of animals, but an oily and balsamous substance; for the fat or tallow, as also the phlegm or watery parts, are cold; whereas the oily and balsamous parts are of a lively heat and spirit.—*Sterne.* Tristram Shandy. Vol. v, Ch. xxxvi.

BARBECUE (bar/be-ku) (*noun*) *a hog roasted whole;*   B8
          (*verb*) *to roast whole*

Barbecue your whole hogs to your palate, steep them in shalots, stuff them out with plantations of the rank and guilty garlic; you cannot poison them, or make them stronger than they are.—*Lamb.* Essays of Elia. "A Dissertation upon Roast Pig."

BARBICAN (bar/bi-kan) *a tower used as a defence to a*   B9
          city or castle

> Within the Barbican a Porter sate,
> Day and night duely keeping watch and ward;
> Nor wight nor worde mote passe out of the gate,
> But in good order, and with dew regard;
> Utterers of secrets he from thence debard,
> Bablers of folly, and blazers of cryme:
> His larumbell might lowd and wyde be hard
> When cause requyrd, but never out of time;
> Early and late it rong, at evening at at prime.
>   —*Spenser.* The Faerie Queene. ii, ix, 25.

Two shafts of soft daylight fell across the flagged floor from the high barbicans: and at the meeting of their rays a cloud of coalsmoke and fumes of fried grease floated, turning.—*James Joyce.* Ulysses. (I). (John Lane).

BARTON (bar/ton) a *farmyard*   B10

>   If someone said on Christmas Eve
> "Come, see the oxen kneel
>
> In the lonely barton by yonder coomb
> Our childhood used to know."
> I should go with him in the gloom,
> Hoping it might be so.—*Thomas Hardy.*

BASHI-BAZOUK (bash/i-ba-zook/)   B11

A Turkish irregular soldier. The bashi-bazouks were a by-word for wildness and ferocity.

BASILISK (baz/il-isk) *a fabulous reptile*   B12

The stare of a basilisk, like a Gorgon, was anciently said
to blast or destroy. Hence the expression " basilisk stare."

There dwell hoary magicians, who have given up their trade and live
sociably as crocodiles on the banks of the Nile. There can one chat with
mummies in a pyramid and breakfast on basilisk's eggs . . .—*Thomas L.
Beddoes. Death's Jest-Book.* Act I, Scene i.

BAVIN (bav/in) *worthless*   B13

Originally used as a noun, meaning waste wood, or
firewood.

KING: The skipping king, he ambled up and down,
With shallow jesters and rash bavin wits,
Soon kindled and soon burnt; carded his state,
Mingled his royalty with capering fools,
Had his great name profaned with their scorns,
And gave his countenance, against his name,
To laugh at gibing boys, and stand the push
Of every beardless vain comparative,
Grew a companion to the common streets,
Enfeoff'd himself to popularity;
That, being daily swallow'd by men's eyes,
They surfeited with honey and began
To loathe the taste of sweetness, whereof a little
More than a little is by much too much.
                    —*Shakespeare.* Henry IV. Pt. i, iii, 2.

BEACONSFIELD (bek/onz-field)   B14

BEAD-ROLL (bede/role) *a list of names*   B15

Originally, a list of names of persons for whom prayers
were to be offered.

Through what fairy land would the man deduce this perpetual bead-
roll of uncontradicted episcopacy?—*Milton.* Animadversions upon a
Defence of the Humble Remonstrance.

BEATIFY (be-at/i-fi) *to make supremely blessed/happy*   B16

Add only that the body of this same rose-stifled beatified Patriarch
cannot get buried except by stealth.—*Carlyle.* The French Revolution.
Pt. i, Bk. ii, Ch. iv.

BEAUCHAMP (be/chum)   B17

BEAULIEU (bu/li)   B18

BEAUNE (bone) *red Burgundy*   B19

BÉCASSE (bay/cas) *an idiot*   B20

BEDEL (bee/del)   B21

A porter, messenger or official, especially of a university.

The academical functionaries, divided between reverence for the King and reverence for the law, were in great distress. Messengers were despatched in all haste to the Duke of Albemarle, who had succeeded Monmouth as Chancellor of the University. He was requested to represent the matter properly to the King. Meanwhile the registrar and bedells waited on Francis, and informed him that, if he would take the oaths according to law, he should instantly be admitted.—*Macaulay.* History of England. Ch. viii.

BEDIZEN (be-dizn/) *to dress up or ornament in a*   B22
                 garish, vulgar way

The May-pole is almost gone out of fashion among us: but May-day, besides its flowering hawthorns and its pearly dews, has still its boasted exhibition of painted chimney-sweepers and the Jack-o'-the-Green, whose tawdry finery, bedizened faces, unwonted gestures, and short-lived pleasures call forth good-humoured smiles and looks of sympathy in the spectators.—*William Hazlitt.* Sketches and Essays. " Merry England."

My great delight in *Compiègne* was the town-hall. I doted upon the town-hall. It is a monument of Gothic insecurity, all turretted, and gargoyled, and slashed, and bedizened with half a score of architectural fancies.—*R. L. Stevenson.* An Inland Voyage. " At Compiègne." (Chatto & Windus).

BED-PRESSER (bed-pres/er) *a lazy person*   B23

The Victorian equivalent of a drone, slug, butterfly, spiv or eel. See the Registration for Employment Order, 1947 (S.R.O. 2409/47).

BEEROCRACY (bere-ok/ra-si) *the clan of ennobled*   B24
                 brewers

BELAMOUR (bel-a-moor/) *lover*   B25

Lo, lo, how brave she decks her bounteous bow'r,
With silken curtain and gold coverlets,
Therein to shrowd her sumptuous belamour.
               —*Spenser.* The Faerie Queene.

BELLEROPHON (be-ler/o-fon)   B26

BENTHAM (ben/tam)   B27

BERKELEY (bark/li)   B28

BERKSHIRE (bark/sher)   B29

BERSERK (ber/serk) *furious*   B30
> Also spelt BARESARK (bar/sark), as in the quotation.
An hour went by, while the day came brighter, and the sun rose and drank up the clouds: an hour of silence in the ship, an hour of agony beyond narration for the sufferers. Brown's gabbling prayers, the cries of the sailors in the rigging, strains of the dead Hemstead's minstrelsy, ran together in Carthew's mind with sickening iteration. He neither acquitted nor condemned himself: he did not think, he suffered. In the bright water into which he stared, the pictures changed and were repeated: the baresark rage of Goddedaal; the blood-red light of the sunset into which they had run forth; the face of the babbling Chinaman as they cast him over; the face of the captain, seen a moment since, as he awoke from drunkenness into remorse. And time passed, and the sun swam higher, and his torment was not abated.—*R. L. Stevenson and Lloyd Osbourne.* The Wrecker. Ch. xxv.

BERYL (ber/il) *a precious stone like an emerald*   B31
> May thy billows rowl ashoar
> The beryl, and the golden ore,
> May thy lofty head be crown'd
> With many a tower and terras round,
> And here and there thy banks upon
> With Groves of myrrhe, and cinnamon.
> —*Milton.* Comus.

BESTEAD* (be-sted/) *to help*   B32
> Hence vain deluding joyes,
> The brood of folly without father bred,
> How little you bested,
> Or fill the fixed mind with all your toyes;
> Dwell in some idle brain,
> And fancies fond with gaudy shapes possess,
> As thick and numberless
> As the gay motes that people the Sun Beams,
> Or likest hovering dreams
> The fickle Pensioners of *Morpheus* train.
> —*Milton.* Il Penseroso. i.

BHAGAVAD-GITA (ba/ga-vad ge/ta)   B33

BIBLIOPHILE (bib/li-o-file) *a lover of books* B34

He was a bit of a book-fancier, and had vied with his brother Angoulême in bringing back the library of their grandfather Charles V, when Bedford put it up for sale in London. The duchess had a library of her own; and we hear of her borrowing romances from ladies in attendance or the blue-stocking Margaret of Scotland. Not only were books collected, but new books were written at the Court of Blois. The widow of one Jean Fougère, a bookbinder, seems to have done a number of odd commissions for the bibliophilous count. She it was who received three vellum-skins to bind the duchess's Book of Hours, and who was employed to prepare parchment for the use of the duke's scribes. And she it was who bound in vermilion leather the great manuscript of Charles's own poems, which was presented to him by his secretary Antony Astesan, with the text in one column, and Astesan's Latin version in the other.—*R. L. Stevenson.* Familiar Studies of Men and Books. " Charles of Orleans." (Chatto & Windus).

In the evening I strolled across the Park, and found myself about six o'clock at the Oxford Street end of Park Lane. A group of loafers upon the pavements, all staring up at a particular window, directed me to the house which I had come to see. A tall, thin man with coloured glasses, whom I strongly suspected of being a plain-clothes detective, was pointing out some theory of his own, while the others crowded round to listen to what he said. I got as near as I could, but his observations seemed to me to be absurd, so I withdrew again in some disgust. As I did so I struck against an elderly deformed man, who had been behind me, and I knocked down several books which he was carrying. I remember that as I picked them up I observed the title of one of them, *The Origin of Tree Worship,* and it struck me that the fellow must be some poor bibliophile, who, either as a trade or as a hobby, was a collector of obscure volumes.—*Sir A. Conan Doyle.* The Return of Sherlock Holmes. " The Adventure of the Empty House." (John Murray).

BIBLIOPOLE (bib/li-o-pole) *bookseller* B35

Davies . . . said [that] Gardner was not properly a bookseller. JOHNSON: " Nay, Sir; he certainly was a bookseller. He had served his time regularly, was a member of the Stationers' Company, kept a shop in the face of mankind, purchased copyright, and was a bibliopole, Sir, in every sense."—*James Boswell.* Life of Johnson A.D. 1775. Ætat. 66.

BICAMERAL (bi-kam/er-al) *having two parts* B36

The only use of this word which we have encountered is in connection with a Parliament. The English Parliament, for example, is bicameral, having a House of Lords and a House of Commons.

A committee of jurists, drawn from the Universities, composed a constitution, providing a bicameral legislature . . .—*Evelyn Waugh.* Scoop. p. 102. (Chapman & Hall).

BICESTER (bis/ter) B37

BISTRE (bis/ter) *a shade of brown*   B38

   . . . the soft seaweed-matted sand seemed endless in its bistre mono-tony.—*Compton Mackenzie.* Gallipoli Memories. Ch. xx.

BLACKAMOOR (blak/a-mor) *a negro*   B39

   A blackamoor in a fit of jealousy kills his innocent white wife.—*Lamb.* Essays of Elia.

   "What's he to Hecuba?" The grinning blackamoors repeated the question, reiterated the answer on a tone of frightful unhappiness. The saxophone warbled on the verge of anguish.—*Aldous Huxley.* Antic Hay. Ch. xv. (Chatto & Windus).

BLACK MASS (blak mas/)   B40

   These horrid rites appear to have sunk into almost un-fathomable obscurity, although there is a slight reference to be found in Aldous Huxley's *Antic Hay* (Ch. V). The blond and bearded Coleman, tapping the pavement with his stick, begins a chant which is referred to as the Black Mass.

BLACK MONDAY (blak mun/di)   B41

   In the 34th of Edw. III the 14th of April, and the morrow after Easter-day, king Edward, with his host, lay before the city of Paris, which day was full dark of mist and hail, and so bitter cold, that many men died on their horses' backs with the cold. Wherefore, unto this day, it has been called the Black-Monday.—*Stowe.* History of England.

BLAZE* (blaze) *a white mark on the face of an animal*   B42

   See the Sherlock Holmes story *Silver Blaze* in the "Memoirs."

BLOWZE (blouz) *a ruddy, fat-faced woman*   B43

   Used as a verb, *blowze* means to make hot and red with exertion.

   AARON: Sweet blowse, you are a beauteous blossom sure.
                Shakespeare. Titus Andronicus. iv. 2.

   I had rather marry a fair one, and put it to the hazard, than be troubled with a blowse.—*Burton.* Anatomy of Melancholy.

   You know the church is two miles off; and I protest I don't like to see my daughters trudging up to their pew all blowzed and red with walking, and looking for all the world as if they had been winners at a smock race.—*Oliver Goldsmith.* The Vicar of Wakefield. Ch. x.

   It was in this manner that my eldest daughter was hemmed in and thumped about, all blowzed, and in spirits, and bawling for fair play, fair play, with a voice that might deafen a ballad-singer, when, confusion on confusion, who should enter the room but our two great acquaintances from town, Lady Blarney and Miss Carolina Wilhelmina Skeggs.—*Ibid.* Ch. xi.

BODEGA (bo-dee/ga) *a wine shop*   B44

From the Spanish. The name has been appropriated specifically to a chain of London taverns.

BŒOTIAN (be-o/shi-an) *stupid*   B45

Note pronunciation.

I was particularly impressed by the spectacle of folly presented in the several militaristic totalitarian régimes that disfigure our world today; for such a régime, enforcing as it does the negation of reason and responsibility, of humane intelligence and the Christian spirit—such a régime, that compels a Spartan discipline for a Bœotian objective, that glorifies reliance on armed force, which, in the light of all the lessons of the last war, is simply reliance on the political efficacy of self-destruction—such a régime, I say, is an object-lesson in popular folly and pure dunderheadedness.— *Eric Linklater.* God Likes Them Plain. "His Majesty The Dentist." (Jonathan Cape).

BOHEA (bo-he/) *inferior grade of tea*   B46

Why should not every member of the New Company be at liberty to export European commodities to the countries beyond the Cape, and to bring back shawls, saltpetre, and bohea to England?—*Macaulay.* History of England. Ch. xxiii.

BOSCAGE (bos/kege) *wood; woodland*   B47

On the other hand, what a day, not of laughter, was that, when he threatened, for lucre's sake, to lay sacrilegious hand on the Palais-Royal Garden! The flower-parterres shall be riven up; the Chestnut Avenues shall fall: time-honoured *boscages,* under which the Opera Hamadryads were wont to wander, not inexorable to men.—*Carlyle.* The French Revolution. Pt. i, Bk. i, Ch. vi.

She lock'd her lips: she left me where I stood:
"Glory to God," she sang, and past afar,
Thridding the sombre boskage of the wood,
Toward the morning-star.
—*Tennyson.* A Dream of Fair Women.

The sun was low down, lolling near the horizon, but there was an astonishing light upon the land. Cottage windows were blocks of solid gold in this lateral brilliance, shafts of shapely shade lay across leagues of fields, he could have counted every leaf among the rumpled boskage of the sycamores. A vast fan of indurated cloud, shell-like and pearly, was wavering over the western sky, but in the east were snowy and rounded masses like fabulous balloons.—*A. E. Coppard.* Clorinda Walks in Heaven. "Craven Arms." (Jonathan Cape).

BOSKY (bos/ki) *with shrubs or trees*   B48

And with each end of thy blue bow dost crown
My bosky acres, and my unshrubb'd down.
—*Shakespeare.* The Tempest. iv. i.

COMUS: I know each lane, and every alley green,
Dingle, or bushy dell, of this wilde Wood,
And every bosky bourn from side to side.
My daily walks and ancient neighbourhood.
                              —*Milton.* Comus. 311.

BOTRYOIDAL (bot-ri-oi/dal) *having the form of a* B49
bunch of grapes

He is a great talker, this man, and a fairly respectable gesticulator, and to him it is we make our first ineffectual tentatives at explaining who indeed we are; but his flow of talk washes that all away again. He has a face of that rubicund, knobby type I have heard an indignant mineralogist speak of as botryoidal, and about it waves a quantity of disordered blond hair.—*H. G. Wells.* A Modern Utopia. Ch. iv. (Nelson).

BOUGAINVILLÆA (boo-gane-vi-lee/a) *a tropical plant* B50

I envied those flowered homes along the Mediterranean out at Montazah and Stanley Bay, with the bougainvillæa climbing over their yellow walls. *Negley Farson.* The Way of a Transgressor. Ch. xlii. (Gollancz).

BOUILLABAISSE† B51

Commercial, smart and vile, dilapidated even in peace-time, Marseilles has the attraction of restlessness, of a post in long-distance travel, of sahibs sweating in clanking trams and lascars sweated on the dockside; of crime, of political assassination (King Alexander was murdered in the Canebière). Bouillabaisse, with its reek of saffron and sea-water is eaten on the quay; saffron mixes with dust and scent in the crowded streets. It is a dirty Mediterranean that washes along the shore.—From The Geographical Magazine, September, 1941. "Provence in Sunlight," by *G. W. Stonier.*

BOUILLON (boo/yon) *broth; soup* B52
THE ECCENTRIC DUCHESS
On one occasion, having lost interest in dinner in the middle of an entrée, she had collected his women guests and herded the hungry but obedient flock into the drawing-room leaving the astonished men to eat the remaining five courses alone. Nobody had ever ventured to draw her attention to this lapse. Miss Anderson, that invaluable woman, had taken care to see that sandwiches and a thermos full of bouillon were put in the bedroom of each of the under-nourished guests . . .—*Barbara Worsley-Gough.* Public Affaires. Ch. vi. (Gollancz).

BOURBON (boor/bon) *an autocrat; a die-hard* B53

Mr. Hugh Dalton, a former Chancellor of the Exchequer, in opening his April Budget of 1947, referred to " the baleful Bourbons of the City."

BOURDON (boor/don) *an undertone; a background noise*   B54

The dim roar of London was like the bourdon note of a distant organ.
—*Oscar Wilde*. The Picture of Dorian Grey.

BOURG (boorg) *a market town*   B55

They take the rustic murmur of their bourg
For the great wave that echoes round the world.
         —*Tennyson*. The Idylls of the King.

BOURGEON (ber/jon) *to blossom*   B56

And lastly came cold February, sitting
In an old wagon, for he could not ride,
Drawne of two fishes, for the season fitting,
Which through the flood before did softly slyde
And swim away: yet had he by his side
His plough and harnesse fit to till the ground,
And tooles to prune the trees, before the pride
Of hasting Prime did make them burgein round.
So past the twelve Months forth, and their dew places found.
         —*Spenser*. The Faerie Queene. vii, 7, 43.

I fear, I shall begin to grow in love
With my dear self, and my most prosperous parts,
They do so spring and burgeon.
         —*Ben Jonson*. Volpone. ii, 1.

In winter this intolerable disinclination to dying—to give it its mildest name—does more especially haunt and beset me. In a genial August noon, beneath a sweltering sky, death is almost problematic. At those times do such poor snakes as myself enjoy an immortality. Then we expand and burgeon. Then are we as strong again, as valiant again, as wise again, and a great deal taller. The blast that nips and shrinks me, puts me in thought of death.—*Charles Lamb*. Essays of Elia. " New Year's Eve."

BOVARY (bo-va-ray/)   B57

BRAGGADOCIO (brag-a-do/shi-o) *bragging, talk*   B58

The meaning of the word used in the quotation is " a man given to bragging."

Boswell was a person whose mean or bad qualities lay open to the general eye; visible, palpable to the dullest . . . . That he was a wine-bibber and gross liver; gluttonously fond of whatever would yield him a little solacement, were it only of a stomachic character, is undeniable enough. That he was vain, heedless, a babbler; had much of the sycophant, alternating with the braggadocio, curiously spiced too with an all-pervading dash of the coxcomb; that he gloried much when the Tailor, by a court-suit, had made a new man of him; that he appeared at the Shakespeare Jubilee with a riband, imprinted " Corsica Boswell," round his hat; and in short, if you will, lived no day of his life without doing or saying more than one pretentious ineptitude; all this unhappily is evident as the sun at noon.—*Carlyle*. Critical and Miscellaneous Essays. " Boswell's Life of Johnson."

BRASSARD (bras/ard) *an arm-band*   B59

CHRISTMAS

The parcel-post became later and later. The delivery of letters passed largely into the hands of odd-looking irregulars with brassards. The pillar-box at the north-east corner was adorned with a threatening announcement about the impossibility of performing its ordinary duties.—*Denis Mackail*. The Square Circle. Ch. v. (Hodder & Stoughton).

BRASSERIE (bras/er-ee) *a beer shop*   B60

Compare BODEGA—a wine shop.

BRAVURA (bra-voor/a) *brilliance*   B61

Or, a song requiring much technical ability in its performance. Compare *coloratura*.

> In Babylon's bravuras—as the home
> Heart-ballads of green Erin or gray Highlands,
> That bring Lochaber back to eyes that roam
> O'er far Atlantic continents or islands.
>
> *Byron*. Don Juan. xvi, 46.

BREAKDOWN (brake/down) *Negro dance*   B62

Tom and Sam Bohee, coloured coons in white duck suits, scarlet socks, upstarched Sambo chokers and large scarlet asters in their button-holes leap out. Each has his banjo slung. Their paler smaller negroid hands jingle the twingtwang wires. Flashing white Kaffir eyes and tusks they rattle through a breakdown in clumsy clogs, twinging, singing, back to back, toe heel, heel toe, with smackfatclacking nigger lips.—*James Joyce*. Ulysses. (John Lane).

BROCADE (bro-kade/) *a rich silken cloth*   B63

. . . nothing can be more unlike than the simplicity of Temple and the richness of Johnson. Their styles differ as plain cloth and brocade.—*James Boswell*. Life of Johnson. A.D. 1750. Ætat 41.

BUCKRAM (buk/rum) *a strong cloth used for bookbinding*   B64

Formerly used by tailors.

Happy indeed would be the state of poetry, would these tickets pass current at the bake-house, the ale-house, and the chandler's shop; but alas! far otherwise; no taylor will take them in payment for buckram.—*Fielding*. The Adventures of Joseph Andrews.

BUGLOSS (bu/gloss) *rough-leaved plant*   B65

The little wilde Buglosse grows upon the dry ditches about Picka-della, and almost everywhere.—*Gerarde*. Herball. p. 199. (Ed. 1633).

BUHL (bool) *inlaid work*   B66

But the house of Glaucus was at once one of the smallest, and yet one of the most adorned and finished, of all private mansions of Pompeii. It would be a model at this day for the house of " a single man in Mayfair," the envy and despair of the cœlibian purchasers of buhl and marquetry.—*Bulwer Lytton.* Last Days of Pompeii. Bk. i, Ch. ii.

They ascended a staircase perfumed with flowers, and on each landing-place was a classic tripod or pedestal crowned with a bust. And then they were ushered into a drawing-room of Parisian elegance; buhl cabinets, marqueterie tables, hangings of the choicest damask suspended from burnished cornices of old carving.—*Disraeli.* Henrietta Temple. Bk. vi, Ch. xix.

BULIMY (bu/li-mi) *morbid craving for food*   B67

We had not disgorged one particle of the nauseous doses with which we were so liberally crammed by the mountebanks of Paris, in order to drug and diet us into perfect tameness. No; we waited till the morbid strength of our boulimia for their physick had exhausted the well-stored dispensary of their empiricism.—*Burke.* Thoughts on a Regicide Peace, 3.

BY-END†   B68

Make not the consequence of Virtue the ends thereof. Be not beneficent for a name or cymbal of applause, nor exact and just in Commerce for the advantages of Trust and Credit, which attend the reputation of true and punctual dealing. For these Rewards, though unsought for, plain Virtue will bring with her. To have other by-ends in good actions sowers Laudable performances, which must have deeper roots, motives, and instigations, to give them the stamp of Virtues.—*Sir Thomas Browne.* Christian Morals. Pt. i, s. x.

CABARET
CABBALISTIC
CABOCHON
CACHEXIA
CACODEMON
CACOPHONY
CADILLAC
CAIN-COLOURED
CALAMITOUS
CALEFACTORY
CALUMNIATE
CAMOMILE
CANAKIN
CANDENT
CANDLEMAS
CANOROUS
CAPRICCIO
CARAPACE
CARAT
CARAVANSARY
CARBUNCLE
CARIOUS
CASEMENT
CASTE
CATAFALQUE
CATAMARAN
CATENERY
CAUDAL
CENOBITE

CENTRIFUGAL
CEPHALALGIC
CERULEAN
CHALICING
CHAMELEON
CHAMPERTY
CHANDOS
CHARYBDIS
CHEVRON
CHICANERY
CHILDE
CHOPINE
CHRYSOLITE
CHRYSOPRASE
CICERONE
CINNABAR
CINQUE-SPOTTED
CIRCUMAMBIENT
CIRCUMVALLATION
CITRINE
CLANRICARDE
CLEMENT
CLERISY
CLOTTED NONSENSE
CLOUD-ECLIPSED
CODDAM
COEVAL
COIFFEUR
COLLYRIUM

COLORATURA
COMMINUTE
COMMONALTY
COMPLIN
CONCATENATION
CONCUPISCENCE
CONDIGN
CONGENER
CONGERIES
CONGLOBULATE
CONJURATION
CONNOTATIVE
CONSTELLATED
CONSUMMATE
CONSUMMATE
CONTUMACY
CONURBATION
CORBEL
CORNUCOPIA
CORVINE
COSMOGONY
COSMOGRAPHY
CREEPING JESUS
CREPUSCULAR
CUBAN HEEL
CULMEN
CURAÇAO
CYNOSURE

CABARET (kab/a-ray) *a tavern*   **C**

Now used to denote a floor-show given in the interval of a dance.

CABBALISTIC (kab-a-lis/tik) *indecipherable*   **C2**

And the windows of Number Thirty grew dirtier and dirtier, and the doorsteps dustier and dustier, and the cabbalistic symbols chalked by children on the side wall which ran down Brereton Place more and more intricate and confusing.—*Denis Mackail.* The Square Circle. Ch. ix. (Hodder & Stoughton).

CABOCHON (ka-bo/shon) *a gem cut and polished but*   **C3**
                without facets

Her eyes, which were fixed disapprovingly upon Cythera, were the colour of the intervening sea. Her little podgy hand clasping the *Saturday Evening Post* displayed a large cabochon sapphire. It was the colour of her eyes.—*Harold Nicolson.* Some People—" Miriam Codd " (1). (Constable).

CACHEXIA (ka-kek/si-a) *a diseased condition*   **C4**

The defects of digestion are the principal cause of scurvy and cachexy. —*Bishop Berkeley.* Siris. § 96.

CACODEMON (kak-o-de/mon) *an evil spirit*   **C5**

If the vultur pick out his right eye first, then they conclude that he is in paradise; if the left, then a cacodæmon vexes him.—*Sir T. Herbert.* Relation of some Years' Travels into Africa and the Great Asia. p. 168.

     QUEEN MARGARET: Hie thee to hell for shame, and leave
         , the world,
                    Thou Cacodemon! there thy kingdom is.
     —*Shakespeare.* All's Well that Ends Well. ii, 3.

CACOPHONY (ka-kof/o-ni) *a discordant noise*   **C6**

. . . the ploughman driving his share straight and glistening through the brown loam was a glory to see as we marched in the pale winter sun. We imitated his cacophonous but delightful orders to his massive horses with joy and thanksgiving.—*Edmund Blunden.* Undertones of War. Ch. xiv.

CADILLAC (ka-de-yak/)   **C7**

CAIN-COLOURED (kane/kul/erd) *reddish-yellow*   C8

QUICKLY: . . . Peter Simple, you say your name is?
SIMPLE: Ay, for fault of a better.
QUICKLY: And Master Slender's your master?
SIMPLE: Ay, foorsooth.
QUICKLY: Does he not wear a great round beard, like a glover's paring knife?
SIMPLE: No, forsooth; he hath but a little wee face, with a little yellow beard—a Cain-coloured beard.
                —*Shakespeare.* The Merry Wives of Windsor. i, iv.

CALAMITOUS (ka-lam/it-us) *unfortunate; woeful*   C9

. . . much rather I shall chuse,
To live the poorest in my Tribe, then richest,
And he in that calamitous prison left.
                —*Milton.* Samson Agonistes. 1478.

O Heav'n! in evil strait this day I stand
Before my Judge, either to undergoe
My self the total Crime, or to accuse
My other self, the partner of my life;
Whose failing, while her Faith to me remaines,
I should conceal, and not expose to blame
By my complaint; but strict necessitie
Subdues me, and calamitous constraint
Least on my head both sin and punishment,
However insupportable, be all
Devolv'd.—*Milton.* Paradise Lost. x.

CALEFACTORY (kal-e-fak/tory) *hot; producing heat*   C10

The air came up off the desert now in great puffs, calefactory as the wind evolved from a hair-drying machine in a barber's shop.—*Osbert Sitwell.* Miracle on Sinai. Bk. i, Ch. ii. (Duckworth).

CALUMNIATE (ka-lum/ni-ate) *to slander*   C11

Though the Quickness of thine Ear were able to reach the noise of the Moon, which some think it maketh in its rapid revolution; though the number of thy ears should equal *Argus* his Eyes; yet stop them all with the wise man's wax, and be deaf unto the suggestions of Tale-bearers, Calumniators, Pickthank or Malevolent Delators, who while quiet Men sleep, sowing the Tares of discord and division, distract the tranquility of Charity and all friendly Society.—*Sir Thomas Browne.* Christian Morals. Pt. i, s. xx.

CAMOMILE (kam/o-mile) *a herb*   C12

Mr. and Mrs. Discobbolos
Climbed to the top of a wall
And they sate to watch the sunset sky
And to hear the Nupiter Piffkin cry
And the Biscuit Buffalo call.

They took up a roll and some Camomile tea,
And both were as happy as happy could be—
Till Mrs. Discobbolos said—
"Oh! W! X! Y! Z!
"It has just come into my head—
"Suppose we should happen to fall! ! ! !"
—*Edward Lear.* Mr. and Mrs. Discobbolos.

CANAKIN (kan/a-kin) *a mug; small can*   C13

And let me the canakin clink.—*Shakespeare.* Othello. ii. 3.

CANDENT (kan/dent) *glowing*   C14

If a wire be heated only at one end, according as that end is cooled upward or downward, it respectively acquires a verticity, as we have declared in wires totally candent.—*Sir Thomas Browne.* Vulgar Errors.

CANDLEMAS (kandl/mas) *2nd February*   C15

"The Feast of the Purification of the Virgin, which was formerly celebrated with many lights in churches."—*Johnson's Dictionary,* Ed.1785.

There is a general tradition in most parts of Europe, that inferreth the coldness of the succeeding winter, upon shining of the sun upon Candlemas day.—*Sir Thomas Browne.* Vulgar Errors.

It beginning to grow a little duskish, *Candlemas* lustily bawled out for lights, which was opposed by all the *Days,* who protested against burning daylight. Then fair water was handed round in silver ewers, and the *same lady* was observed to take an unusual time in *washing* herself.—*Charles Lamb.* Essays of Elia. "Rejoicings upon the New Year's coming of Age."

CANOROUS (kan-or/us) *melodious*   C16

Birds that are most canorous, and whose notes we most commend, are of little throats, and short.—*Sir Thomas Browne.* Vulgar Errors.

. . . the high canorous note of the North-easter . . .—*R. L. Stevenson.* "Ordered South." (Chatto & Windus).

CAPRICCIO (ka-pre/cho) *a caprice*   C17

BERTRAM: . . . war is no strife
            To the dark house and the detested wife.
PAROLLES: Will this capriccio hold in thee, art sure?
            —*Shakespeare.* All's Well that Ends Well. ii, 3.

He was just closing the front door behind him, when he remembered something. He turned round. "I say," he called after the retreating pink kimono. "It's rather absurd. But how can I write? I don't know your name. I can't just address it 'Rosie'."

The great lady laughed delightedly. This had the real *capriccio* flavour. "Wait," she said, and she ran into the sitting-room. She was back again in a moment with an oblong of pasteboard. "There," she said, and dropped it into his great-coat pocket. Then blowing a kiss she was gone.—*Aldous Huxley.* Antic Hay. Ch. ix. (Chatto & Windus).

CARAPACE (kar/a-pace) *shell of tortoise or other*   C18
　　　　　crustacean

　　He worms down through a coalhole, his brown habit trailing its tether over rattling pebbles. After him toddles an obese grandfather rat on fungus turtle paws under grey carapace. Dignam's voice, muffled, is heard baying under ground: *Dignam's dead and gone below.* Tom Rochford, robinredbreasted, in cap and breeches, jumps from his two-columned machine.—*James Joyce.* Ulysses. (John Lane).

CARAT (kar/at) *1/24th part of pure gold*   C19

　　Thus a piece of 18 carat gold ware contains 18/24 parts of pure gold. The authorized standards of fineness in this country are 22, 18, 14 and 9 carats. With certain exceptions, any gold ware made in the U.K. or imported and sold must be of one of the authorized standards and hall-marked by the Wardens of the Goldsmiths' Company before sale. The unit known as a carat which is used for valuing precious stones is a weight and not a proportion.

　　The term carat is said to be derived from the name of a bean, the produce of a species of Erythrina, a native of the district of the Shangallas, in Africa, a famous mart for gold dust. The tree is called kuara, a word signifying " sun " in the language of the country; because it bears flowers and fruit of a flame colour. As the dry seeds of the fruit are nearly always of uniform weight, the savages have used them from time immemorial to weigh gold. The beans were transported into India at an ancient period, and have long been employed there for weighing diamonds. The carat of the civilized world is an imaginary weight, consisting of four nominal grains, a little lighter than four grains troy.—*Ure.* Dictionary of Arts, Manufactures, and Mines, " Diamond."

CARAVANSARY (kar-a-van/sar-i) *an inn*   C20

　　. . . the great caravansary which at that time was the chief glory of the town of Monterey.—*R. B. Cunninghame Graham.* Thirteen Stories. " A Hegira." (Heinemann).

CARBUNCLE (kar/bunkl) *a precious stone of a red or*   C21
　　　　　fiery colour

　　　　So spake the Enemie of Mankind, enclos'd
　　　In Serpent, Inmate bad, and toward *Eve*
　　　Address'd his way, not with indented wave,
　　　Prone on the ground, as since, but on his reare,
　　　Circular base of rising foulds, that tour'd
　　　Fould above fould a surging Maze, his Head
　　　Crested aloft, and Carbuncle his Eyes;
　　　With burnisht Neck of verdant Gold, erect
　　　Amidst his circling Spires, that on the grass
　　　Floted redundant: pleasing was his shape,
　　　And lovely, never since of Serpent kind
　　　Lovelier.—*Milton.* Paradise Lost. ix.

CARIOUS (ka/ri-us) *decayed or ulcerated* C22

. . . it was not only the Dictator who suffered from carious teeth. By a fortunate dispensation of Providence ninety per cent. of the inhabitants of Baltland were afflicted . . .—*Eric Linklater.* God Likes Them Plain. "His Majesty the Dentist." (Jonathan Cape).

CASEMENT (kase/ment) *a hinged window* C23

SNOUT: Doth the moon shine that night we play our play?
BOTTOM: A calendar, a calendar! look in the almanac; find out moonshine, find out moonshine.
QUINCE: Yes, it doth shine that night.
BOTTOM: Why, then may you leave a casement of the great chamber window, where we play, open, and the moon may shine in at the casement.
—*Shakespeare.* A Midsummer-Night's Dream. iii, i.

And I arose, and I released
The casement, and the light increased
With freshness in the dawning east.
—*Tennyson.* The Two Voices.

CASTE (karst) *a privileged class* C24

In the days of Popish ascendancy he had taken refuge among his friends here; he had returned to his home when the ascendancy of his own caste had been re-established: and he had been chosen to represent the University of Dublin in the House of Commons.—*Macaulay.* History of England. Ch. xxiii.

CATAFALQUE (kat/a-falk) *a platform for a coffin* C25

. . . six professional female mourners who grouped themselves about the catafalque in attitudes of exquisite melancholy.—*Michael Sadleir.* Blessington-D'Orsay. Ch. II (iii). (Constable).

CATAMARAN* (kat-a-ma-ran/) *a raft* C26

Here and there over the surface of the sea moved what the natives called *patini*—catamarans made of a pair of boxed-in pontoons joined together near the ends and with a high seat for the rower in the middle. —*Aldous Huxley.* Those Barren Leaves. (Chatto & Windus).

CATENERY (ka-tee/nar-i) *(adjective) curved like a* C27
hanging chain; (noun) such a curve

Where water takes its first leap from the top, it is cool, and collected, and uninteresting, and mathematical; but it is when it finds that it has got into a scrape, and has farther to go than it thought for, that its character comes out: it is then that it begins to writhe, and twist, and sweep out, zone after zone, in wilder stretching as it falls, and to send down the rocket-like, lance-pointed, whizzing shafts at its sides, sounding for the bottom. And it is this prostration, this hopeless abandonment of its ponderous power to the air, which is always peculiarly expressed by Turner, and especially in the case before us; while our other artists, keeping to the parabolic line, where they do not lose themselves in smoke and foam, make their cataract look muscular and wiry, and may consider themselves fortunate if they can keep it from stopping. I believe the majesty of motion which Turner has given by these concentric catenary lines must be felt even by those who have never seen a high waterfall, and therefore cannot appreciate their exquisite fidelity to nature.—*John Ruskin.* Modern Painters. Vol. I (15). " Turner's Water-Painting."

A row of seventeen glorious diamonds, as large almost as filberts, encircle, not too tightly, the neck, a first time. Looser, gracefully fastened thrice to these, a three-wreathed festoon, and pendants enough (simple pear-shaped, multiple star-shaped, or clustering amorphous) encircle it, enwreath it, a second time. Loosest of all, softly flowing round from behind, in priceless catenary, rush down two broad threefold rows; seem to knot themselves, round a very Queen of Diamonds . . .—*Carlyle.* Critical and Miscellaneous Essays. " The Diamond Necklace."

CAUDAL (kaw/dal) *pertaining to the tail*   C28

> In a dark garden, by a dreadful tree
> The Druid Toms were met. They numbered three,
> Tab Tiger, Demon Black and Ginger Hate.
> Their forms were tense, their eyes were full of fate;
> The horror was that they should sit so still,
> Save for the involuntary caudal thrill.—*Lilliput.* May, 1942.

CENOBITE (see/no-bite) *a monk*   C29

With the south-wester tied under his chin the bosun's face, in the dawn, was that of a cenobite. It was refined, even ascetic.—*H. M. Tomlinson.* All Hands. Ch. xliii. (Heinemann).

CENTRIFUGAL (sen-trif/u-gal) *tending to fly outwards*   C30

I climbed into the rigging, stood on the board, and eagerly scanned that ring of coral reef and bursting breaker, and the blue lagoon which they enclosed. The two islets within began to show plainly—Middle Brooks and Lower Brooks Island, the Directory named them; two low, bush-covered, rolling strips of sand, each with glittering beaches, each perhaps a mile or a mile and a half in length running east and west, and divided by a narrow channel. Over these, innumerable as maggots, there hovered, chattered, screamed, and clanged, millions of twinkling sea-birds; white and black; the black by far the largest. With singular scintillations, this vortex of winged life swayed to and fro in the strong sunshine, whirled continually through itself, and would now and again burst asunder and scatter as wide as the lagoon: so that I was irresistibly reminded of nebular convulsions. A thin cloud overspread the arena of the reef and the adjacent sea—the dust, as I could not but fancy, of earlier explosions. And. a little apart, there was yet another focus of centrifugal and centripetal flight, where, hard by the deafening line of breakers, her sails (all but the tattered topsail) snugly furled down, and the red rag that marks Old England on the seas beating, union down, at the main—the Flying

Scud, the fruit of so many toilers, a recollection in so many lives of men, whose tall spars had been mirrored in the remotest corners of the sea— lay stationary at last and for ever, in the first stage of naval dissolution.— *R. L. Stevenson and Lloyd Osbourne. The Wrecker.* Ch. xiii. (Chatto & Windus).

CEPHALALGIC (sef-al-al/jik) *headache, or remedy for headache*   C31

Administer to each of them lenitives, aperitives, abstersives, corrosives, restringents, palliatives, laxatives, cephalalgics, icterics, apoplegmatics, acoustics, as their several cases required.—*Swift.* Gulliver's Travels. Pt. iii, Ch. vi.

CERULEAN (se-ru/le-an) *sky coloured; blue*   C32

The Moon was shining slobaciously from the star-bespangled sky, while her light irrigated the smooth and shiny sides and wings and backs of the Blue-Bottle-Flies with a peculiar and trivial splendour, while all nature cheerfully responded to the ceruléan and conspicuous circumstances. —*Edward Lear.* The Story of the Four Little Children Who Went Round the World.

. . . when I look back across the years to that cerulean voyage I surrender anew to the drowsy enchantment of it . . .—*Compton Mackenzie.* Gallipoli Memories. Ch. xxi.

CHALICING (chal/i-sing) *scenting*   C33

O Blest unfabled Incense Tree,
That burns in glorious Araby!
With red scent chalicing the air,
Till earth-life grow Elysian there!
—*G. Darley.* Nepenthe. i, 147.

CHAMELEON (ka-me/le-on) *a kind of lizard*   C34

I can add colours to the chameleon,
Change shapes with Proteus for advantages.
— *Shakespeare.* Henry VI. Pt. iii, iii, 2.

CHAMPERTY (cham/per-ti)   C35

Unlawful agreement to pay the cost of maintaining a cause of action for another person; the latter agreeing to pay over either a specified sum or a proportion of any damages awarded.

Maintenance is a similar unlawful agreement without the promise of any reward.

CHANDOS (shan/dos)   C36

CHARYBDIS (ka-rib/dis)   C37

CHEVRON (shev/ron)   C38

A zig-zag mark employed in architecture and heraldry, and
also used as a distinguishing badge of non-commissioned officers.

CHICANERY (shi-kane/er-i) *trickery; disingenuous*   C39
conduct

The weakest part of mankind have this saying commonest in their
mouth. It is the trite consolation administered to the easy dupe, when he
has been tricked out of his money or estate, that the acquisition of it will
do the owner *no good*. But the rogues of this world—the prudenter part
of them, at least—know better; and if the observation had been as true as
it is old, would not have failed by this time to have discovered it. They
have pretty sharp distinctions of the fluctuating and the permanent.
"Lightly come, lightly go," is a proverb, which they can very well afford
to leave, when they leave little else, to the losers. They do not always find
manors, got by rapine or chicanery, insensibly to melt away, as the poets
will have it; or that all gold glides, like thawing snow, from the thief's
hand that grasps it. Church land, alienated to lay uses, was formerly
denounced to have this slippery quality. But some portions of it somehow
always stuck so fast, that the denunciators have been fain to postpone the
prophecy of refundment to a late posterity.—*Charles Lamb*. Last Essays
of Elia. "That Ill-Gotten Gain Never Prospers."

But in the same letter the ambassador thought it necessary to hint to
his master that the diplomatic chicanery which might be useful in other
negotiations would be all thrown away here.—*Macaulay*. History of
England. Ch. xxiii.

CHILDE (child) *the eldest son of a nobleman*   C40

Every knight had after him riding
Three henchmen [each] on him awaiting:—
And every childe ware of leaves grene
A fresh chapelet.
                              —*Chaucer*. Flower and Leaf.
The noble childe, preventing his desire,
Under his club with wary boldnesse went,
And smote him on the knee that never yet was bent.
                    —*Spenser*. The Faerie Queene. vi, 8, xv.

CHOPINE (cho-pene/) *a high shoe*   C41

Your ladyship is nearer heaven than when I saw you last, by the
altitude of a chopine.—*Shakespeare*. Hamlet. ii, 2.

Nor are those short-legged ladies thought less godly, who fly to
chopines.—*Jeremy Taylor*. Artificial Handsomeness. p. 60.

CHRYSOLITE (kris/o-lite) *a precious stone, green and*   C42
translucent

> Such another world,
> Of one entire and perfect chrysolite,
> I'd not have sold her for.
> —*Shakespeare.* Othello. v. 2.
> If metal, part seem'd gold, part silver clear:
> If stone, carbuncle most, or chrysolite.
> —*Milton.* Paradise Lost. iii, 595.

CHRYSOPRASE (kris/o-praze) *an apple-green chalcedony*   C43

Stand for half an hour beside the fall of Schaffhausen, on the north side where the rapids are long, and watch how the vault of water first bends, unbroken, in pure, polished velocity, over the arching rocks at the brow of the cataract, covering them with a dome of crystal twenty feet thick—so swift that its motion is unseen except when a foam globe from above darts over it like a falling star; and how the trees are lighted above it under all their leaves, at the instant that it breaks into foam; and how all the hollows of that foam burn with green fire like so much shattering chrysoprase.—*John Ruskin.* Modern Painters. Vol. i (14). "The Wonders of Water."

. . . Kuo, like a column of apple-green chrysoprase, stood waiting for them . . . Miss Min, a little column of ‚flaming porphyry, stood in the background.—*Eric Linklater.* Juan in China. (Jonathan Cape).

CICERONE (sis-a-ro/ne) *a guide*   C44

He was disappointed—rather amazed; but Madame Colonna having sent for him to introduce her to some of the scenes and details of Eton life, his vexation was soon absorbed in the pride of acting in the face of his companions as the cavalier of a beautiful lady, and becoming the cicerone of the most brilliant party that had attended Montem.—*Disraeli.* Coningsby. Bk. i, Ch. ii.

CINNABAR (sin/a-bar) *vermilion*   C45

Woody mountains hemmed the place all round; the barrier to the east was particularly steep and leafy, the lower parts of it, along the sea, falling in sheer cliffs streaked with cinnabar.—*R. L. Stevenson.* The Beach of Falesá. Ch. iv. (Heinemann).

. . . the fruitful clay-pit, which had yielded, through many blendings and experimental bakings, bricks of a lovely soft pale rose, making his mission a symphony in cinnabar.—*A. J. Cronin.* The Keys of the Kingdom. Ch. iv (4). (Gollancz).

CINQUE-SPOTTED (sink-spot/ed) *with five spots*   C46

> On her left breast
> A mole; cinque-spotted, like the crimson drops
> I' th' bottom of a cowslip.
> —*Shakespeare.* Cymbeline. ii, 2.

CIRCUMAMBIENT (ser-kum-am/bi-ent) *surrounding* C47

. . . which of us but remembers, as one of the sunny spots in his existence, the day when he opened these airy volumes, fascinating him by a true natural magic! It was as if the curtains of the past were drawn aside, and we looked mysteriously into a kindred country, where dwelt our Fathers; inexpressibly dear to us, but which had seemed forever hidden from our eyes. For the dead night had engulfed it; all was gone, vanished as if it had not been. Nevertheless, wondrously given back to us, there once more it lay; all bright, lucid, blooming; a little island of Creation amid the circumambient Void.—*Carlyle.* Critical and Miscellaneous Essays. " Boswell's Life of Johnson."

CIRCUMVALLATION (ser-kum-val-ay/shun) C48

a fortification; an encirclement

A few hours after Boufflers had entered the place the besieging forces closed round it on every side; and the lines of circumvallation were rapidly formed.—*Macaulay.* History of England. Ch. xxi.

For there is something in marriage so natural and inviting, that the step has an air of great simplicity and ease; it offers to bury for ever many aching preoccupations; it is to afford us unfailing and familiar company through life; it opens up a smiling prospect of the blest and passive kind of love, rather than the blessing and active; it is approached not only through the delights of courtship, but by a public performance and repeated legal signatures. A man naturally thinks it will go hard with him if he cannot be good and fortunate and happy within such august circumvallations.—*R. L. Stevenson.* Virginibus Puerisque. (Chatto & Windus).

Now the chief circumstance in the life of Lady Harman was Sir Isaac. Indeed, as she grew to a clear consciousness of herself and her position, it seemed to her he was not so much a circumstance as a circumvallation. There wasn't a direction in which she could turn without immediately running up against him.—*H. G. Wells.* The Wife of Sir Isaac Harman. Ch. v. (Collins).

CITRINE (sit/rine) *lemon coloured* C49
C.f. CAIN-COLOURED.

CLANRICARDE (klan-rik/ard) C50

CLEMENT (klem/ent) *tender; compassionate* C51

" . . . you are clearly the most clement and skilful dentist in the world."—*Eric Linklater.* God Likes Them Plain. " His Majesty The Dentist." (Jonathan Cape).

CLERISY (kler/i-si) *the intelligentsia* C52

The clerisy of a nation, that is, its learned men, whether poets, or philosophers, or scholars, are these points of relative rest. There could be no order, no harmony of the whole, without them.—*Coleridge.* Table Talk.

CLOTTED NONSENSE (klot/id non/sens) *nonsense with*   C53
    a distinguishing epithet

Another Great Victorianism. The expression has a weight and size that make it convenient to hurl at the head of an offender. While it is effective as a missile it is yet not heavy enough to inflict a serious injury.

CLOUD-ECLIPSED (kloud e-klip/zd) *hidden by clouds*   C54

    But durst not ask of her audaciously
    Why her two suns were cloud-eclipsed so
    Nor why her fair cheeks over-wash'd with woe.
            —*Shakespeare*. The Rape of Lucrece.

CODDAM (kod/am)   C55

Perhaps the nadir of all sport. A coin or other small article is held in the hand. Another individual guesses which hand it is in.

COEVAL (ko-e/val) *(1) of the same age or generation;*   C56
    (2) existing at the same time

COIFFEUR (kwa-fer/) *hairdresser*   C57

COLLYRIUM (ko-lir/i-um) *eye-salve*   C58

There are surely few that have belief to swallow or hope enough to experiment, the collyrium of Albertus, which promiseth a strange effect, and such as theories would count inestimable, that is to make one see in the dark; yet thus much, according unto his receipt, will the right eye of an hedge-hog, boiled in oil, and preserved in a brazen vessel, effect. —*Sir Thomas Browne*. Vulgar Errors. 28.

COLORATURA (kul-er-a-toor/a) *a singer who adds trills,*   C59
    etc. to give brilliance to the music

It is a moot point whether the coloratura singer or the fashionable fiddler is the bigger fool. To be compelled to decide between the broken melodies of Vieuxtemps and Wieniawski and the unbroken insipidity of Shadow Song and Mad Scena is like having to choose between the rescue of wife or mother. There *is* no choice.—*James Agate* Playgoing. (i). (Jarrolds).

COMMINUTE (kom/i-nute) *reduce to minute particles*   C60

Parchments, skins and cloth drink in liquors, though themselves be intire bodies, and not comminuted, as sand and ashes.—*Bacon.* Natural and Experimental History.

COMMONALTY (kom/un-al-ti) *the common people*   C61

There is in every state, as we know, two portions of subjects, the nobles and the commonalty.—*Bacon.* Essays. xvi.

COMPLIN (kom/plin) *last Catholic daily service*   C62

If a man were but of a day's life, it is well if he lasts till even song, and then says his compline an hour before the time.—*Jeremy Taylor.* Holy Living.

CONCATENATION (kon-kat-e-nay/shun) *connexion;*   C63
                        series of ideas, events, etc.

Seek the consonancy and concatenation of truth.—*Ben Jonson.* Discoveries.

Meanes are not meanes, but in their concatenation, as they depend, and are chained together.—*Donne.* Devotions.

CONCUPISCENCE (con-ku/pi-sens) *excessive greed or*   C64
                        desire

The touch of these costly crystals sent a shiver of emotion through the man's stalwart frame; his face was transfigured, and his eyes shone with concupiscence; indeed it seemed as if he luxuriously prolonged his occupation, and dallied with every diamond that he handled.—*R. L. Stevenson.* New Arabian Nights. " The Rajah's Diamond." (Chatto & Windus).

CONDIGN (kon-dine/) *deserved; suitable; merited*   C65

GLOUCESTER :   Unless it were a bloody murderer,
                Or foul felonious thief that fleeced poor passengers,
                I never gave them condign punishment.
                        —*Shakespeare.* Henry VI. Pt. ii, 3, i.

Boldly she bid the Goddesse downe descend,
And let her selfe into that Ivory throne;
For she her selfe more worthy thereof wend,
And better able it to guide alone;
Whether to men, whose falls she did bemone,
Or unto Gods, whose state she did maligne,
Or to th' infernall Powers her need give lone
Of her faire light and bounty most benigne,
Her selfe of all that rule she deemed most condigne.
                        —*Spenser.* The Faerie Queene. vi, 6, xi.

CONGENER (kon/jen-er) *thing (person or animal) of the same kind* C66

Might not Canary birds be naturalized to this climate, provided their eggs were put, in the spring, into the nests of some of their congeners, as goldfinches, greenfinches, etc.? Before winter perhaps they might be hardened and able to shift for themselves.—*White.* Natural History of Selborne. Letter xii to Thomas Pennant.

CONGERIES† C67

. . . his cab hurried away from the unspeakable hideousness of Euston Station and turned into that congeries of tombstone-makers' yards and unsavoury lodging-houses which constitutes the Euston Road . . .—*Ian Hay.* A Knight on Wheels. Ch. xvi. (Hodder & Stoughton).

CONGLOBULATE (kon-glob/u-late) *to cluster together in a round mass* C68

He seemed pleased to talk of natural philosophy. "That woodcocks, (said he) fly over the northern countries is proved, because they have been observed at sea. Swallows certainly sleep all the winter. A number of them conglobulate together, by flying round and round, and then all in a heap throw themselves under water, and lye in the bed of a river."—*James Boswell.* Life of Johnson. A.D. 1768. Ætat. 59.

This dictum of Johnson's has been criticized by that excellent writer Mr. C. E. Vulliamy in " Ursa Major " (a study of Dr. Johnson). He says: " Although Johnson was inordinate in his mockery of the credulous and the ignorant, he himself believed in many absurdities, and in certain matters allowed his credulity to overcome his reason. At Oxford in 1768, after he had been expatiating on the supposed advantages of that place as a seat of learning, he incautiously ventured upon the subject of ' natural philosophy ' . . ." Mr. Vulliamy then proceeds to quote from the passage reproduced above. While it is clear that Johnson's statement is incorrect, it should be remembered that his error was by no means an absurdity in his own generation, and for proof of this the reader is referred to Gilbert White's 12th letter to Pennant, the relevant portion of which is quoted above under the word AIT. It appears from this letter, which is dated 4th November 1767, that White would not have opposed Johnson's view, and might even have shared it.

CONJURATION (kon-joor-ay/shun) *solemn entreaty; incantation* C69

What drugs, what charms,
What conjuration, and what mighty magick,
For such proceeding I am charg'd withal,
I won his daughter with.—*Shakespeare.* Othello. i, 3.

CONNOTATIVE (kon-no/ta-tive) *implying; denoting*   C70
(*indirectly*)

Cardinal Newman, proposing the idea of a University to the Roman Catholics of Dublin, lamented that the English language had not, like the Greek, " Some definite words to express, simply and generally, intellectual proficiency or perfection, such as ' health,' as used with reference to the animal frame, and ' virtue,' with reference to our moral nature." Well, it is a reproach to us that we do not possess the term : and perhaps again a reproach to us that our attempts at it—the world " culture " for instance —have been apt to take on some soil of controversy, some connotative damage from over-preaching on the one hand and impatience on the other. —*Sir Arthur Quiller-Couch.*   The Art of Writing.   Lecture i.

CONSTELLATED (kon/stel-ay-ted) *illuminated with*   C71
many lights, as with stars

The familiar nocturnal pageant of the West Riding was all round us. This is the region of mountaineering trams; you see them far away at night, climbing the hills, like luminous beetles. You will go through mile after mile of streets, climbing all the time, and then suddenly arrive at a stretch of open country that seems nearly as wild and cold as Greenland. From such heights you look across at hills that are constellated and twinking with street lamps.—*J. B. Priestley.*   English Journey.   Ch. vi (1). (Heinemann and Gollancz).

CONSUMMATE (kon/su-mate) (*verb*) *to complete*   C72

Yourself, myself, and other lords,
If you think meet, this afternoon will post
To consummate this business happily.
                    —*Shakespeare.*   King John.   v, 7.

There shall we consummate our spousal rites.—Titus Andronicus. ii, 2.

The person was cunning enough to begin the deceit in the weaker, and the weaker sufficient to consummate the fraud in the stronger.—*Sir Thomas Browne.*   Vulgar Errors.

CONSUMMATE (kon-sum/at) (*adjective*) *complete;*   C73
perfect

I do but stay till your marriage be consummate.
                    —*Shakespeare.*   Much Ado about Nothing.   iii. ii.

Earth, in her rich attire
Consummate, lovely smil'd.
                    —*Milton.*   Paradise Lost.   vii, 601.

CONTUMACY (kon/tu-ma-si) *disobedience*   C74

Such acts
Of contumacy will provoke the Highest
To make death in us live.
                    —*Milton.*   Paradise Lost.   x, 1026.

CONURBATION (kon-ur-bay/shun) *a large town or a*   C75
         group of contiguous towns

THE MUNICIPAL ELECTIONS
Of the Conservatives who stood for election 74 per cent. were successful compared with 28 per cent. of the Socialists. With the seats went
control of 23 borough councils in every part of England. The defection
of the great industrial conurbations of Lancashire from the Socialist cause
and the swing to the right in Birmingham were noteworthy.—*Evening
Standard* editorial, 3rd November, 1947.

CORBEL (kor/bel) *stone or timber projection from a wall*   C76

      The corbels that ribbed each massive aisle,
      Were a fleur-de-lis or a quatre-feuille.
         —*Sir Walter Scott.* The Lay of the Last Minstrel.

CORNUCOPIA (kawr-nu-ko/pi-a) *horn of plenty*   C77

     Ten streets give on to the Piazza, and at either end of its ellipse the
water of sumptuous fountains ceaselessly blows aloft and falls. Commerce,
in that to the north of the Exchange holds up her cornucopia, and from
the midst of its grapes and apples the master jet leaps up . . .—*Aldous
Huxley.* Antic Hay. Ch. xi. (Chatto & Windus).

CORVINE (kor/vin) *like a crow*   C78

     " Who exactly does run that Works?" asked Stephen, encouraged at
last to put into words a question that had occupied his mind for some
while past. " Mr. Hopkin or Alec Bone?"
     Mr. Cuffings emitted his corvine laugh.—*Hugh McGraw.* The Boon
Companions. Ch. xii. (Heinemann).

COSMOGONY* (kos-mog/o-ni) *theory of the origin of*   C79
         the universe

     The world is in its dotage, and yet the cosmogony or creation of the
world has puzzled philosophers of all ages.—*Oliver Goldsmith.* The Vicar
of Wakefield. Ch. xiv.

COSMOGRAPHY (kos-mog/ra-fi) *description or mapping*   C80
         of universe or earth

     I never travelled but in map or card, in which mine unconfined
thoughts have freely expatiated, as having ever been especially delighted
with the study of cosmography.—*Burton.* Anatomy of Melancholy.

CREEPING JESUS   C81

     A modern term of inexact meaning. A sly, hypocritical
person; a twirp. A person with soft manners and oleaginous
speech who is suspected of turpitude by reason of his outward
correctness; a spoil-sport.

CREPUSCULAR (kre-pus/ku-lar) *dark or half-lit*   C82

. . . crepuscular depths of personality.—*William James.* The Will to Believe.

CUBAN HEEL *a high straight heel without any curves*   C83
Cf. CHOPINE.

CULMEN (kul/men) *height*   C84

Burke is here at the culmen of a long sustained argument, and his language has soared with it, as his way was—logic and emotion lifting him together as upon two balanced majestic wings.—*Sir Arthur Quiller-Couch.* The Art of Writing. Lecture ii.

CURACAO (ku-ra-so/) *a liqueur*   C85

In England, for example, this cordial has been well known for at least three centuries, but more especially since King George IV set the fashion for it by defying his gout and drinking large quantities of curaçao every night after dinner, in the conditions of tropical heat within doors which he always favoured, under the carved palm-leaves and among the dragons and twisting serpents of the Royal Pavilion at Brighton.—*Osbert Sitwell.* Sing High! Sing Low! "Still Life" (2). (Macmillan).

CYNOSURE†   C86

If the most exquisite orchestral music could be continued without a pause for a series of years, and children brought up and educated in the room in which it was perpetually resounding, I believe their enjoyment of music, or understanding of it, would be very small. And an accurately parallel effect seems to be produced upon the powers of contemplation, by the redundant and ceaseless loveliness of the high mountain districts. The faculties are paralyzed by the abundance, and cease, as we before noticed of the imagination, to be capable of excitement, except by other subjects of interest than those which present themselves to the eye. So that it is, in reality, better for mankind that the forms of their common landscape should offer no violent stimulus to the emotions—that the gentle upland, browned by the bending furrows of the plough, and the fresh sweep of the chalk down, and the narrow winding of the copse-clad dingle, should be more frequent scenes of human life than the Arcadias of cloud-capped mountain or luxuriant vale; and that, while humbler (though always infinite) sources of interest are given to each of us around the homes to which we are restrained for the greater part of our lives, these mightier and stranger glories should become the objects of adventure —at once the cynosures of the fancies of childhood, and themes of the happy memory, and the winter's tale of age.—*John Ruskin.* Modern Painters. Vol. iv. "Man and the Mountains."

DAEDAL

DAGUERREOTYPE

DALMATIC

DALZIEL

DÉBUT

DECADE

DECADENT

DECAHEDRON

DE CRESPIGNY

DEFERVESCENCE

DELIQUESCE

DELIQUIUM

DÉMENTI

DEMONIAC

DEMOTIC

DENIGRATE

DÉNOUEMENT

DERACINATE

DESCARTES

DESCENSION

DÉTENTE

DEVOIR

DEWBESPRENT

DEWFALL

DIABLERIE

DIABOLISM

DIÆRESIS

DIAGNOSTIC

DIALECTIC

DIALYSIS

DIAPASON

DIAPEPHRADIZING

DIDACTIC

DIES IRÆ

DIFFLUENT

DIGAMMA

DIONYSIAC

DIORAMA

DIOSCURI

DISANCHOR

DISCANDY

DISEMBOGUE

DISHABILLE

DISPITEOUS

DISSONANT

DITHYRAMB

DIURNAL

DON JUAN

DONNE

DON QUIXOTE

DORP

DOVE-EYED

DOWN PLATFORM

DUBIETY

DUDINE

DÜRERESQUE

DAEDAL (dee/dal) *of mysterious complexity or skill*   **D**

      Language is a perpetual Orphic song,
      Which rules with Dædal harmony a throng
      Of thoughts and forms . . .
              —*Shelley*. Prometheus. iv, 400.

DAGUERREOTYPE (da-ger/ro-tipe) *primitive photograph* **D2**

    Alexander von Humboldt, the German scientist and geographer, in one of his letters to his friend Fox Talbot wrote: " Daguerre is my Chimborasso!"—*Lucia Moholy*. A Hundred Years of Photography. (Penguin).

DALMATIC (dal-mat/ik) *royal or ecclesiastical vestment*   **D3**

    BLOOM (*in dalmatic and purple mantle, to the bishop of Down and Connor, with dignity*): Thanks, somewhat eminent sir.—*James Joyce*. Ulysses.

DALZIEL (dee-el/)   **D4**

DÉBUT (de-bu/) *first appearance*   **D5**

      Compare: débutant (Masc.); débutante (Fem.).

DECADE (dek/ade) *a period of 10 years; a group of 10*   **D6**

DECADENT (dek/a-dent) *growing worse*   **D7**

    But of those decadent ages in which no ideal either grows or blossoms? When belief and loyalty have passed away, and only the cant and false echo of them remain; and all solemnity has become pageantry; and the creed of persons in authority has become one of two things: an imbecility of a Machiavelism? Alas, of these ages World-History can take no notice.—*Carlyle*. The French Revolution. Pt. i, Bk. i, Ch. ii.

DECAHEDRON (dek-a-hee/dron) *a solid figure with 10 sides* **D8**

DE CRESPIGNY (dekrep/ini)   **D9**

DEFERVESCENCE (de-fer-ves/ens) *a cooling down*   **D10**

    Most commonly young beginners are zealous and high, and not so easily tempted to a recession, till after a long time by a revolution of affections, they are abated by a deferverscency in holy actions.—*Jeremy Taylor*. Great Exemplar of Sanctity and Holy Life.

DELIQUESCE (de-li-kwes/) *liquify; melt away* D11

The almost cataclysmal development of new machinery, the discovery of new materials, and the appearance of new social possibilities through the organised pursuit of material science has given enormous and unprecedented facilities to the spirit of innovation. The old local order has been broken up or is now being broken up all over the earth, and everywhere societies deliquesce, everywhere men are afloat amidst the wreckage of their flooded conventions, and still tremendously unaware of the thing that has happened.—*H. G. Wells.* A Modern Utopia. Ch. ii.

DELIQUIUM (de-lik/wi-um) *faintness; fainting* D12

If he be locked in a close room, he is afraid of being stifled for want of air; and carries bisket, aqua vitæ, or some strong waters about him, for fear of deliquiums of being sick.—*Burton.* Anatomy of Melancholy.

DÉMENTI (day-mahn/ti) *official denial of rumour* D13

DEMONIAC (de-mo/ni-ak) *person possessed with a devil* D14

. . . raving and blaspheming incessantly, like a demoniac . . .— *Macaulay.* History of England.

> . . . he, all unarm'd
> Shall chase thee with the terror of his voice
> From thy Demoniak holds, possession foul,
> Thee and thy Legions, yelling they shall flye . . .
> —*Milton.* Paradise Regained. iv, 626.

FLEEMING JENKIN

His manner is dry, brisk and pertinacious, and the choice of words not much. The point about him is his extraordinary readiness and spirit. You can propound nothing but he has either a theory about it readymade, or will have one instantly on the stocks, and proceed to lay its timbers and launch it in your presence. " Let me see," he will say. " Give me a moment. I *should* have some theory for that." A blither spectacle than the vigour with which he sets about the task, it were hard to fancy. He is possessed by a demoniac energy, welding the elements for his life, and bending ideas, as an athlete bends a horse-shoe, with a visible and lively effort.—*R. L. Stevenson.* Talk & Talkers. (i) (Chatto & Windus).

DEMOTIC (de-mot/ik) *popular* D15

In Egyptian writing the demotic or enchorial system is a corruption of the heiratic, which is a degeneration of the heiroglyphic, which is but a modification of the pictorial.—*Farrar.* Chapters on Language. Ch. xiii.

> Twit twit twit
> Jug jug jug jug jug jug
> So rudely forc'd.
> Tereu
> Unreal City.
> Under the brown fog of a winter noon

Mr. Eugenides, the Smyrna merchant
Unshaven, with a pocket full of currants
C.i.f. London: documents at sight,
Asked me in demotic French
To luncheon at the Cannon Street Hotel
Followed by a weekend at the Metropole.
—*T. S. Eliot.* The Fire Sermon, from " The Waste Land."

(Faber & Faber).

DENIGRATE (den/i-grate) *blacken* D16

By suffering some impression from fire, bodies are casually or arti-
ficially denigrated in their natural complexion: thus are charcoals made
black by an infection of their own suffitus.—*Sir Thomas Browne.* Vulgar
Errors.

BATH CONTROL

Opinions are apt to come round in cycles, and it sometimes happens
that those which in one generation belonged to established age are later
held by insurgent youth. It was, roughly speaking, in the early eighteen-
thirties that Pendennis and Warrington, not long down from St. Boniface,
set up together in Temple Chambers, and old Mr. Grump of the Norfolk
Circuit, disturbed by the roaring of their shower baths, cursed the practice
as " an absurd, new-fangled, dandified folly." Now some 115 years later
the converse is seen: the almost venerable LEADER of the OPPOSITION
is the champion of the bath, while the relatively juvenile MINISTER of
FUEL and POWER denigrates it.—" *The Times,*" 31st October, 1947.

An extract from the relevant speech by the Leader of the Opposition,
Mr. Winston Churchill, is subjoined. (*See Parliamentary Debates, House
of Commons,* 28*th October,* 1947, col. 711):

I will conclude my strictures in the social and domestic field—
I have a large field to cover and will endeavour to distribute them
evenly—by reading the latest economies proposed by the new Minister
of Fuel and Power, who represents, I believe, Socialist intellectualism
and the old school tie. He advocated—according to what I read in
the public Press, and I have made some enquiries about its authenticity
—he advocated a policy of fewer baths. I really must read the words
which he is reported to have used, as I think they constitute almost
a record :

" Personally, I have never had a great many baths myself, and I
can assure those who are in the habit of having a great many that it
does not make a great difference to their health if they have less. As
for your appearance "—

said this representative of His Majesty's Government—

" most of that is underneath and nobody sees it."

When Ministers of the Crown speak like this on behalf of His Majesty's
Government, the Prime Minister and his friends have no need to
wonder why they are getting increasingly into bad odour. I had even
asked myself, when meditating upon these points whether you, Mr.
Speaker, would admit the word " lousy " as a Parliamentary expression
in referring to the Administration, provided, of course, it was not
intended in a contemptuous sense but purely as one of factual
narration.

"Come, come," said Mr. Porteous. "I do a little teaching myself; I must stand up for the profession."

Gumbril Senior let go his beard and brushed back the hair that the wind of his own vehemence had brought tumbling into his eyes. "I don't denigrate the profession," hc said. "Not at all. It would be an excellent profession if every one who went into it were as much interested in teaching as you are in your job, Porteous, or I in mine. It's these un-decided creatures like Theodore, who ruin it by drifting in. Until all teachers are geniuses and enthusiasts, nobody will learn anything, except what they teach themselves."—*Aldous Huxley.* Antic Hay. Ch. ii. (Chatto & Windus).

DÉNOUEMENT (day-noo/mahn) *explanation; unravelling*   D17

DERACINATE (de-ras/i-nate) *to uproot*   D18
    BURGUNDY: Her vine, the merry cheerer of the heart,
               Unpruned dies; her hedges even-pleach'd,
               Like prisoners wildly overgrown with hair,
               Put forth disorder'd twigs; her fallow leas
               The darnel, hemlock and rank fumitory
               Doth root upon, while that the coulter rusts
               That should deracinate such savagery;
                   —*Shakespeare.* Henry V. Act v, Sc. ii.

DESCARTES (day-kart/)   D19

DESCENSION (de-sen/shun) *act of descending; degradation* D20
        From a god to a bull? A heavy descension!
        It was Jove's case. From a prince to a 'prentice?
        A low transformation! that shall be mine.
              —*Shakespeare.* Henry IV. Pt. II, ii, 2.

DÉTENTE (day-tant/) *relaxation of international tension* D21

DEVOIR (dev-wahr/) *duty; act of civility*   D22
        Madam, if any service or devoir
    Of a poor errant knight may right your wrongs,
    Command it.
    —*Beaumont and Fletcher.* The Knight of the Burning Pestle.

DEWBESPRENT (du/be-sprent) *sprinkled with dew*   D23
        This evening late by then the chewing flocks
    Had ta'n their supper on the savoury Herb
    Of Knot-grass dew-besprent and were in fold,
    I sate me down to watch upon a bank
    With Ivy canopied, and interwove
    With flaunting Hony-suckle, and began
    Wrapt in a pleasing fit of melancholy
    To meditate upon my rural minstrelsie.
    Till fancy had her fill, but ere a close
    The wonted roar was up amidst the Woods,
    And fill'd the Air with barbarous dissonance.
              —*Milton.* Comus.

DEWFALL (du/fawl) *the time when dew falls*   D24

Expanding while the dew-fall flows.—*Moore*. Lalla Rookh.

DIABLERIE (di-ab/ler-i) *occult or evil traits or associations*   D25

Ever since I first listened to McTaggart at Cambridge I have been either fascinated or amused by metaphysics . . . . Ever since there has been to me about all metaphysics a suggestion of McTaggart's peculiar atmosphere of childlike diablerie.—*J. B. Priestley*. Rain Upon Godshill. Ch. xiv. (Heinemann).

DIABOLISM (di-ab/o-lizm) *evil conduct; worship of evil*   D26

While thou so hotly disclaimest the devil, be not guilty of diabolism. —*Sir Thomas Browne*. Christian Morals. i, 16.

Aubrey Beardsley, although he died a saint, represents a diabolonian incident in British art.—*Holbrook Jackson*. The Eighteen Nineties. Ch. v. (Jonathan Cape).

Mr. Boldero's bird-like eyes twinkled very brightly. " We shall get them," he repeated, and he laughed a happy little laugh, full of such a childlike diabolism, such an innocent gay malignity that it seemed as though a little leprechaun had suddenly taken the financier's place in Gumbril's best arm-chair.—*Aldous Huxley*. Antic Hay. Ch. x. (Chatto & Windus).

DIÆRESIS (di-er/e-sis)   D27

Two dots placed over a vowel indicating that the vowel is to be pronounced separately.

DIAGNOSTIC* (di-ag-nos/tik) *a distinguishing mark*   D28

Sir Thomas Millington, who was physician in ordinary to the King, thought that she [Queen Mary] had the measles. But Radcliffe, who, with coarse manners and little book learning, had raised himself to the first practice in London chiefly by his rare skill in diagnostics, uttered the more alarming words, small pox.—*Macaulay*. History of England. Ch. xx.

SAN FRANCISCO

The street for which we were now bound took its rise among blowing sands, somewhere in view of the Lone Mountain Cemetery; ran for a term across that rather windy Olympus of Nob Hill, or perhaps just skirted its frontier; passed almost immediately after through a stage of little houses, rather impudently painted, and offering to the eye of the observer this diagnostic peculiarity, that the huge brass plates upon the small and highly-coloured doors bore only the first names of ladies—Nora or Lily or Florence; traversed China Town, where it was doubtless undermined with opium cellars, and its blocks pierced, after the similitude of rabbit-warrens, with a hundred doors and passages and galleries.—*R. L. Stevenson and Lloyd Osbourne*. The Wrecker. Ch. x.

DIALECTIC (di-a-lek/tik) *logical argument; reasoning*   D29

The essence . . . of " dialectic " in all its forms, as its very name denotes, is dialogue, the habit of seeking truth by means of question and answer, primarily with one's self.—*Walter Pater*. The Doctrine of Plato. Lecture vii from " Plato and Platonism." (Macmillan).

DIALYSIS (di-al/i-sis) *separation; diæresis*   D30

But the fact of chief interest to us here, is that the relatively small-atomed crystalloids have immensely greater diffusive power than the relatively large-atomed colloids. Among the crystalloids themselves, there are marked differences of diffusibility; and among the colloids themselves there are parallel differences, though less marked ones. But these differences are small compared with that between the diffusibility of the crystalloids as a class, and the diffusibility of the colloids as a class. Hydrochloric acid is seven times as diffusible as sulphate of magnesia; but it is fifty times as diffusible as albumen, and a hundred times as diffusible as camomel. These differences of diffusibility manifest themselves with nearly equal distinctness, when a permeable septum is placed between the solution and the water. And the result is, that when a solution contains substances of different diffusibilities, the process of dialysis, as Professor Graham calls it, becomes a means of separating the mixed substances: especially when such mixed substances are partly crystalloids and partly colloids.—*Herbert Spencer*. Data of Biology.

DIAPASON†   D31

That we on earth, with undiscording voice,
May rightly answer that melodious noise;
As once we did, till disproportion'd sin
Jarr'd against Nature's chime, and with harsh din
Broke the fair musick that all creatures made
To their great Lord, whose love their motion sway'd
In perfect diapason, whilst they stood
In first obedience, and their state of good.
—*Milton*. Ode at a Solemn Musick. (Blest pair of Syrens).

DIAPEPHRADIZING (di-a-pep/a-di-sing) *talking with the fingers*   D32

There my guide led me into a large room, where a great many peasants were eating soup with macaroni in it, and some few, meat. But I was too exhausted to eat meat, so I supped up my broth and then began diapephradizing on my fingers to show the great innkeeper what I wanted. —*Hilaire Belloc*. The Path to Rome. (Allen & Unwin).

DIDACTIC (di-dak/tik) *instructive; dogmatic*   D33

We shall not need here to describe, out of their didactical writings, what kind of prayers, and what causes of confidence they teach towards the Blessed Virgin Mary and all Saints.—*Jeremy Taylor*. Dissuasive against Popery. Ch. ii, s. 9.

[Hogarth's] persons, in many instances, seem too much taken away from their proper indifference to effect, and to be made too much of conscious agents and joint contributors. He " o'er-informs his tenements." His very goods and chattels are didactic.—*Leigh Hunt.* Essays. "On Washerwomen."

BERNARD SHAW

. . . mere " brilliance," critical or otherwise, was rarely for him an end in itself, as was the wit of Oscar Wilde and Max Beerbohm. His cleverness subserved a creative end, an end which looked forward towards a new and resplendent civilisation. It was the sharp edge of the sword of purpose. He did not scruple to enlist the forces of art in his service, and his plays, therefore, are invariably didactic. . . —*Holbrook Jackson.* The Eighteen Nineties. Ch. xiv. (Jonathan Cape).

DIES IRÆ (di/eze i/re) *day of reckoning* D34

The main controlling influence was exerted by Mr. Bevan, who stood in much the same relation to his Estimators as De Treville to his Musketeers. They abused him freely and filthily among themselves, but woe betide the incautious outsider who should venture a word of criticism. And Mr. Bevan, for his part, stood firmly by his men on those *dies iræ* when lightning flashed from the brows of the august Mr. North and the sackcloth and ashes of repenting estimators littered the carpet in the Managing Director's office.—*Hugh P. McGraw.* Rude Society. Ch. iv. (Heinemann).

DIFFLUENT (dif/lu-ent) (1) *dissolving;* (2) *flowing away* D35

Ice is water congealed by the frigidity of the air, whereby it acquireth no new form; but rather a consistence or determination of its diffluency. —*Sir Thomas Browne.* Vulgar Errors.

DIGAMMA (di-gam/a) *a letter of the early Greek alphabet* D36
Represented by the figure *F*.

> Towering o'er your alphabet like Saul,
> Stands our digamma, and o'ertops them all.
> —*Pope.* Dunciad.

DIONYSIAC (di-o-niz/i-ak) *intoxicating; relating to* D37
strong drink

THE " KING WILLIAM IV "

. . . its long periods of idleness seemed to have plunged the upstairs dining-room into a state of dejection which it was determined to communicate to any one who entered it . . . Grimmest and gauntest of all by night, when the row of paraffin lamps seemed to illuminate themselves and nothing else, it exercised a most powerful dionysiac influence on the benevolent societies, who drank deeply in their efforts to shake off the surrounding gloom . . .—*Denis Mackail.* The Flower Show. (Heinemann).

DIORAMA (di-o-rah/ma) *a changing scene*   D38
THE STYLE OF LORD MACAULAY
The style of Macaulay . . . is a diorama of political pictures. You seem to begin with a brilliant picture,—its colours are distinct, its lines are firm; on a sudden it changes, at first gradually, you can scarcely tell how or in what, but unmistakably,—a slightly different picture is before you, then the second vision seems to change,—it too is another and yet the same; then the third shines forth and fades; and so without end.—*Walter Bagehot*. Essays. " Thomas Babington Macaulay."

DIOSCURI (di-os-ku/ri) *Castor and Pollux*   D39
At other times the Dioscuri might occupy themselves in Mending the Radiator or Having a Look at the Kettle. The electric radiator, an ancient and battle-scarred relic, which was kicked over on an average twice a day, used for boiling eggs for Thursday's lunch and making toast for afternoon tea, had long since decided to rebel against its lot.—*Hugh P. McGraw*. Rude Society. Ch. iv. (Heinemann).

DISANCHOR (dis-ang/kor) *to leave*   D40

DISCANDY (dis-kan/di) *to dissolve*   D41
> The hearts
> That spaniel'd me at heels, to whom I gave
> Their wishes, do discandy, melt their sweets
> On blossoming Cæsar.
> —*Shakespeare*. Antony and Cleopatra. iv, 10.

DISEMBOGUE (dis-em-bogue/) *to come forth; to flow out*   D42
> If I get in adoors, not the power o' th' country,
> Nor all my aunt's curse shall disembogue me.
> —*Beaumont and Fletcher*. The Little Thief.

DISHABILLE (dis-a-beal/) *a negligent or incomplete*   D43
state of dress
A woman who would preserve a lover's respect to her person, will be careful of her appearance before him when in dishabille.—*Richardson*. Clarissa.

The wife at last made her appearance, at once a slattern and a coquette . . . . She made twenty apologies for being seen in such an odious dishabille.—*Oliver Goldsmith*. Essays. 11.

The lodgers of each inn form a distinct society, that eat together; and there is a commodious public room, where they breakfast in dishabille, at separate tables, from eight o'clock till eleven, as they chance or choose to come in. Here also they drink tea in the afternoon, and play at cards or dance in the evening.—*Smollett*. Humphrey Clinker.

DISPITEOUS (dis-pit/e-us) *pitiless*   D44

Spurring so hot with rage dispiteous.
—*Spenser.* The Faerie Queene.

DISSONANT (dis/o-nant) *discordant*   D45

You are too harsh, too dissonant;
There's no true musick in your words, my lord.
—*Beaumont and Fletcher.* The Woman-Hater.

Questionless this was a hard-heartedness of divorcing, worse than that in the Jews, which they say extorted the allowance from Moses, and is utterly dissonant from all the doctrine of our Saviour.—*Milton.* Doctrine and Discipline of Divorce.

DITHYRAMB (dith/i-ram) *wild or rambling speech*   D46
or song

The words lack the authentic note of the greatest English poetry, but they had a dithyrambic inspiration for youth and it is sad they are now no longer sung.—*Compton Mackenzie.* The Windsor Tapestry. (Chatto & Windus).

DIURNAL (di-urn/al) *constituting a day; daily; in or*   D47
of the day; occupying a day

JOHNSON ON AVIATION

You . . . will easily conceive with what pleasure a philosopher, furnished with wings and hovering in the sky, would see the earth and all its inhabitants rolling beneath him, and presenting to him successively by its diurnal motion, all the countries within the same parallel. How must it amuse the pendent spectator to see the moving scene of land and ocean, cities and deserts; to survey with equal security the marts of trade and the fields of battle.—*Dr. Johnson.* Rasselas.

It was then the height of the season and the summer; the weather was serene and cloudless; and as he paced under the blinded houses and along the vacant streets, the chill of the dawn had fled, and some of the warmth and all the brightness of the July day already shone upon the city. He walked at first in a profound abstraction, bitterly reviewing and repenting his performances at whist; but as he advanced into the labyrinth of the south-west, his ear was gradually mastered by the silence. Street after street looked down upon his solitary figure, house after house echoed upon his passage with a ghostly jar, shop after shop displayed its shuttered front and its commercial legend; and meanwhile he steered his course, under day's effulgent dome and through this encampment of diurnal sleepers, lonely as a ship.—*R. L. Stevenson.* The Dynamiter. " The Squire of Dames." (Heinemann).

DON JUAN ((1) don joo/an; (2) doan huan)   D48

The name can be pronounced straightforwardly don joo/an. If, however, the second, or Spanish pronunciation is preferred, the breathed *huan,* then the full name must be given as *doan* huan and not don huan.

DONNE (dun)   D49

DON QUIXOTE (don kwik/set; done kwik/sote;   D50
          doan ke-ho/tay)
    See note to DON JUAN.

DORP (dorp) *small town*   D51
          What should they do, beset with dangers round,
          No neighbouring dorp, no lodging to be found,
          But bleaky plains, and bare unhospitable ground?
                    —*Dryden.* The Hind and the Panther.

DOVE-EYED (duv/ide) *gentle looking*   D52
          dove-eyed pity.—*Shelley.* Prometheus. iii, 3.

DOWN PLATFORM (down plat/fawm)   D53
    The down platform is the platform adjoining the line
running to the main terminus.

DUBIETY (du-by/e-ti) *doubtfulness*   D54
    The last verse of Susan was to be got rid of, at all events. It threw
a kind of dubiety upon Susan's moral conduct. Susan is a servant maid.
I see her trundling her mop, and contemplating the whirling phenomenon
through blurred optics; but to term her "a poor outcast" seems as much
as to say that poor Susan was no better than she should be, which I trust
was not what you meant to express.—*Charles Lamb.* Letter to Wordsworth.

DUDINE (du-dene/) *fashionable woman*   D55

DÜRERESQUE (du-rer-esk/) *like a painting by Dürer*   D56
    The brilliant lights and sooty shades which struggled upon the skin
and clothes of the persons standing round caused their lineaments and
general contours to be drawn with Düreresque vigour and dash. · Yet the
permanent moral expression of each face it was impossible to discover,
for as the nimble flames towered, nodded, and swooped through the
surrounding air, the blots of shade and flakes of light upon the counten-
ances of the group changed shape and position endlessly. All was
unstable; quivering as leaves, evanescent as lightning. Shadowy eye-
sockets, deep as those of a death's head, suddenly turned into pits of
lustre: a lantern-jaw was cavernous, then it was shining; wrinkles were
emphasized to ravines, or obliterated entirely by a changed ray. Nostrils
were dark wells; sinews in old necks were gilt mouldings; things with no
particular polish on them were glazed; bright objects, such as the tip of a
furze-hook one of the men carried were as glass; eyeballs glowed like
little lanterns. Those whom Nature had depicted as merely quaint became
grotesque, the grotesque became preternatural; for all was in extremity.—
Thomas Hardy. The Return of the Native. Bk. i (3). (Macmillan).

EAR-WITNESS

EAU DE NIL

EBBW

EBRIETY

ECARTÉ

ÉCLAT

ECLECTIC

ECLIPTIC

ECLOGUE

EDENTATE

EFFLORESCENCE

EFFULGENCE

ELECTRO-BIOLOGY

ELLIPSIS

EMBATHE

EMBEZZLE

EMBRASURE

EMBRYO

EMIR

EMPIRIC

ENCAUSTIC

ENDEMIC

ENSAFFRONED

EPHYDRIAD

EPICENE

EPITOME

EQUIVOCAL

EREMITE

EROTOMANIA

ESCULENT

ESTHER

ESURIENT

ETERNIZE

ETIOLATION

EULENSPIEGEL

EUNICE

EUPEPSIA

EVANESCENCE

EXANIMATE

EXEGESIS

EXEQUIES

EXIGIBLE

EXILITY

EXORDIAL

EXOTERIC

EXPATIATE

EXSUCCOUS

EXTOL

EX-VOTO

EAR-WITNESS (ere/wit-nes) *one who attests anything*   E
        heard by himself

    All present were made earwitnesses, even of each particular branch of a common indictment.—*Hooker*. Ecclesiastical Polity.

EAU DE NIL (o der neel/)   E2

    Literally, Nile water, which suggests, to the Western mind, an Eastern perfume.

EBBW (eb/oo)   E3

EBRIETY (e-bri/e-ti) *drunkenness*   E4

    Bitter almonds, as an antidote against ebriety, hath commonly failed. —*Sir Thomas Browne*. Vulgar Errors.

ECARTÉ (ay-kar/tay) *card game*   E5

    All eyes were on a very pretty woman, with fifteen thousand a-year, and only twenty-three. The Duke of Shropshire wished he was disembarrassed. Such a player of ecarté might double her income.—*Disraeli*. The Young Duke. Bk. ii, Ch. iv.

ÉCLAT (e-klah/) *splendour; success*   E6

    Nothing more contributes to the variety, surprize and éclat of Homer's battles, than that artificial manner of gaging his heroes by each other.—*Pope*. Essay on Homer.

ECLECTIC (ek-lek/tik) *selective*   E7

    . . . British philosophy, tracing it from Duns Scotus to Dugald Stewart, has now gone through the first and second of these stages, the scholastic and the eclectic, and in considerable honour. With our amiable Professor Stewart, than whom no man, not Cicero himself, was ever more entirely eclectic, that second or eclectic class may be considered as having terminated; and now philosophy is at a stand among us, or rather there is now no philosophy in these islands. It remains to be seen whether we also are to have our " third stage," and how that new and highest " class " will demean itself here. The French philosophers seem busy studying Kant, and writing of him; but we imagine Novalis would pronounce them still only in the eclectic stage. He says afterwards that all eclectics are essentially and at bottom sceptics; the more comprehensive, the more sceptical.—*Carlyle*. Critical and Miscellaneous Essays. " Novalis."

    All these old palaces [in Antigua] have fine iron grilles over their windows, and doors of smooth cypress wood with ornate bosses and designs of iron nails and studs, almost Byzantine in appearance. And several of them, of which the finest example is perhaps the former university and present museum, were designed by an eclectic architect from Seville, who lived here during the 40's and 50's of the eighteenth century and whose declared aim it was to invent a manner which would represent the style wherein the descendants of the Moorish builders in Andalusia, *would have* worked, had their ancestors never been turned out by the Spaniards! And this ingenious adaptation of Saracenic, embodying rococo themes, which he deliberately evolved, is singularly delightful and to be seen nowhere else, even in Guatemala. The resemblance between, let us say, certain courts of the Alhambra and that of the university here, with its gaily fretted arcade and its lion fountain, is unmistakable; though, in addition, since all the workmen employed were peons, the Indian influence is again to be felt.—*Osbert Sitwell.* Sing High! Sing Low! " Still Life." (1). (Macmillan).

ECLIPTIC (e-klip/tik) *the apparent path of the sun*   E8

All stars, that have their distance from the eclipstick northwards not more than twenty-three degrees and a half, may, in progression of time, have declination southward, and move beyond the equator.—*Sir Thomas Browne.* Vulgar Errors. iv, 13.

ECLOGUE†   E9

John Davidson is as varied as he is excellent, and as charming in moments of light-heartedness as he is noble in his tragic moods. Time probably will favour his ballads, but it will by no means neglect the magic poetry of his eclogues, nor the grandeur of certain passages in his poetic dramas.—*Holbrook Jackson.* The Eighteen Nineties. Ch. xiii. (Jonathan Cape).

EDENTATE (e-den/tate) *toothless*   E10
OF HENRY JAMES
His intricate mind, as persistent and endentate as a pseudopodium . . .—*H. G. Wells.* Experiment in Autobiography. Ch. vii, s. 5. (Gollancz).

EFFLORESCENCE (ef-flo-res/ens) *blossoming; eruption*   E11

In no other branch of pictorial art was there so much activity during the whole of the period, and, on the whole, so much undisputed excellence, as in the various pen and pencil drawings which blossomed from innumerable books and periodicals. To a considerable extent this remarkable efflorescence of an art which had remained passive for so many years was an off-shoot of the renaissance of decorative art.—*Holbrook Jackson.* The Eighteen Nineties. Ch. xxi. (Jonathan Cape).

EFFULGENCE†   E12
THE TOWN OF FRIBOURG IN SWITZERLAND
It is not redeemed from desertness, but unrestrained in fruitfulness— a generous land, bright with capricious plenty, and laughing from vale to vale in fitful fulness, kind and wild; nor this without some sterner element

mingled in the heart of it. For along all its ridges stand the dark masses of innumerable pines, taking no part in its gladness, asserting themselves for ever as fixed shadows, not to be pierced or banished, even in the intensest sunlight; fallen flakes and fragments of the night, stayed in their solemn squares in the midst of all the rosy bendings of the orchard boughs, and yellow effulgence of the harvest, and tracing themselves in black network and motionless fringes against the blanched blue of the horizon in its saintly clearness.—*John Ruskin*. Modern Painters. Vol. iv.

ELECTRO-BIOLOGY (e-lek/tro bi-ol/o-ji)   E13

The study of electrical phenomena in living creatures.

ELLIPSIS (el-lips/is) *the omission of a word or phrase*   E14
MAX BEERBOHM
He pays you a delicate compliment by leaving you something to tell yourself; the end of his ellipsis, as in all the great essayists, is yourself.—*Holbrook Jackson*. The Eighteen Nineties. Ch. vii. (Jonathan Cape).

EMBATHE (em-bathe/) *to bathe*   E15

The water Nymphs that in the bottom plaid,
Held up their pearled wrists and took her in,
Bearing her straight to aged *Nereus* Hall,
Who piteous of her woes, rear'd her lank head,
And gave her to his daughters to imbathe
In nectar'd lavers strew'd with Asphodil,
And through the porch and inlet of each sense
Dropt in Ambrosial Oils till she reviv'd,
And underwent a quick immortal change
Made Goddess of the River; still she retains
Her maid'n gentlenes, and oft at Eeve
Visits the herds along the twilight meadows,
Helping all urchin blasts, and ill luck signes
That the shrewd medling Elfe delights to make,
Which she with pretious viold liquors heals.
      —*Milton*. Comus.

Methinks a sovran and reviving joy must needs rush into the bosom of him that reads or hears, and the sweet odour of the returning gospel imbathe his soul with the fragrancy of Heaven.—*Milton*. Of Reformation in England. Bk. i.

EMBEZZLE (em-bezl/)   E16
When Orford had nothing to gain by doing what was wrong, he did what was right, and did it ably and diligently. Whatever Torrington did not embezzle he wasted. Orford may have embezzled as much as Torrington; but he wasted nothing.—*Macaulay*. History of England. Ch. xxiv.

The very fine distinction between embezzlement and larceny has existed since the beginning of the 19th century.

Embezzlement is the taking of property by a clerk or servant on behalf of his employer and the subsequent misappropriation of such property before it has reached the possession of the employer, *e.g.* if a bank clerk who receives money at the counter puts the money into his own pocket.   In such cases, since the thing embezzled has never been in the possession of the employer there can, technically, be no larceny.   Larceny occurs where property is unlawfully taken out of the possession of the person who owns it.

EMBRASURE (em-bray/zhur) (*1*) *an opening through*   E17
which cannon are pointed; (*2*) *a space*
within a window or door

Gaudy dollwomen loll in the lighted doorways, in window embrasures, smoking birdseye cigarettes.   The odour of the sicksweet weed floats towards him in slow round ovalling wreaths.—*James Joyce.*   Ulysses. (John Lane).

EMBRYO (em/bri-o) *the rudimentary form of an*   E18
animal, etc.

I have been told that the oak-tree raises in the Muslim mind much the same funereal association as do the yew and cypress in ours; but I cannot say what tradition or psychological twist is behind this.   I have often wondered whether our own ideas about yews are not coloured by the severely practical measures of our rustic ancestors.   Each village would want its yew-trees from which to cut bows (though the best and most expensive, such as won us Agincourt, were probably made of the more reliable yew that was imported from Spain).   But no village would want its embryo arsenal dotted about in the unfenced fields, or strips of field, where cows could nibble at the dark green foliage, and, if they did not poison themselves, certainly poison the taste of their milk.   Since the churchyard was probably the only walled enclosure available, it was the obvious place to plant the yews.   They may have acquired from this alone their associations with graves and worms and epitaphs.—*Evan John.*   Time in the East.   (Heinemann).

EMIR (e-mere/) *an Arab chief*   E19

The book of Job shows that, long before letters and arts were known to Ionia, these vexing questions were debated with no common skill and eloquence, under the tents of the Idumean emirs; nor has human reason in the course of three thousand years, discovered any satisfactory solution of the riddles which perplexed Eliphaz and Zophar.—*Macaulay.*   Critical and Historical Essays.   " Ranke's History of the Popes."

EMPIRIC* (em-pir/ik) *one who is guided by or reasons*   E20
     from experience or observation

   . . . by fire
Of sooty coal, the Empirick Alchymist
Can turn, or holds it possible to turn,
Metals of drossiest Ore to perfet Gold.
        —Milton. Paradise Lost. v. 439.

But you must now notice especially one flower, that here is bought either for decoration or to be eaten. This is the yucca; large spikes, clustering spires of cup-like blossom, creamy and green, ivory and white. The petals, cool, crisp and aromatic, of these flowers, sprinkled with their golden centres shredded over them, dressed with oil and vinegar, and rubbed with garlic, form one of the usual dishes of this country [Guatemala]. Texture and flavour are both excellent. . . . I cannot say whether these yuccas, though they look precisely the same, only larger and more florescent, are identical with those grown in English gardens, and I have not dared to find out empirically.—*Osbert Sitwell.* Sing High! Sing Low! " Still Life." (Macmillan).

" I admire your wisdom, sir," said Gumbril. The old gentleman was delighted. " And I have been much impressed by your philosophical reflections," he said. " Tell me, are you at all interested in old brandy?" " Well, not philosophically," said Gumbril. " As a mere empiric only." " As a mere empiric!" The old gentleman laughed. " Then let me beg you to accept a case. I have a cellar which I shall never drink dry, alas! before I die. My only wish is that what remains of it shall be distributed among those who can really appreciate it."—*Aldous Huxley.* Antic Hay. Ch. xvii. (Chatto & Windus).

ENCAUSTIC (en-kaw/stik) *form of painting in which the*   E21
     colours are fixed by heat, usually on to a
     surface of earthenware

   May also be used, in a wider sense, to mean burnt on or burnt in, as in the second quotation.

But what interested them more than the gallery or the rich saloons, or even the baronial hall, was the chapel. . . . The walls and vaulted roofs painted in encaustic by the first artists of Germany, and representing the principal events of the second Testament, produced an effect that stifled them into silence.—Disraeli. The Young Duke. Bk. ii, Ch. iv.

Johnson could write accomplished and even elegant verses; his powers of satire, intensified as they were by encaustic bitterness, were often formidable in action; but he was not a poet, and it is doubtful whether many people could now read his poems for pleasure, or indeed, read them at all.—*C. E. Vulliamy.* Ursa Major. (Michael Joseph).

ENDEMIC (en-dem/ik) *recurring; common; contagious;*   E22
     widespread

Spy fever was endemic on the peninsula, and seldom a day passed without an excitable Brigadier's telephoning that he had caught some ruffian red-handed, the ruffian always turning out on investigation either

to be a Greek cook who had wandered from a Brigade nearby, or an
interpreter with a long and honourable career of service behind him.—
Compton Mackenzie.   Gallipoli Memories.

[In Egypt] justice, like cholera, was a visitation of a mysterious and
very unpleasant kind . . .   No sane men would expect, much less accept,
an invitation to assist in making it endemic.—*Lord Lloyd.*   Egypt Since
Cromer.   Vol. i, p. 12.

ENSAFFRONED (en-saf/rond) *of a saffron hue*   E23

. . . a stratum of ensaffroned light was imposed on a stratum of deep
blue, and behind these lay still remoter scenes wrapped in frigid grey.—
Thomas Hardy.   The Return of the Native.   Bk. ii (2).   (Macmillan).

EPHYDRIAD (ef-e-dry/ad) *a wood nymph*   E24

. . . the verdant valley, even then a haunt of every leafy spirit and
the blue-eyed ephydriads . . .—*Edmund Blunden.*   Undertones of War.
(xiii).

EPICENE (ep/i-sene) *sexless; hermaphroditic*   E25

Ostrorog had been pouring into the ears of Miriam Codd the secrets
of what I fear must have been a troubled and an epicene past.—*Harold
Nicolson.*   Miriam Codd, from " Some People." (vii).   (Constable).

A habit of dress, a tone of voice, an elegant humorous deportment
that had been admired and imitated, a swift epicene felicity of wit, the art
of dazzling and confusing those he depised—these had been his, and now
they were the current exchange of comedians; there were only a few
restaurants, now, which he could frequent without fear of ridicule and
there he was surrounded, as though by distorting mirrors, with gross reflections and caricatures of himself.   Was it thus that the rich passions of
Greece and Arabia and the Renaissance had worn themselves out?—
Evelyn Waugh.   Put Out More Flags.   Ch. i (5) .   (Chapman & Hall).

EPITOME (e-pit/o-mi) *summary; abstract*   E26

The great man does, in good truth, belong to his own age; nay, more so
than any other man; being properly the synopsis and epitome of such age
with its interests and influences: but belongs likewise to all ages, otherwise he is not great.—*Carlyle.*   Critical and Miscellaneous Essays.
" Boswell's Life of Johnson."

EQUIVOCAL (e-kwiv/o-kul) *ambiguous*   E27

Lady Burghersh was a woman of severe social principle, who later
contrived to copy out portions of Byron's memoirs and then, curiosity
satisfied, to destroy her copy with much public indignation.   Virtue so
ingenious and so inquisitive could be trusted to detect an equivocal Mrs.
Farmer behind the legitimate splendours of Lord Blessington's wife.—
Michael Sadleir.   Blessington-D'Orsay.   Ch. iii.   (Constable).

EREMITE (er/e-mite) *a hermit*   E28

Yeobright preaching to the Egdon eremites that they might rise to a serene comprehensiveness without going through the process of enriching themselves, was not unlike arguing to ancient Chaldeans that in ascending from earth to the pure empyrean it was not necessary to pass first into the intervening heaven of ether.—*Thomas Hardy.* The Return of the Native. Bk. iii (2). (Macmillan).

EROTOMANIA (e-ro-to-may/ni-a) *melancholia or insanity*   E29
        caused by love

ESCULENT (es/ku-lent) *eatable; good for food*   E30

In those days one dined at noon and supped at seven, and for those two meals alone James Farey catered, and the fare was as English and as old as Wedbury. Chops, steaks, baked or roast potatoes, home-made bread, Stilton cheese and butter. That was all . If you wanted fish or fowl or sweets you might go elsewhere for such esculent fripperies. And for drink there was ale in silver tankards.—*Neil Bell.* The Man who believed in Farey's. (Collins).

ESTHER (es/ter)   E31

ESURIENT (e-su/ri-ent) *hungry*   E32

Unparalleled Cagliostro! Looking at thy so attractively decorated private theatre, wherein thou actedst and livedst, what hand but itches to draw aside thy curtain; overhaul thy paste-boards, paint-pots, paper-mantles, stage-lamps, and turning the whole inside out, find *thee* in the middle thereof! For there of a truth wert thou; though the rest was all foam and sham, there sattest *thou,* as large as life, and as esurient; warring against the world, and indeed conquering the world, for it remained thy tributary, and yielded daily rations.—*Carlyle.* Critical and Miscellaneous Essays. " Count Cagliostro."

. . . such vicious and esurient atoms . . .—*Compton Mackenzie.* Gallipoli Memories.

ETERNIZE (e-tern/ize) *to make eternal*   E33

In these and such-like passions Rosader did every day eternize the name of his Rosalynd; and this day especially when Aliena and Ganimede (inforced by the heat of the sun to seeke for shelter) by good fortune arrived in that place, where this amorous forrester registred his melancholy passions. They saw the sodaine change of his looks, his folded armes, his passionate sighs: they heard him often abruptly cal on Rosa-lynd, who (poore soule) was as hotly burned as himselfe, but that shee shrouded her paines in the cinders of honourable modesty.—*Thomas Lodge.* Ganimede and Rosader.

ETIOLATION (e-te-o-lay/shun) *whitening*   E34

His face, except for the underlying suggestion of feebleness and etiolation, was in its concave tendency rather beautiful, its hollows clearly cut, but his skull was too visible beneath the drawn skin, and in his whole frame was something that told one of his stock and how in the past it had already supplied too much achievement, both intellectual and artistic. —*Osbert Sitwell*.   Miracle on Sinai.   Bk. i, Ch. ii.   (Duckworth).

EULENSPIEGEL (oi/len-spe-gel)   E35

EUNICE (u/nis; u-ni/se)   E36

EUPEPSIA (u-pep/si-a) *good digestion*   E37

An easy, laconic gentleman; of grave politeness; apt to lose temper at play; yet, on the whole, good-humoured, eupeptic and eupractic . . . —*Carlyle*. Critical and Miscellaneous Essays. " Diderot."

THE HALL OF THE 500 CHINESE GODS
 . . . All except a few were united by the family likeness of remote amusement and well-fed peace, they were gods in clover, and their eupeptic superiority was more unnerving than all the torture and bloody wounds of the Christian hagiarchy.—*Eric Linklater*.   Juan in China. (Jonathan Cape).

EVANESCENCE†   E38

It will be found on observation that under a bank—suppose with dark trees above showing spaces of bright sky, the bright sky is reflected distinctly, and the bottom of the water is in those spaces not seen; but in the dark spaces of reflection we see the bottom of the water, and the colour of that bottom and of the water itself mingles with and modifies that of the colour of the trees casting the dark reflection.

This is one of the most beautiful circumstances connected with water surface, for by these means a variety of colour and a grace and evanescence are introduced in the reflection otherwise impossible. Of course at great distances even the darkest objects cast distinct images, and the hue of the water cannot be seen; but in near water the occurrence of its own colour modifying the dark reflections while it leaves light ones unaffected is of infinite value.—*John Ruskin*. Modern Painters. Vol. i, Ch. xiv. " The Wonders of Water."

EXANIMATE (eg-zan/i-mate) *lifeless; depressed*   E39

On thother side they saw that perilous Rocke,
Threatning it selfe on them to ruinate,
On whose sharp cliftes the ribs of vessels broke;
And shivered ships, which had beene wrecked late,
Yet stuck with carkases exanimate
Of such, as having all their substance spent
In wanton joyes and lustes intemperate,
Did afterwards make shipwrack violent
Both of their life and fame, for ever fowly blent.
                    —*Spenser*. The Faerie Queene. Bk. II, xii, 5, vii.

EXEGESIS (eks-e-je/sis) *science of interpretation*   E40

The modern clergyman has acquired in his study of the science which I believe is called exegesis an astonishing facility for explaining things away.—*W. Somerset Maugham.* The Moon and Sixpence. (Heinemann).

EXEQUIES (eks/e-kwiz) *funeral rites*   E41

TALBOT: . . . let's not forget
          The noble Duke of Bedford late deceas'd,
          But see his exequies fulfill'd in Rouen.
                    —*Shakespeare.* Henry VI. Pt. I, iii, 2.

EXIGIBLE (eks/i-ji-bl) *capable of being demanded*   E42

The paper currencies of North America consisted not in bank notes payable to the bearer on demand, but in a government paper, of which the payment was not exigible till several years after it was issued.—*Adam Smith.* The Wealth of Nations. i, 232.

EXILITY (eg-zil/i-ti) *thinness; scantiness*   E43

It is with great propriety that subtlety, which, in its original import, means exility of particles, is taken, in its metaphorical meaning, for nicety of distinction.—*Dr. Johnson.* The Lives of the Poets. " Cowley."

EXORDIAL (egz-or/di-al) *introductory; introduction*   E44

The greatest underweening of this life is to undervalue that, unto which this is but exordial, or a passage leading unto it.—*Sir Thomas Browne.* Christian Morals. iii, 25.

EXOTERIC (ex-o-ter/ik) *popular; intelligible*   E45

Among the habitual dwellers in these delicate halls, there was a tacit understanding, a prevalent doctrine that required no formal exposition, no proofs and illustrations, no comment and no gloss; which was indeed rather a traditional conviction than an imparted dogma; that the exoteric public were on many subjects the victims of very vulgar prejudices, which these enlightened personages wished neither to disturb nor to adopt.— *Disraeli.* Coningsby.

EXPATIATE (ek-spa/shi-ate) *to dilate; to speak or write*   E46
                copiously on a subject

Goldsmith expatiated on the common topick, that the race of our people was degenerated, and that this was owing to luxury. JOHNSON: " Sir, in the first place, I doubt the fact; for, Sir, consider to how very small a proportion of our people luxury can reach."—*James Boswell*. Life of Johnson. A.D. 1773. Ætat. 64.

We dined at an excellent inn at Chapel-house, where he expatiated on the felicity of England in its taverns and inns . . .—*James Boswell*. Life of Johnson. A.D. 1776. Ætat. 67.

EXSUCCOUS (ex-suk/us) *dry; destitute of juice*   E47

Most men expected to find a consumed kell, empty and bladder-like guts, livid and marbled lungs, and a withered pericardium in this exsuccous corpse . . .—*Sir Thomas Browne*. Letter to a Friend.

EXTOL (ek-stol/) *to praise; to glorify*   E48

. . . Heav'n and Earth shall high extole
Thy praises, with th' innumerable sound
Of Hymns, and sacred Songs, wherewith thy Throne
Encompass'd shall resound thee ever blest.
                    —*Milton*. Paradise Lost. iii, 146.

After extolling their strength and spirit he proceeded to explain why it was that, with all their strength and spirit, they were constantly beaten.—*Macaulay*. History of England. Ch. xiv.

EX-VOTO (eks-vo/to) *a thank-offering; an offering in   E49
                pursuance of a vow*

. . . *ex-voto* pictures, like sign-boards, of naked souls in purgatory, grinning with anguish in the middle of high red and yellow flames.—*Robert Graves*. Good-bye to All That. Ch. iv. (Jonathan Cape).

The church at *Creil* was a nondescript place in the inside, splashed with gaudy lights from the windows, and picked out with medallions of the *Dolorous Way*. But there was one oddity, in the way of an *ex voto*, which pleased me hugely: a faithful model of a canal boat, swung from the vault, with a written aspiration that *God* should conduct the *Saint Nicolas* of *Creil* to a good haven. The thing was neatly executed, and would have made the delight of a party of boys on the waterside. But what tickled me was the gravity of the peril to be conjured. You might hang up the model of a sea-going ship. and welcome: one that is to plough a furrow round the world, and visit the tropic or the frosty poles, runs dangers that are well worth a candle and a mass. But the *Saint Nicolas* of *Creil,* which was to be tugged for some ten years by patient draught horses, in a weedy canal, with the poplars chattering over-head, and the skipper whistling at the tiller; which was to do all its errands in green, inland places, and never got out of sight of a village belfry in all its cruising; why, you would have thought if anything could be done without the intervention of Providence, it would be that! But perhaps the skipper was a humourist: or perhaps a prophet, reminding people of the seriousness of life by this preposterous token.—*R. L. Stevenson*. An Inland Voyage. " Down the Oise." (Chatto & Windus).

FABULIST	FINICAL
FACILE	FLAGITIOUS
FAIENCE	FLAMEN
FAMILY GROCER	FLASH HOUSE
FAMULUS	FLEXILE
FARTHINGALE	FLOCCULENT
FASCINE	FLORET
FAUN	FLOWERET
FEAST-WON	FORECASTLE
FECULENT	FORENSIC
FENCIBLE	FREMESCENCE
FEU DE JOIE	FRENETIC
FEUILLETON	*FRÖBEL*
FIDELIO	FRORE
FIELD-NIGHT	FUGACIOUS
FIESOLE	FULGOROUS
FIGURINE	FUNAMBULIST
FINALE	

FABULIST†   F

I do not think we ever enough endeavour to enter into what a Greek's real notion of a god was. We are so accustomed to the modern mockeries of the classical religion, so accustomed to hear and see the Greek gods introduced as living personages, or invoked for help, by men who believe neither in them nor in any other gods, that we seem to have infected the Greek ages themselves with the breath, and dimmed them with the shade, of our hypocrisy; and are apt to think that Homer, as we know that Pope, was merely an ingenious fabulist; nay, more than this, that all the nations of past time were ingenious fabulists also, to whom the universe was a lyrical drama, and by whom whatsoever was said about it was merely a witty allegory, or a graceful lie, of which the entire upshot and consummation was a pretty statue in the middle of the court, or at the end of the garden.—*John Ruskin*. Modern Painters. "The Greek Notion of a God."

FACILE (fas/il) *(1) easy to be done; (2) pliant; easily led;*   F2
    (3) skilful; (4) fluent; (5) ready; (6) good-tempered

FAIENCE (fa/yahns) *glazed earthenware or porcelain*   F3

He stood for a moment still as a faience statuette.—*Compton Mackenzie*. Gallipoli Memories.

FAMILY GROCER (fam/i-li gro/ser)   F4

A grocer who serves families and who is not a purveyor to the military, etc.

FAMULUS (fam/u-lus) *sorcerer's assistant*   F5

The great gulf of Tophet, and tenth of August, opened itself at the magic of your eloquent voice; and lo now, it will not close at your voice! It is a dangerous thing such magic. The magician's famulus got hold of the forbidden book, and summoned a goblin: "Plait-il," What is your will? said the goblin. The famulus, somewhat struck, bade him fetch water: the swift goblin fetched it, pail in each hand; but lo, would not cease fetching it! Desperate, the famulus shrieks at him, smites at him, cuts him in two; lo, two goblin water-carriers ply; and the house will be swum away in Deucalion deluges.—*Carlyle*. The French Revolution. Pt. iii, Bk. iii, Ch. iii.

FARTHINGALE (far/thing-gale) *hooped petticoat worn*   F6
    in the 16th century

With silken coats, and caps, and golden rings,
With ruffs, and cuffs, and farthingales.
    —*Shakespeare*. The Taming of the Shrew. iv., 3.

FASCINE (fa-sene/) *a bundle of brushwood used for making*   F7
    earthworks, etc.

    Ramparts were made of sandbags, and fascines of barbed wire disposed across the frontier streets.—*Eric Linklater.* "Juan in China." (Jonathan Cape).
    "Fascine" in this quotation, evidently means a cylindrical roll—a clear example of extension of meaning.

FAUN (fawn) *fabulous semi-human creature*   F8

        Rough, Satyrs danc'd, and Fauns with cloven heel
   From the glad sound would not be absent long.
                  —*Milton*. Lycidas. 34.

FEAST-WON (feast/wun) *bribed by entertainment*   F9

FECULENT (fek/u-lent) *dirty; containing sediment; turbid*   F10

        But both his hands, most filthy feculent,
   Above the water were on high extent,
   And feign'd to wash themselves incessantly,
   Yet nothing cleaner were for such intent.
                —*Spenser*. The Faerie Queene.

FENCIBLE (fen/si-bl) *soldier enlisted for home service only* F11
    As, the Home Guard.

FEU DE JOIE (fer de zhwa) *salvos of gunfire in token of*   F12
    national rejoicing

FEUILLETON (fu-ye/ton) *serial story in newspaper*   F13

FIDELIO (fi-day/li-o)   F14

FIELD-NIGHT (field/nite) *an evening or night marked by*   F15
    some important meeting, business or event

FIESOLE (fe/az-ol-e)   F16

FIGURINE (fig-ur-ene/) *statuette* F17

ARNOLD BENNETT

Never have I known anyone else so cheerfully objective as Bennett. His world was as bright and hard surfaced as crockery—his *persona* was, as it were, a hard, definite china figurine.—*H. G. Wells.* Experiment in Autobiography. Ch. viii, s. 5. (Gollancz).

FINALE (fi-nay/li) *the last part; the end* F18

Note pronunciation. Not *fi-nar/li.*

It was arranged that the two horsemen should first occupy the arena: . . . that Glaucus and the lion should next perform their part in the bloody spectacle; and the tiger and the Nazarene be the grand finale.— *Bulwer Lytton.* The Last Days of Pompeii. Bk. v, Ch. ii.

" A little gamble and a little thrill at week-ends, when the green Finale comes round, and, of course, the hope that some day that little dream business of mine might come true. But win or lose I always look forward to Saturdays and the Green Finale."—*First Year's Work* (1937-38) by Mass Observation. (Lindsay Drummond).

[This appears to refer to the final edition of an evening paper].

FINICAL (fin/i-kal) *fastidious* F19

A whoreson, glassgazing, superserviceable, finical rogue.—*Shakespeare.* King Lear. ii, 2.

FLAGITIOUS (fla-jish/us) *extremely wicked* F20

FLAMEN (flay/men) *priest* F21

A drear and dying sound
Affrights the flamens at their service quaint.
—*Milton.* Ode on the Nativity.

FLASH HOUSE (flash hous) F22

The business address of a receiver of stolen goods.

FLEXILE (fleks/ile) *pliable* F23

Every flexile wave
Obeys the blast; the aerial tumult swells.
—*Thomson.* Seasons. " Summer."

FLOCCULENT (flok/u-lent) *in small flakes* F24

The night was overcast, and through the flocculent grey of the heaped clouds there filtered a faint half-light of dawn. Just at the edge of the sky the cloud-canopy had a blood-red rim.—*H. G. Wells.* The Late Mr. Elvesham, from " The Country of the Blind." (Collins).

FLORET (flor/et) *a small flower; part of a composite*   F25
flower

For what can we conceive of that first Eden which we might not yet win back, if we chose? It was a place full of flowers, we say. Well: the flowers are always striving to grow wherever we suffer them; and the fairer, the closer. There may indeed have been a Fall of Flowers, as a Fall of Man; but assuredly creatures such as we are can now fancy nothing lovelier than roses and lilies, which would grow for us side by side, leaf overlapping leaf, till the earth was white and red with them, if we cared to have it so. And Paradise was full of pleasant shades and fruitful avenues. Well: what hinders us from covering as much of the world as we like with pleasant shade and pure blossom, and goodly fruit? Who forbids its valleys to be covered over with corn till they laugh and sing? Who prevents its dark forests, ghostly and uninhabitable, from being changed into infinite orchards, wreathing the hills with frail-floretted snow, far away to the half-lighted horizon of April, and flushing the face of all the autumnal earth with glow of clustered food?—*John Ruskin.* Modern Painters. Vol. v, 53.

FLOWERET (flour/et) *small flower; floret*   F26

Sometimes her head she fondly would aguise
With gaudy garlands of fresh flow'rets dight,
About her neck, or rings of rushes plight.
                    —*Spenser.* The Faerie Queene.

That same dew, which sometime on the buds
Was wont to swell, like round and orient pearls,
Stood now within the pretty flow'ret's eyes,
Like tears that did their own disgrace bewail.
        —*Shakespeare.* A Midsummer Night's Dream. iv. 1.

. . . so to the sylvan lodge
They came, that like Pomona's arbour smil'd,
With flow'rets deck'd, and fragrant smells.
                    —*Milton.* Paradise Lost. v. 377.

FORECASTLE (foke/sl) *short raised deck at bow; forward*   F27
part under deck in merchant ship
Often spelt FO'C'SLE.

FORENSIC (for-en/sik) *legal*   F28

The legal learning of Mackenzie was not profound: but, as a scholar, a wit, and an orator, he stood high in the opinion of his countrymen; and his renown had spread even to the coffeehouses of London and to the cloisters of Oxford. The remains of his forensic speeches prove him to have been a man of parts, but are somewhat disfigured by what he doubtless considered as Ciceronian graces, interjections which show more art than passion, and elaborate amplifications, in which epithet rises above epithet in wearisome climax.—*Macaulay.* History of England. Ch. vi.

FREMESCENCE (fre-mes/ens) *noisy; tumultuous; riotous*   F29

Rumour, therefore, shall arise; in the Palais Royal and in broad France. Paleness sits on every face; confused tremor and fremescence; waxing into thunder-peals, of fury stirred on by fear.—*Carlyle*. The French Revolution. Pt. i, Bk. v, Ch. iv.

FRENETIC†   F30

British Governments had not yet decided that gambling is immoral, except for Cabinet Ministers and the rich, and regular State lotteries with big prizes afforded the British masses, a proverb all over dice-mad Europe throughout this century as frenetic gamblers, the same thrills as their betters experienced nightly at White's and Boodle's and the Cocoa-Tree.—*D. B. Wyndham Lewis*. The Hooded Hawk. Ch. vi. (Eyre & Spottiswoode).

FRÖBEL (frer/bel)   F31

FRORE (fror) *frosty*   F32

. . . the parching air,
Burns frore, and cold performs th' effect of fire.
—*Milton*. Paradise Lost. ii, 594.
But Mr. Beeston stood in a frore and fearful silence. His brittle dreams of happy power lay splintered within him, his very breath was occluded.—*Eric Linklater*. God Likes Them Plain. " His Majesty The Dentist." (Jonathan Cape).

FUGACIOUS (fu-gay/shus) *fleeting; elusive*   F33

A thing so fine and fugacious as to escape our nicest search.—*Bishop Berkeley*. Siris. s. 43.

FULGOROUS (ful/gor-us) *flashing*   F34

. An amateur reporter . . . declares that he heard him talk one day, in nightgown and slippers, for the space of two hours, concerning earth, sea and air, with a fulgorous impetuosity almost beyond human, rising from height to height.—*Carlyle*. Critical & Miscellaneous Essays. " Diderot."

FUNAMBULIST (fu-nam/bu-list) *a rope dancer*   F35

Tread softly and circumspectly in this funambulatory track and narrow Path of Goodness.—*Sir Thomas Browne*. Christian Morals. Pt. i, 1.

GALA	GITANO
GALACTIC	GLAUCOUS
GALACTOPHAGIST	GLOZE
GALANTINE	*GODAVARI*
GALBANUM	*GOETHE*
GALILEO	GOLUPTIOUS
GALLIPOT	GRACIOSITY
GARNITURE	GRAVAMEN
GAZEBO	GRAVID
GELID	GRAVIGRADE
GENERIC	GREEN-SICKNESS
GEODESIC	GREGARIOUS
GEOGHEGAN	GRINGO
GEORGIC	GROTESQUE
GERMINAL	*GUADELOUPE*
GIAOUR	GUERDON
GIGLOT	GULES
GIGOT	GULOSITY
GIOTTO	GYMNOSOPHIST
GIOVANNI	GYNÆOSYNCRASY

GALA (gar/la) *a festival*   G

They dressed as if for a gala at Versailles, ate off plate, drank the richest wines, and kept harems on board, while hunger and scurvy raged among the crews, and while corpses were daily flung out of the portholes. —*Macaulay*. History of England. Ch. iii.

Why is Paris dancing, and flinging fire-works? They are gala-nights, these last of September; Paris may well dance, and the universe: the edifice of the constitution is completed! . . . And now by such illumination, jubilee, dancing and fire-working, do we joyously handsel the new social edifice, and first raise heat and reek there, in the name of Hope.— *Carlyle*. The French Revolution. Pt. ii, Bk. v, Ch. i.

GALACTIC (ga-lak/tik) *relating to the Milky Way;*   G2
or to milk

The nebulæ are not dispersed with anything like uniformity; but are abundant around the poles of the galactic circle, and rare in the neighbourhood of its plane.—*Herbert Spencer*. The Instability of the Homogeneous.

GALACTOPHAGIST (ga-lak-tof/a-jist) *one who drinks*   G3
milk, or lives on a diet of milk

In the feeding-houses of Cheapside, through which the red buses run, the pale galactophagists enter their rooms. There reading a midday edition, they absorb their thin and lukewarm diet, while a yard or so away the life of the busy, crowded street like a river, rushes on. The street is a river, and they sit upon its bank.

GALANTINE (gal/an-tene) *prepared boned white meat*   G4
AN INTELLIGENCE SUMMARY
. . . I know that Grave's well-prepared galantine will more than compensate for the amateurishly chopped and somewhat stringy dish of mincemeat I offered.—*Compton Mackenzie*. Gallipoli Memories.

GALBANUM (gal/ba-num) *a scented resin*   G5

And the Lord said unto Moses, Take unto thee sweet spices, stacte, and onchya, and galbanum [khelbenah]; these sweet spices with pure frankincense: of each shall there be a like weight: and thou shalt make it a perfume, a confection after the art of the apothecary, tempered together pure and holy.—*Exodus*. xxx, 34, 35.

GALILEO (gal-i-lee/o)   G6

GALLIPOT (gal/li-pot) *a glazed pot*   G7

Plato said his master Socrates was like the apothecary's gallipots, that had on the outsides apes, owls, and satyrs; but within precious drugs. —*Bacon*.   Apophthegms.

. . . the long rows of them, bottles and gallipots in hand, some tattered and dirty, others decent enough, sitting in the dimness, men and women of all ages, children, gave one an impression which was weird and horrible.   They suggested the grim drawings of Daumier.—*W. Somerset Maugham*. Of Human Bondage. Ch. lxxxi. (Heinemann).

GARNITURE (gar/ni-cher) *furniture; ornament; trimmings;*   G8
embellishment; costume; etceteras

Her education in youth was not much attended to; and she happily missed all that train of female garniture, which passeth by the name of accomplishments.—*Charles Lamb*.   Essays of Elia.   "Mackery End, in Hertfordshire."

GAZEBO†   G9

Any person who loves, as we do, such forgotten places, will find delight and poetry in Oporto in the old convent of Santa Clara.   This town of camellias, for nowhere else are they so smooth and beautiful as in the quintas of the Douro, must be looked down on from above, from a church tower in its midst, because of its tiled roofs.   Each old house would seem to have a staircase well that is carried up into a pavilion or gazebo, even if it be no bigger than a large birdcage.—*Sacheverell Sitwell*. acred & Profane Love.   Bk. v, Pt. v.   (Faber & Faber).

GELID†   G10

From the deep oose and gelid cavern rous'd
They flounce.—*Thomson*.   Seasons.   "Spring."

GENERIC (je-ner/ik) *characteristic of genus or class;*   G11
not specific

These men—whom modern writers set down as the Sophists, and denounce as the moral pestilence of their age—were not distinguished in any marked or generic way from their predecessors.—*Grote*.   History of Greece.   Pt. ii, Ch. lxvii.

GEODESIC (je-o-des/ik)   G12
Probably a curved surface; a wide curve.

Mr. Cardan was a middle-sized, thickly built man.   The upper hem of his trousers followed an ample geodesic; his shoulders were very broad, his neck short and powerful.—*Aldous Huxley*.   Those Barren Leaves. (Chatto and Windus).

GEOGHEGAN (gay/gan)   G13

GEORGIC†   G14
  Much less ought the low phrases and terms of art, that are adapted
to husbandry, have any place in such a work as the Georgick, which is
not to appear in the natural simplicity and nakedness of its subject, but
in the pleasantest dress that poetry can bestow upon it.—*Addison*. On
Virgil's Georgicks.

GERMINAL (zhar-me-na!/) *seventh month of Republican*   G15
                year—21st March to 19th April

GIAOUR (jowr) *Turkish name for infidel, esp. Christian* G16
      Cf. GRINGO.

GIGLOT (gig/lot) *a foolish girl*   G17
            . . . young Talbot was not born
          To be the pillage of a giglot wench.
                —*Shakespeare*. Henry VI. Pt. i, iv, 7.
          The fam'd Cassibelan, who was once at point
        (O giglot fortune!) to master Cæsar's sword.
                —*Shakespeare*. Cymbeline. iii, 1.

GIGOT (jig/ot) *a leg of mutton*   G18
  . . . cut the slaves to giggets.—*Beaumont and Fletcher*. Double
Marriage.

GIOTTO (jot/o)   G19

GIOVANNI (jo-var/ne)   G20

GITANO (ji-tar/no) *a gipsy*   G21

GLAUCOUS†   G22
  The green world slid past her half-shut eyes. Green darkness of
trees overarching the olive shadows and tawny-glaucous lights of water;
and between the twilight stretches of green vaulting, the wide gold-green
meadows, islanded with elms. And always the faint weedy smell of the
river; and the air so soft and warm against the face that one was hardly
aware any longer of the frontiers between self and not-self, but lay there,
separated by no dividing surfaces, melting, drowsily melting into the
circumambient summer.—*Aldous Huxley*. Eyeless In Gaza. Ch. xvi.
(Chatto & Windus).

GLOZE (gloze) *to flatter*   G23

> For man will hearken to his glozing lyes,
> And easily transgress.
>> —*Milton*. Paradise Lost. iii, 93.
>> So gloz'd the Tempter, and his Proem tun'd;
> Into the Heart of *Eve* his words made way:
>> —*Ibid*. ix, 549.

GODAVARI (go-da/ver-i)   G24

GOETHE (ger/te)   G25

" You are expressing a very general opinion," said I.
" Is that so, indeed, sir?" he exclaimed, with unmistakable excitement. " Is the book well known? and who was *Go-eath?* I am interested
in that, because upon the title-page the usual initials are omitted, and it
runs simply ' by Go-eath.' Was he an author of distinction? Has he
written other works?"—*R. L. Stevenson and Lloyd Osbourne.* The
Wrecker. Ch. XIX.

GOLUPTIOUS (go-lup/shus) *delicious*   G26

GRACIOSITY (gras-i-os/it-i) *benevolence*   G27

Blessed old marquis—or else accursed! He is there, with his broad
bull-brow; with the huge cheekbones; those deep eyes, glazed as in
weariness; the lower visage puckered into a simpering graciosity, which
would pass itself off for a kind of smile.—*Carlyle*. Critical & Miscellaneous Essays. " Mirabeau."

GRAVAMEN (gra-vay/men) *essence (of accusation);*   G28
        grievance

GRAVID (grav/id) *pregnant*   G29

Coleman exploded with delight. " Gravid," he kept repeating,
" gravid, gravid. The laws of gravidy, first formulated by Newton, now
recodified by the immortal Einstein. God said, Let Newstein be, and
there was light. And God said, Let there be Light; and there was darkness o'er the face of the earth." He roared with laughter.—*Aldous
Huxley*. Antic Hay. Ch. v. (Chatto & Windus).

GRAVIGRADE (grav/i-grade) *walking heavily*   G30

GREEN-SICKNESS (gren-sik/nes) *a disease affecting*   G31
        young and delicate women and due to deficiency
        of colouring matter in the blood

Sir Thomas Browne's *Urn Burial* is the only panacea for all the
nauseas occasioned by Mr. Arlen's green-sickness.—*James Agate*. Playgoing. v. (Jarrolds).

GREGARIOUS (gre-gare/i-us) *herding together*   G32

Without intelligence, man is not social, he is only gregarious.—
Dr. Johnson. Journey to the Western Islands of Scotland.

GRINGO (gring/go) *a contemptuous name for an*   G33
        Englishman or Anglo-American, used in Mexico
Cf. GIAOUR.

GROTESQUE (gro-tesk/) *distorted; unnatural*   G34

So on he fares, and to the border comes
Of *Eden,* where delicious Paradise,
Now nearer, Crowns with her enclosure green,
As with a rural mound the champain head
Of a steep wilderness, whose hairie sides
With thicket overgrown, grottesque and wilde,
Access deni'd; and over head up grew
Insuperable highth of loftiest shade,
Cedar, and Pine, and Firr, and branching Palm,
            —Milton. Paradise Lost. iv.

GUADELOUPE (gwa-de-loop/)   G35

GUERDON (ger/don) *a reward*   G36

Fame is the spur that the clear spirit doth raise
To scorn delights, and live laborious days;
But the fair guerdon when we hope to find,
And think to burst out into sudden blaze,
Comes the blind fury with the abhorred shears,
And slits the thin-spun life.
            —Milton. Lycidas. 71.

GULES (gulz) *red*   G37

Lord Ollebeare had a face like a coat of arms. His nose might have
been a fist, clenched and mailed, gules. In fact, he was one of those men
you sometimes see in the street. His moustaches were two dolphins
argent, his eyes two étoiles azur.—*John Collier.* Defy the Foul Fiend.
(Macmillan).

GULOSITY (gu-los/i-ti) *gluttony*   G38

At supper this night he talked of good eating with uncommon satis-
faction. "Some people (said he) have a foolish way of not minding, or
pretending not to mind, what they eat. For my part, I mind my belly
very studiously, and very carefully; for I look upon it, that he who does
not mind his belly, will hardly mind anything else." . . . Yet I have
heard him, upon other occasions, talk with great contempt of people who
were anxious to gratify their palates; and the 206th number of his Rambler
is a masterly essay against gulosity.—*James Boswell.* Life of Johnson.
A.D. 1763. Ætat. 54.

How has our Countess managed with Cagliostro? Cagliostro, gone from Strasburg, is as yet far distant, winging his way through dim space; will not be here for months: only his predictions in "cipher" are here. Here or there, however, Cagliostro, to our Countess, can be useful. At a glance, the eye of genius has described him to be a bottomless slough of falsity, vanity, gulosity and thick-eyed stupidity; of foulest material, but of fattest;—fit compost for the plant she is rearing. Him who has deceived all Europe she can undertake to deceive.—*Carlyle*. Critical and Miscellaneous Essays. "The Diamond Necklace."

Is the solving of crosswords a recreation or an educational process? Or is it both? Professor Walter Murdoch, of the University of Western Australia, was recently invited to pronounce on the educational value of the crossword puzzle. In order to equip himself for an answer he spent 20 minutes' hard labour on one of these problems published in an American paper, and he reports that at the end of it he found his vocabulary the richer by half a dozen words. He now knows that there is a South American monkey called a titi and a brilliantly coloured tropical fish called an opah; that a névé is an expanse of granular snow; that there is an Indian shrub called a lequirity whose seeds are used for decoration; that a glutton is afflicted with gulosity; and that a person given to writing is scribacious.—*Manchester Guardian*. May, 1947.

GYMNOSOPHIST (jim-nos/o-fist) *a Hindu fakir*   G39

Those seven wise men of Greece, those British druids, Indian brachmanni, Aethiopian gymnosophists, magi of the Persians.—*Burton*. Anatomy of Melancholy. (To the Reader).

"How can any man complain of hunger," said Peter, "in a country where such excellent sallads are to be gathered in almost every field? or of thirst, where every river and stream produces such delicious potations? And as for cold and nakedness, they are evils introduced by luxury and custom. A man naturally wants cloths no more than a horse or any other animal, and there are whole nations who go without them; but these are things, perhaps, which you, who do not know the world—" "You will pardon me, sir," returned Adams, "I have read of the gymnosophists." —"A plague of your jehosophats!" cried Peter.—*Fielding*. Adventures of Joseph Andrews.

HENRY DAVID THOREAU

Thus this singularly eccentric and independent mind, wedded to a character of so much strength, singleness, and purity, pursued its own path of self-improvement for more than half a century, part gymnosophist, part backwoodsman; and thus did it come twice, though in a subaltern attitude, into the field of political history.—*R. L. Stevenson*. Familiar Studies of Men and Books.

But there is this about some women, which overtops the best gymnosophist among men, that they suffice to themselves, and can walk in a high and cold zone without the countenance of any trousered being. I declare, although the reverse of a professed ascetic, I am more obliged to women for this ideal than I should be to the majority of them, or indeed to any but one, for a spontaneous kiss. There is nothing so encouraging as the spectacle of self-sufficiency.—*R. L. Stevenson*. An Inland Voyage. "Antwerp to Boom." (Chatto & Windus).

GYNÆOSYNCRASY (ge-ne-o-sin/kra-si)   G40

This is a word which we have invented. Its meaning is obvious. It denotes the curious eccentricity and perversity of the female species.

HARUN-AL-RASCHID	HIGH TEA
HAWARDEN	HIPPOGRIFF
HAY	HIRSUTE
HEAVY-BELLY	HISTORIETTE
HEBDOMADAL	HISTORIOGRAPHER
HEBE	HISTORY, ANCIENT
HEBETUDE	HISTORY, MEDIÆVAL
HECATE	HISTORY, MODERN
HECATOMB	*HOBART*
HEINOUS	HOLOCAUST
HELICAL	HOLOGRAPH
HELIOLATRY	HONG
HELOÏSE	HORRENT
HEMICYCLE	HOURI
HERMENEUTIC	HOY
HERVEY	HUSBANDRY
HETEROCLITE	HYALINE
HETEROGENEOUS	HYDROCEPHALIC
HETEROPATHIC	HYPERBATON
HEXAMETER	HYPERBOLE
HIERARCHY	HYPERBOREAN
HIEROGLYPH	HYPODERMIC
HIEROPHANT	HYPOSTASIS

HARUN-AL-RASCHID (ha/roon al rash/id)   H

HAWARDEN (har/den)   H2

HAY (hay) *country dance*   H3
GAVESTON :   Music and poetry is his delight;
Therefore I'll have Italian masks by night,
Sweet speeches, comedies, and pleasing shows;
And in the day, when he shall walk abroad,
Like sylvan nymphs my pages shall be clad;
My men, like satyrs grazing on the lawns,
Shall with their goat-feet dance the antic hay.
—*Christopher Marlowe.* Edward the Second.

HEAVY-BELLY (hev/i bel/i) *an abdominous person*   H4

HEBDOMADAL (heb-dom/a-dal) (1) *weekly;*   H5
(2) *consisting of 7 days*

HEBE (he/be) *Goddess of Youth*   H6

HEBETUDE (heb/e-tude) *bluntness; dullness*   H7

HECATE (hek/a-te)   H8

HECATOMB (hek/a-tomb) *a public sacrifice; a hundred;*   H9
the sacrifice of one hundred oxen, etc.
The senators celebrated the happy restoration with hecatombs and public rejoicings.—*Edward Gibbon.* The Decline and Fall of the Roman Empire. Ch. xii.
We lunched on a meadow inside a parallelogram of poplars. The leaves danced and prattled in the wind all round about us. The river hurried on meanwhile, and seemed to chide at our delay. Little we cared. The river knew where it was going; not so we: the less our hurry, where we found good quarters and a pleasant theatre for a pipe. At that hour, stockbrokers were shouting in *Paris* Bourse for two or three per cent; but we minded them as little as the sliding stream, and sacrificed a hecatomb of minutes to the gods of tobacco and digestion. Hurry is the resource of the faithless. Where a man can trust his own heart, and those of his friends, to-morrow is as good as to-day. And if he die in the meanwhile, why then, there he dies, and the question is solved.—*R. L. Stevenson.* An Inland Voyage. " Down the Oise: to Moy." (Chatto & Windus).

HEINOUS (hay/nus) *atrocious; abominable*   H10

To abrogate or innovate the gospel of Christ, if men or angels should attempt, it were most heinous and accursed sacrilege.—*Hooker*. Ecclesiastical Polity.

PEMBROKE: This is the man should do the bloody deed:
He show'd his warrant to a friend of mine
The image of a wicked heinous fault
Lives in his eye.
               —*Shakespeare*. King John. iv, 2.

HELICAL (hel/i-kal) *spiral*   H11

The talking ceased, and Fairway gave a circular motion to the rope as if he were stirring batter. At the end of a minute a dull splashing reverberated from the bottom of the well; the helical twist he had imparted to the rope had reached the grapnel below.—*Thomas Hardy*. The Return of the Native. Bk. iii (3). (Macmillan).

HELIOLATRY (he-li-ol/a-tri) *sun worship*   H12

HELOÏSE (a-lo-ez/)   H13

HEMICYCLE (hem/i-sikl) *a semicircle*   H14

The carriages turned into the Avenue Montagne and drew up before the Palais des Beaux Arts. The scene was most lively here as great crowds had gathered near the entrance, and the Queen received a tremendous ovation when the Emperor assisted her from the carriage. The hemicycle before the building was ablaze with flowers, and all round stood poles ornamented with escutcheons, flags and oriflammes of the French and English colours. Victoria, holding Louis Napoleon's arm, and followed by her husband, the two children and their suite, stepped forward toward the door. She wore a dress of Royal Stuart tartan and a white mantle. or so says the *Morning Post.—Edith Saunders*. A Distant Summer. Ch. vii. (Sampson Low, Marston & Co.).

HERMENEUTIC (her-me-nu/tik) *explanatory; explanation*   H15

. . . ev'n the Greeks themselves, supreme in making as in thinking, never of their own art found the true hermeneutic.—*Robert Bridges*. The Testament of Beauty. Bk. ii. (The Clarendon Press).

HERVEY (har/vi)   H16

HETEROCLITE (het/er-o-klete) *anomalous; irregular*   H17

. . . to relish the unusual, the grotesque and the heteroclite was one of his more notable faculties.—*Eric Linklater*. Juan in China. (Jonathan Cape).

And now . . . think of the Tassos and older or later Racines, struggling to raise their office from its pristine abasement of court-jester; and
teach and elevate the world, in conjunction with that other quite heteroclite
task of solacing and glorifying some *Pullus Jovis,* in plush cloak and other
gilt or golden king-tackle, that they in the interim might live thereby!—
Carlyle. Critical and Miscellaneous Essays. " Diderot."

HETEROGENEOUS† H18

The Contradiction which yawns wide enough in every Life, which it is
the meaning and task of Life to reconcile, was in Johnson's wider than in
most. Seldom, for any men, has the contrast between the ethereal heaven-
ward side of things, and the dark sordid earthward, been more glaring:
whether we look at Nature's work with him or Fortune's from first to last,
heterogeneity, as of sunbeams and miry clay, is on all hands manifest.—
Carlyle. Critical and Miscellaneous Essays. " Boswell's Life of Johnson."

HETEROPATHIC (het-er-o-path/ik) *regulating by a* H19
different action, force or law

In medicine, the opposite of homœopathic. See D.U.W.(A).
Treatment by inducing action of a different kind.

Again, laws which were themselves generated in the second mode, may
generate others in the first. Though there be laws which, like those of
chemistry and physiology, owe their existence to a breach of the principle
of composition of causes, it does not follow that these peculiar, or as they
might be termed, heteropathic laws, are not capable of composition with
one another. The causes which by one combination have had their laws
altered, may carry their new laws with them unaltered into their ulterior
combinations. And hence there is no reason to despair of ultimately
raising chemistry and physiology to the condition of deductive sciences; for
though it is impossible to deduce all chemical and physiological truths from
the laws or properties of simple substances or elementary agents, they may
possibly be deducible from laws which commence when these elementary
agents are brought together into some moderate number of not very complex combinations.—*J. S. Mill.* System of Logic. Bk. iii, Ch. vi, s. 2.

HEXAMETER (heks-am/e-ter) *line of six metrical feet* H20

Mr. Chiswick was inflexible. He thought the years which had already
been wasted on hexameters and pentameters quite sufficient.—*Macaulay.*
Critical and Historical Essays. " Warren Hastings."

HIERARCHY (hi/er-ark-i) *grade; order of authority* H21
See HIERATIC in D.U.W.(A).

. . . whom the supreme King
Exalted to such power, and gave to rule,
Each in his Hierarchie, the Orders bright.
—*Milton.* Paradise Lost. i, 735.

It is worth remembering that card games, like almost everything else
in this land of social hierarchies, are not without their class distinctions.

Whist was once the favourite card game of the upper classes. Now that those people play bridge, auction or contract, whist has found its devotees in a very different set of people, chiefly the small shop-keeping, artisan, and working classes.—*J. B. Priestley*. English Journey. Ch. iv. (4). (Heinemann & Gollancz).

Our use of the term "hierarchy" must not be misunderstood. No doubt the earliest usage, many centuries ago, was to employ this word with a theological implication, relating to the "heavenly host"; or to this or that form of church establishment or priestly order. In English usage the term long ago came to be applied to non-theological organisations, but often with an implication of formation and control from the top. The use of the term in modern logic, or in contemporary science, now implies no necessary ascendancy or pre-eminence, any more than any theological reference, but merely "a body of persons or things ranked in grades, orders or classes, one above another"; or "a system or series of terms of successive rank (as classes, orders, genera, species, etc.) used in classification" (*New English Dictionary*). It is in this purely neutral sense of classification, implying neither dictatorship nor popular election, that we use the term in this book.—*S. & B. Webb*. Soviet Communism. Vol. i, p. v (footnote). (Gollancz).

HIEROGLYPH (hi-er-o-glif/) *a symbol in ancient*   H22
Egyptian writing

From the cigar divan he proceeded to parade the streets, still heated with the fire of his eloquence, and scouting upon every side for the offer of some fortunate adventure. In the continual stream of passers-by, on the sealed fronts of houses, on the posters that covered the hoardings, and in every lineament and throb of the great city he saw a mysterious and hopeful hieroglyph.—*R. L. Stevenson*. The Dynamiter. "The Superfluous Mansion." (Heinemann).

HIEROPHANT (hi/er-o-fant) *a priest; one who teaches*   H23
the rules of religion

Upon the established religions of Europe the East had renewed her encroachments, and was pouring forth a family of rites which in various ways attracted the attention of the luxurious, the political, the ignorant, the restless, and the remorseful. Armenian, Chaldee, Egyptian, Jew, Syrian, Phrygian, as the case might be, was the designation of the new hierophant; and magic, superstition, barbarism, jugglery, were the names given to his rite by the world.—*Cardinal Newman*. Essay on the Development of Christian Doctrine.

Further, as he drew nearer, through the darkling air, it seemed as if light emanated from his whole body. His expression was transfigured, and in his new bearing there was a suggestion of the hierophant. Moreover, he spoke exultingly a language which no one, not even his own children, could understand . . .—*Osbert Sitwell*. Miracle on Sinai. Bk. iii, Ch. ii. (Duckworth).

HIGH TEA (hi te) *tea at which meat is eaten*   H24

HIPPOGRIFF (hip/o-grif) *fabulous creature with*   H25
horse's body

> . . . he caught him up, and without wing
> Of *Hippogriff* bore through the Air sublime.
>   —*Milton.* Paradise Regained. iv, 541.

In truth, much of Bacon's life was passed in a visionary world, amidst things as strange as any that are described in the Arabian Tales . . . amidst buildings more sumptuous than the palace of Aladdin, fountains more wonderful than the golden water of Parizade, conveyances more rapid than the hippogryph of Ruggiero, arms more formidable than the lance of Astolfo, remedies more efficacious than the balsam of Fierabras. Yet in his magnificent day-dreams there was nothing wild, nothing but what sober reason sanctioned.—*Macaulay.* Critical and Historical Essays. " Lord Bacon."

Wo the day when they mounted thee, a peaceable pedestrian, on that wild hippogryff of a democracy; which, spurning the firm earth, nay lashing at the very stars, not yet known Astolpho could have ridden!—*Carlyle.* The French Revolution. Pt. i, Bk. iv, Ch. iv.

God is as much a general term to the Christian or the Jew as to the Polytheist; and dragon, hippogriff, chimera, mermaid, ghost, are as much so as if real objects existed, corresponding to those names.—*J. S. Mill.* System of Logic. Bk. i, Ch. vii, s. 1.

HIRSUTE (her/sute) *rough; hairy*   H26

There are bulbous, fibrous, and hirsute roots: the hirsute is a middle sort, between the bulbous and fibrous; that besides the putting forth sap upwards and downwards, putteth forth in round.—*Bacon.* Natural and Experimental History.

An hirsute beggar's brat, that lately fed on scraps.—*Burton.* Anatomy of Melancholy. (To the Reader).

Their bodies, that are affected with this universal melancholy, are most part black;—hirsute they are and lean.—*Burton.* Anatomy of Melancholy.

HISTORIETTE (his-tor-i-et/) *a tale*   H27

Nobody had a chance against him; he answered all your questions before you asked them; contradicted everybody with the intrepidity of a Rigby; annihilated your anecdotes by historiettes infinitely more piquant; and if anybody chanced to make a joke which he could not excel, declared immediately it was a Joe Miller.—*Disraeli.* Coningsby.

HISTORIOGRAPHER (his-tor-i-og/ra-fer) *writer of history*   H28

Far, far exceeding the bonhomie of Macheath, the Duke could not resist remembering, that had it been his fortune to have lived in the land in which his historiographer will soon be wandering, in short to have been a pacha instead of a peer, he might have married all three.—*Disraeli.* The Young Duke.

He now, having determined to apply himself vigorously to the discharge of the duties which belonged to him as historiographer of France, came to see the great events which it was his office to record.—*Macaulay.* History of England, Ch. xix.

HISTORY, ANCIENT *history to the end of the Western*   H29
   Empire

HISTORY, MEDIÆVAL *from 476 A.D. to the*   H30
   Reformation

HISTORY, MODERN *from 1517 A.D. onwards*   H31

HOBART (hub/art)   H32

HOLOCAUST (hol/o-kawst) *wholesale destruction*   H33
  Offer not only Peace-Offerings but Holocausts unto God.—*Sir Thomas Browne.* Christian Morals. Pt. i, s. 1.

HOLOGRAPH (hol/o-graf) *a deed or testament written*   H34
   wholly by the grantor's or testator's own hand

HONG (hong) *a Chinese factory*   H35

HORRENT (hor/ent) *bristling; erect*   H36
    The Stygian Councel thus dissolv'd; and forth
  In order came the grand infernal Peers,
  Midst came thir mighty Paramount, and seemd
  Alone th' Antagonist of Heav'n, nor less
  Then Hells dread Emperour with pomp Supream,
  And God-like imitated State; him round
  A Globe of fierie Seraphim inclos'd
  With bright imblazonrie, and horrent Arms.
      —*Milton.* Paradise Lost. ii.

HOURI (hoo/ri) *attractive female*   H37
  Other girls, very heavily made-up, emerged from the cloakroom, and passed on into the ballroom examining Peter with unconcealed interest as they went.
  He heard one houri remark to her friend:
  " That's Connie's Chap."—*Hugh McGraw.* Rude Society. xvii (2). (Heinemann).

HOY†   H38
    He sent to Germany, strange aid to rear:
  From whence eftsoons arrived here three hoys
  Of Saxons, whom he for his safety employs.
      —*Spenser.* The Faerie Queene.

HUSBANDRY† H39

 . . . poor and mangled Peace . . .
Hath from France too long been chased,
And all her husbandry doth lie on heaps,
Corrupting in its own fertility.
    —*Shakespeare.* Henry V. v. 2.

HYALINE† H40

  Who seekes
To lessen thee, against his purpose serves
To manifest the more thy might: his evil
Thou usest, and from thence creat'st more good.
Witness this new-made World, another Heav'n
From Heaven Gate not farr, founded in view
On the cleer Hyaline, the Glassie Sea;
Of amplitude almost immense, with Starr's
Numerous, and every Starr perhaps a World
Of destind habitation.
    —*Milton.* Paradise Lost. vii.

HYDROCEPHALIC (hi-dro-ce-fal/ik) *dropsical* H41

 A hobgoblin in the image of Punch Costello, hipshot, crook-backed, hydrocephalic, prognathic with receding forehead and Ally Sloper nose tumbles in somersaults through the gathering darkness.—*James Joyce.* Ulysses (ii). (John Lane).

HYPERBATON (hi-per/ba-ton) *inversion of the order* H42
of words

 . . . if your meaning be with a violent hyperbaton to transpose the text.—*Milton.* Animadversions upon a Defence of the Humble Remonstrance.

HYPERBOLE† H43

  Taffata phrases, silken terms precise,
Three-pil'd hyperboles, spruce affectation,
Figures pedantical, these summer flies,
Have blown me full of maggot ostentation.
    —*Shakespeare.* Love's Labour Lost. v. 2.

 They lived, not in an afterglow, but just before the colour died, in a mount of hyperbole, of exaggerated stillness, when no one moved, and all eyes watched the sunset.—*Sacheverell Sitwell.* Sacred & Profane Love. Book v, Pt. v. (Faber & Faber).

HYPERBOREAN†   H44

Returning home in triumph, he can express himself contented, charmed with his reception; has mineral specimens, and all manner of hyperborean memorials for friends; unheard of things to tell . . .—*Carlyle.* Critical and Miscellaneous Essays. " Diderot."

HYPODERMIC (hi-po-der/mik) *injection through*   H45
the skin

HYPOSTASIS* (hi-pos/ta-sis) *basis; substance; personality*   H46
OF THE NATURE OF SPIRITS

. . . they have knowledge not only of the specifical, but numerical forms of individuals, and understand by what reserved difference each single Hypostasis (besides the relation to its species), becomes its numerical self.—*Sir Thomas Browne.* Religio Medici. First Part.

IAGO	INDURATE
ICHTHYOLOGY	INEFFABLE
IMBRICATE	INELUCTABLE
IMBROGLIO	INENARRABLE
IMMEDICABLE	INEXIGENT
IMMINENT	INGRESS
IMMITIGABLE	INGURGITATE
IMMOLATE	INSOUCIANT
IMPARADISE	INTEGUMENT
IMPLEX	INTERREGNUM
IMPRESARIO	INTROIT
IMPRIMATUR	INURBANE
INCONDITE	*IQUIQUE*
INCRASSATE	IRASCIBLE
INCULCATE	*IRENE*
INCURVATE	IRREFRAGABLE
INDICT	ITALIAN WAREHOUSEMAN
INDICTION	

IAGO (e-a/go)   I

ICHTHYOLOGY (ik-thi-ol/o-ji) *study of fish*   I2

Of the value of this principle of harmony, some idea may be formed from the circumstance, that on it Agassiz has based the whole of that celebrated classification, of which he is the sole author, and by which fossil ichthyology has for the first time assumed a precise and definite shape.— *Buckle.* History of Civilization in England. Vol. i, Ch. xiv.

"I was once in love with an ichthyologist," said Juan encouragingly. "But she always had damp clothes and I used to catch cold."—*Eric Linklater.* Juan in China. (Jonathan Cape).

IMBRICATE†   I3

The fans consisted of the trains of peacocks whose quills were set in a long stem so as to imbricate the plumes in the gradation of their natural growths.—*Beckford.* Vathek.

IMBROGLIO†   I4

It was appointed of Fate that, in this wide-weltering, strangely growing, monstrous, stupendous imbroglio of Convention business, the grand first-parent of all the questions, controversies, measures and enterprises which were to be evolved there to the world's astonishment, should be this question of King Louis.—*Carlyle.* The French Revolution. Pt. iii, Bk. ii, Ch. iii.

Long experience of Ukridge's ingenious schemes had given me a fatalistic feeling with regard to them. With whatever fair prospects I started out to co-operate with him on these occasions, I almost invariably found myself entangled sooner or later in some nightmare imbroglio.—*P. G. Wodehouse.* Ukridge. Ch. vii. (Herbert Jenkins).

IMMEDICABLE (i-med/i-kabl) *incurable*   I5

> My griefs not only pain me
> As a lingring disease,
> But finding no redress, ferment and rage,
> Nor less then wounds immedicable
>Ranckle, and fester, and gangrene,
> To black mortification.
>
>   —*Milton.* Samson Agonistes.

IMMINENT†   I6

What dangers at any time are imminent, what evils hang over our heads, God doth know, and not we.—*Hooker.* Ecclesiastical Polity.

IMMITIGABLE (i-mit/i-gabl) *incapable of being softened*   I7

And I remember being taken at the age of nine to see Sarah [Bernhardt] in some piece of immitigable woe. The old gentleman who took me wept long and loud into the red silk handkerchief which it was at that time fashionable to tuck into the waistcoat. Recovering somewhat, he said with a voice still shaking with emotion: " Rachel was better!" I have always regarded this as, in the circumstances, a masterpiece of dramatic criticism.—*James Agate*. Playgoing. (iv). (Jarrolds).

IMMOLATE (im/mo-late) *to sacrifice*   I8
THE POET DAVIDSON
He saw the phenomena of field and hedgerow and woodland with clear eye and appreciative exactitude. But he did not immolate his personality at the shrine of Nature after the manner of Wordsworth or Shelley.—*Holbrook Jackson*. The Eighteen Nineties Ch. xiii. (Jonathan Cape).

Mr. Marion Crawford has immolated himself upon the altar of local colour.—*Oscar Wilde*. The Decay of Lying.

IMPARADISE (im-par/a-dice) *to make supremely happy*   I9

thus these two
Imparadis't in one anothers arms
The happier *Eden,* shall enjoy thir fill
Of bliss on bliss, while I to Hell am thrust
Where neither joy nor love, but fierce desire,
Among our other torments not the least.
—*Milton*. Paradise Lost. iv, 506.

IMPLEX (im/pleks) *intricate; complicated*   I10

Every poem is, according to Aristotle's division either simple or implex: it is called simple when there is no change of fortune in it; implex, when the fortune of the chief actor changes from bad to good, or from good to bad.—*Addison*. Spectator, No. 297.

IMPRESARIO (im-pre-za/ri-o) *organizer of entertainment*   I11

IMPRIMATUR (im-pri-may/tur) *(1) licence to print and   I12
   publish; (2) mark of approval*

Sometimes five imprimaturs are seen together dialogue-wise in the piatza of one title-page.—*Milton*. Areopagitica.

Thus shall my title pass a sacred seal,
Receive an imprimatur from above,
While angels shout. An infidel reclaim'd!
—*Young*. Night Thoughts. vii.

. . . he bellowed aloud . . . on the occasion of a prize day, that our little magazine showed signs of considerable talent, though it was an unofficial publication on which he " might have hesitated to set his *Imprimatur*." Somehow we felt it would have been even more crushing if he had set his *Imprimatur*. It sounded like the thumb of a giant.—*G. K. Chesterton*. " Autobiography." Ch. iii. (Hutchinson).

INCONDITE (in-kon/dit) *unfinished; crude; irregular*   I13

They . . . use inarticulate, incondite voices, speeches, obsolete gestures, &c.—*Burton.* Anatomy of Melancholy.

INCRASSATE (in-kras/ate) *to thicken*   I14

And even that seeds themselves in their rudimentall discoveries, appear in foliaceons surcles, or sprouts within their coverings, in a diaphanous gellie, before deeper incrassation, is also visibly verified in Cherries, Acorns, Plums.—*Sir Thomas Browne.* Garden of Cyrus. Ch. iii.

INCULCATE (in-kul/kate) *to enforce; to urge*   I15

I profess myself to have ever entertained a profound veneration for the astonishing force and vivacity of mind which the Rambler exhibits. That Johnson had penetration enough to see, and, seeing, would not disguise the general misery of man in this state of being may have given rise to the superficial notion of his being too stern a philosopher. But men of reflection will be sensible that he has given a true representation of human existence, and that he has, at the same time, with a generous benevolence displayed every consolation which our state affords us; not only those arising from the hopes of futurity, but such as may be attained in the immediate progress through life. He has not depressed the soul to despondency and indifference. He has every where inculcated study, labour, and exertion.—*James Boswell.* Life of Johnson. A.D. 1750. Ætat. 41.

The importance of strict and scrupulous veracity cannot be too often inculcated. Johnson was known to be so rigidly attentive to it, that even in his common conversation the slightest circumstance was mentioned with exact precision. The knowledge of his having such a principle and habit made his friends have a perfect reliance on the truth of everything that he told, however it might have been doubted if told by many others. As an instance of this, I may mention an odd incident which he related as having happened to him one night in Fleet Street. "A gentlewoman (said he) begged I would give her my arm to assist her in crossing the street, which I accordingly did; upon which she offered me a shilling, supposing me to be the watchman. I perceived that she was somewhat in liquor." This, if told by most people, would have been thought an invention; when told by Johnson, it was believed by his friends as much as if they had seen what passed.—*James Boswell.* Life of Johnson. A.D. 1776. Ætat. 67.

INCURVATE (in-ker/vate) *to bend* (*inwards*)   I16

But age doth not rectify, but incurvate our natures, turning bad dispositions into worser habits . . .—*Sir Thomas Browne.* Religio Medici. First Part.

INDICT (in-dite/) *to accuse; to charge with an offence*   I17

DESDEMONA: I was, unhandsome warrior as I am,
                 Arraigning his unkindness with my soul;
                 But now I find I had suborn'd the witness,
                 And he's indicted falsely.
                     —*Shakespeare.* Othello. iii. 4.

INDICTION (in-dik/shun) (1) *declaration;* (2) *a cycle of*   I18
        15 years

INDURATE (in/du-rate) *to harden; grow hard*   I19

Dried, souced, indurate fish.—*Burton.* Anatomy of Melancholy.

There was a wide margin of grass along here, and Gabriel's footsteps were deadened by its softness, even at this indurating period of the year.— *Thomas Hardy.* Far From the Madding Crowd. Ch. vi. (Macmillan).

And as they got up into the highlands beyond Scutari they began to realise the deceitfulness of Podgoritza and the real truth about khans. Their next one they reached after a rainy evening, and it was a cavernous room with a floor of indurated mud and full of eye-stinging wood-smoke and wind and the smell of beasts, unpartitioned, with a weakly hostile custodian from whom no food could be got but a little goat's flesh and bread.— *H. G. Wells.* The Research Magnificent. Ch. iv. (Collins).

INEFFABLE†   I20

> To whom the Son, with calm aspect and cleer
> Light'ning Divine, ineffable, serene,
> Made answer.
> > —*Milton.* Paradise Lost. v, 733.

INELUCTABLE†   I21

> Now Love, the ineluctable, with bitter sweetness
> Fills me, overwhelms me, and shakes my being.
> > —*Edwin Marion Cox.* The Poems of Sappho.

INENARRABLE (in-e-nar/abl) *unspeakable; indescribable*   I22

. . . the 'cello meditated those Mohammedan ecstasies that last, under the green palms of Paradise, six hundred inenarrable years apiece.—*Aldous Huxley.* Antic Hay. Ch. xv. (Chatto & Windus).

INEXIGENT (in-ex/i-gent) *unexacting; undemanding*   I23

BYRON AND LADY BLESSINGTON
He, conquered by her swift inexigent intelligence, forgot the female in the sympathetic feminine.—*Michael Sadleir.* Blessington D'Orsay. Ch. ii. (Constable).

INGRESS (in/gres) *entrance*   I24

. . . to light a fire is the instinctive and resistant act of man when, at the winter ingress, the curfew is sounded throughout Nature.—*Thomas Hardy.* The Return of the Native. Bk. i (2). (Macmillan).

INGURGITATE (in-ger/ji-tate) *to swallow* I25

Nothing pesters the body and mind sooner, than to be still fed, to eat and ingurgitate beyond all measure, as many do.—*Burton.* Anatomy of Melancholy.

INSOUCIANT (in-soo/ci-ant) *careless* I26

The ladies of Watteau, gay and insouciant, seemed to wander with their cavaliers among the great trees, whispering to one another careless, charming things, and yet somehow oppressed by a nameless fear.—*W. Somerset Maugham.* Of Human Bondage. Ch. xlvii. (Heinemann).

INTEGUMENT (in-teg/u-ment) *skin; husk* I27

If, with Cuvier, we compare and class them [animals] according to the structure of the skeleton, or, with Blainville, according to the nature of their outward integuments, the agreements and differences which are observable in these respects are not only of much greater importance in themselves, but are marks of agreements and differences in many other important particulars of the structure and mode of life of the animals.—*J. S. Mill.* System of Logic. Pt. iv, Ch. ii, s. 4.

INTERREGNUM (in-ter-reg/num) *interval; pause* I28

A great meeting of noblemen and gentlemen who had property in Ireland was held, during the interregnum at the house of the Duke of Ormond in Saint James's Square.—*Macaulay.* History of England. Ch. xii.

INTROIT (in-tro/it) I29

A psalm sung by a priest approaching the altar to begin Mass or Communion.

INURBANE (in-ur-bane/) *discourteous* I30

IQUIQUE (e-key/kay) I31

IRASCIBLE (i-ras/ibl) *irritable* I32

IRENE (i-re/ne) I33

IRREFRAGABLE (i-ref/ra-gabl) *unanswerable* I34

. . . such irrefragable logic . . .—*Compton Mackenzie.* Gallipoli Memories. Ch. x.

ITALIAN WAREHOUSEMAN   *a grocer*   I35

After them march the guilds and trades and train-bands with flying colours: coopers, bird fanciers, millwrights, newspaper canvassers, law scriveners, masseurs, vintners, trussmakers, chimney sweeps, lard refiners, tabinet and poplin weavers, farriers, Italian warehousemen, church decorators, bootjack manufacturers, undertakers, silk mercers, lapidaries, salesmasters, corkcutters, assessors of fire losses, dyers and cleaners, export bottlers, fellmongers, ticketwriters, heraldic seal engravers, horse repository hands, bullion brokers, cricket and archery outfitters, riddlemakers, egg and potato factors, hosiers and glovers, plumbing contractors. After them march gentlemen of the bed chamber, Black Rod, Deputy Garter, Gold Stick, the master of horse, the lord great chamberlain, the earl marshal, the high constable carrying the sword of state, Saint Stephen's iron crown, the chalice and bible. Four buglers on foot blow a sennet. Beefeaters reply, winding clarions of welcome. Under an arch of triumph Bloom appears bareheaded, in a crimson velvet mantle trimmed with ermine, bearing Saint Edward's staff, the orb and sceptre with the dove, the curtana. He is seated on a milkwhite horse with long flowing crimson tail, richly caparisoned, with golden headstall. Wild excitement. The ladies from their balconies throw down rosepetals. The air is perfumed with essences. The men cheer. Bloom's boys run amid the bystanders with branches of hawthorn and wrenbushes.—*James Joyce*. Ulysses. p. 471. (John Lane).

JACINTH

JACK TOWEL

JINN

JOCUND

JONQUIL

JOUST

JOWETT

JUBILEE

JACINTH (jas/inth) *a precious stone, orange-red in colour;*   **J**
    a variety of zircon

> Then drew he forth the brand Excalibur,
> And o'er him, drawing it, the winter moon
> Brightening the skirts of a long cloud, ran forth,
> And sparkled keen with frost against the hilt;
> For all the haft twinkled with diamond sparks,
> Myriads of topaz-lights, and jacinth-work
> Of subtlest jewellery.
> > —*Tennyson.* Morte d'Arthur.

JACK TOWEL (jak towl) *a roller towel*   **J2**

JINN (gin) *an evil spirit; a demon*   **J3**

. . . the monstrous shapes of bursting shells, fierce jinn of livid green and black and foul yellow smoke . . .—*Compton Mackenzie.* Gallipoli Memories.

JOCUND (jok/und) *merry*   **J4**

MACBETH: O, full of scorpions is my mind, dear wife!
                        Thou know'st that Banquo, and his Fleance,
                        lives.
LADY MACBETH: But in them nature's copy's not eterne.
MACBETH: There's comfort yet; they are assailable;
                        Then be thou jocund: ere the bat hath flown
                        His cloister'd flight; ere to black Hecate's
                            summons
                        The shard-borne beetle with his drowsy hums
                        Hath rung night's yawning peal, there shall be
                            done
                        A deed of dreadful note.
> > —*Shakespeare.* Macbeth. III, iii.

JONQUIL (jong/kwil) *(1) a kind of daffodil; (2) pale yellow*   **J5**

> Nor gradual bloom is wanting,
> Nor hyacinths of purest virgin white,
> Low bent and blushing inward; nor jonquilles
> Of potent fragrance.
> > —*Thomson.* Seasons. " Spring."

But amid all this solid splendour there were certain intimations of feminine elegance in the veil of finely-cut pink paper which covered the nakedness of the empty but highly polished fire-place, and in the hand-screens, which were profusely ornamented with ribbon of the same hue, and one of which afforded a most accurate if not picturesque view of Margate, while the other glowed with a huge wreath of cabbage-roses and jonquils.—*Disraeli* Henrietta Temple. Bk. vi, Ch. x.

JOUST (joost) *fight on horseback*   J6

> . . . or to describe Races and Games,
> Or tilting Furniture, emblazon'd Shields,
> Impreses quaint, Caparisons and Steeds;
> Bases and tinsel Trappings, gorgious Knights
> At Joust and Torneament; then marshal'd Feast
> Serv'd up in Hall with Sewers, and Seneshals;
>
> —*Milton.* Paradise Lost. ix.

JOWETT (jou/et)   J7

JUBILEE (joo/bi-lee) *a time of commemoration and*   J8
         rejoicing

> Angels uttering joy, heaven rung
> With jubilee, and loud hosannas filled
> The eternal regions.
>
> —*Milton.* Paradise Lost. iii, 347.

Sunderland was able: he was useful: he was unprincipled indeed: but so were all the English politicians of the generation which had learned, under the sullen tyranny of the saints, to disbelieve in virtue, and which had, during the wild jubilee of the Restoration, been dissolved in vice.— *Macaulay.* History of England. Ch. xxii.

KALEIDOSCOPE

KAVANAGH

KEDLESTON

KEENING

KINGCUP

KNOLLYS

KALEIDOSCOPE (ka-li/do-skope) *an instrument through*   K
which an object is seen multiplied, the images being arranged in a symmetrical pattern

If I show you that such an event or reign was an obliquity to the right hand, and how produced, and such other event or reign a deviation to the left, and whence originating,—that the growth was stopped here, accelerated there,—that such a tendency is, and always has been, corroborative, and such other tendency destructive, of the main progress of the idea towards realization;—if this idea, not only like a kaleidoscope, shall reduce all the miscellaneous fragments into order, but shall also minister strength, and knowledge, and light to the true patriot and statesman for working out the bright thought, and bringing the glorious embryo to a perfect birth;—then, I think, I have a right to say that the idea which led to this is not only true, but the truth, the only truth.—*Coleridge.* Table Talk.

When I look at a candle through a multiplying glass, I see what seems a dozen candles instead of one: and if the real circumstances of the case were skilfully disguised, I might suppose that there were really that number; there would be what is called an optical deception. In the kaleidoscope there really is that deception: when I look through the instrument, instead of what is actually there, namely, a casual arrangement of coloured fragments, the appearance presented is that of the same combination several times repeated in symmetrical arrangement round a point. The delusion is of course effected by giving me the same sensations, which I should have had if such a symmetrical combination had really been presented to me.—*J. S. Mill.* System of Logic.

KAVANAGH (kav/a-na)   K2

KEDLESTON (kel/son)   K3

KEENING (kee/ning) *lamentation*   K4

But upon Wiseman and Wishart the significance of that barbaric keening was lost. Full of bread and drink, they rollicked along unconcerned, embraced the girls who had scarce energy to repel them, took up and joined (with drunken voices) in the death wail, and at last (on what they took to be an invitation) entered under the roof of a house in which was a considerable concourse of people sitting silent. They stooped below the eaves, flushed and laughing; within a minute they came forth again with changed faces and silent tongues; and as the press severed to make way for them, Taveeta was able to perceive, in the deep shadow of the house, the sick man raising from his mat a head already defeatured by disease. The two tragic triflers fled without hesitation for their boat, screaming on Taveeta to make haste.—*R. L. Stevenson.* The Ebb Tide. Ch. v.

KINGCUP (king/kup) *marsh marigold*   K5

>   Bring hither the pink and purple collumbine
> With gillyflowers;
> Bring coronations, and sops in wine,
> Worn of paramours;
> Strow me the ground with daffadowndillies,
> And cowslips, and kingcups, and loved lillies:
> The pretty pance,
> And the chevisance
> Shall match with the fair flower-delice.
>   —*Spenser*. Shepherd's Calendar. iv.

KNOLLYS (nolz)   K6

LABYRINTHIAN	LEMAN
LACHRYMA CHRISTI	LEMMA
LACKADAISICAL	LENITIVE
LACONISM	*LEOMINSTER*
LACUSTRINE	*LEONCAVALLO*
LADY DAY	*LE QUEX*
LAMBENT	LEVIATHAN
LAMMAS	LEVIN
LAOCOÖN	LIBERTICIDE
LAO-TSZE	LIGHT-YEAR
LAPIDARY	LITERATI
LARBOARD	LITTORAL
LA ROCHEFOUCAULD	LORIMER
LASCAR	LUCULENT
LATITUDINARIAN	LUSH
LAVEROCK	LUSKISH
LAZZARONE	LUSTRATION
LEE	LUSTRUM
LEFEBVRE	LYCEUM
LE FEUVRE	LYDIAN
LEIBNITZ	*LYSAGHT*

LABYRINTHIAN (lab-i-rinth/i-an) *winding; intricate*   L

> Mark how the labyrinthian turns they take,
> The circles intricate, and mystic maze,
> Weave the grand cipher of Omnipotence.
> —*Young.* Night Thoughts. ix, 1131.

LACHRYMA CHRISTI (lak/ri-ma kris/ti) *a sweet red*   L2
     wine from South Italy

LACKADAISICAL (lak-a-day/zi-kal) *languid; careless*   L3

LACONISM (lak/on-ism) *a pithy phrase or expression*   L4

The hand of Providence writes often by abbreviatures, heiroglyphicks, or short characters, which, like the laconism on the wall [Daniel, iii, 25] are not to be made out but by a hint or key from that Spirit which indicted them.—*Sir Thomas Browne.* Christian Morals. i, 25.

LACUSTRINE (la-kus/trine) *relating to lakes*   L5

It may be that prehistoric man lived in this valley in truly lacustrine fashion and shaped for himself, as in the recently discovered marsh village of Glastonbury, a home on sunken piles.—*H. W. Tompkins.* Highways & Byways in Hertfordshire. Ch. v. (Macmillan).

LADY DAY (la/di day) *the 25th March*   L6

LAMBENT†   L7

This last picture is a study of sea whose whole organization has been broken up by constant recoils from a rocky coast. The Laugharne gives the surge and weight of the ocean in a gale, on a comparatively level shore; but the Land's End, the entire disorder of the surges when every one of them, divided and entangled among promontories as it rolls in, and beaten back part by part from walls of rock on this side and that side, recoils like the defeated division of a great army, throwing all behind it into disorder, breaking up the succeeding waves into vertical ridges, which in their turn, yet more totally shattered upon the shore, retire in more hopeless confusion; until the whole surface of the sea becomes one dizzy whirl of rushing, writhing, tortured, undirected rage, bounding, and crashing, and coiling in an anarchy of enormous power; subdivided into myriads of waves, of which every one is not, be it remembered, a separate surge, but part and portion of a vast one, actuated by internal power, and giving in every direction the mighty undulation of impetuous line which glides over the rocks and writhes in the wind, overwhelming the one, and piercing the other with the form, fury, and swiftness of a sheet of lambent fire.—*John Ruskin.* Modern Painters. Ch. xv.

LAMMAS (lam/mas) *the 1st August*   L8

> Even or odd, of all days in the year,
> Come lammas eve at night, shall she be fourteen.
> > —*Shakespeare.* Romeo and Juliet. i, 3.

LAOCOÖN (lay-ok/o-on)   L9

LAO-TSZE (la/ot zer)   L10

LAPIDARY (lap/i-dar-i) (*1*) *relating to stone;* (*2*) *a person*   L11
      who cuts and polishes precious stones, or who
      deals in precious stones

The writer of an epitaph should not be considered as saying nothing
but what is strictly true. Allowance must be made for some degree of
exaggerated praise. In lapidary inscriptions a man is not upon oath.—
James Boswell. Life of Johnson. A.D. 1775. Ætat. 66.

As I walked upon the edge I could see far and wide over the sandy
bottom of the bay; the sun shone clear and green and steady in the
deeps; the bay seemed rather like a great transparent crystal, as one sees
them in a lapidary's shop; there was naught to show that it was water but
an internal trembling, a hovering within of sun-glints and netted shadows,
and now and then a faint lap and a dying bubble round the edge. The
shadows of the rocks lay out for some distance at their feet, so that my
own shadow, moving, pausing, and stooping on the top of that, reached
sometimes half across the bay.—*R. L. Stevenson.* The Merry Men. Ch. iii.

LARBOARD†   L12

> . . . or when Ulysses on the larboard shunn'd
> Charybdis, and by the other whirlpool steer'd.
> > —*Milton.* Paradise Lost. ii, 1019.

LA ROCHEFOUCAULD (la rosh-foo-ko/)   L13

LASCAR (las/kar) *East Indian seaman*   L14
   This term formerly included a native Indian soldier.

Nine new battalions of sepoys were raised, and a corps of native
artillery was formed out of the hardy lascars of the Bay of Bengal.—
Macaulay. Critical and Historical Essays. "Warren Hastings."

LATITUDINARIAN (lat-i-tud-i-nare/i-an) *an agnostic;*   L15
      a person of liberal views

The golden days of Harley would return. The Somersets, the Lees,
and the Wyndhams would again surround the throne. The latitudinarian
prelates, who had not been ashamed to correspond with Doddridge and to
shake hands with Whiston, would be succeeded by divines of the temper
of South and Atterbury.—*Macaulay.* Critical and Historical Essays.
"Earl of Chatham."

LAVEROCK (lav/rock) *lark*   L16

> There, see a black-bird feed her young,
> Or a leverock build her nest.
> > —*Izaak Walton*. The Compleat Angler.

LAZZARONE (lats-a-ro/nay) *beggar*   L17

. . . no longer was Florence an affair of cathedrals, museums and lazzaroni, but a social stage whereon intellect, gaiety and fashion played their several parts.—*Michael Sadleir*. Blessington-d'Orsay. Ch. iii (ii). (Constable).

LEE†   L18

Another resultant phenomenon is the formation of cloud in the calm air to leeward of a steep summit; cloud whose edges are in rapid motion, where they are affected by the current of the wind above, and stream from the peak like the smoke of a volcano, yet always vanish at a certain distance from it as steam issuing from a chimney.—*John Ruskin*. Modern Painters. Ch. ix.

I am sure I would rather be a bargee than occupy any position under Heaven that required attendance at an office. There are few callings, I should say, where a man gives up less of his liberty in return for regular meals. The bargee is on shipboard—he is master of his own ship—he can land whenever he will—he can never be kept beating off a lee-shore a whole frosty night when the sheets are as hard as iron; and so far as I can make out, time stands as nearly still with him as is compatible with the return of bed-time or the dinner-hour. It is not easy to see why a bargee should ever die.—*R. L. Stevenson*. An Inland Voyage. " On the Willebroek Canal." (Chatto & Windus).

LEFEBVRE (le fevr)   L19

LE FEUVRE (le fevr)   L20

LEIBNITZ (lip/nits)   L21

LEMAN (lce/man) *sweetheart; mistress*   L22

> Hold for my sake, and do him not to dye;
> But vanquish'd, thine eternal bondslave make,
> And me, thy worthy meed, unto thy leman take.
> > —*Spenser*. The Faerie Queene.

> A cup of wine,
> That's brisk and fine,
> And drink unto the leman mine.
> > —*Shakespeare*. Henry IV. Part ii, v. 3.

LEMMA (lem/ma) *an assumption*   L23

I shall premise the following lemma: If with a view to demonstrate
any proposition, a certain point is proposed, by virtue of which certain
other points are attained; and such supposed point be itself afterwards
destroyed or rejected by a contrary supposition; in that case, all the other
points, attained thereby and consequent thereupon, must also be destroyed
and rejected, so as from thence forward to be no more supposed or
applied in the demonstration.—*Bishop Berkeley*. Analyst. s. xii.

LENITIVE (len/it-iv) *assuasive*   L24

An apothecary's shop, wherein are remedies . . . alternatives, corro-
boratives, lenitives.—*Burton*. Anatomy of Melancholy.

LEOMINSTER (lem/ster)   L25

LEONCAVALLO (lay-on-ka-val/o)   L26

LE QUEX (le ku/)   L27

LEVIATHAN (le-vi/a-than) *huge creature or object*   L28

KING HENRY: What rein can hold licentious wickedness
                When down the hill he holds his fierce career?
                We may as bootless spend our vain command
                Upon the enraged soldiers in their spoil
                As send precepts to the leviathan
                To come ashore.
                            —*Shakespeare*. Henry V. iii, 3.

LEVIN (lev/in) *lightning*   L29

            As when the flashing Levin haps to light
        Uppon two stubborne oakes, which stand so neare
        That way betwixt them none appeares in sight;
        The Engin, fiercely flying forth, doth teare
        Th' one from the earth, and through the aire doth bear;
        The other it with force doth overthrow
        Uppon one side, and from his rootes doth reare:
        So did the Championesse those two there strow,
        And to their sire their carcasses left to bestow.
                —*Spenser*. The Faerie Queene. Bk. v, vi, 40.

Mankind, you would have thought, might have remained content with
what Prometheus stole for them and not gone fishing the profound heaven
with kites to catch and domesticate the wild-fire of the storm. Yet here
we have the levin brand at our doors, and it is proposed that we should
henceforward take our walks abroad in the glare of permanent lightning.
—*R. L. Stevenson*. "A Plea for Gas Lamps." (Chatto & Windus).

LIBERTICIDE (li-ber/ti-side) *enemy of liberty* L30

The priest, the slave, and the liberticide.
—*Shelley*. Adonais.

LIGHT-YEAR L31

The distance travelled by light in the space of one year, namely 6,000,000,000,000 miles.

LITERATI (lit-er-ay/ti) *learned people; literary people* L32

The unwearied Richter tried other plans. He presented Magazine editors with essays, some one in ten of which might be accepted; he made joint-stock with certain provincial literati of the Hof district, who had cash and published for themselves.—*Carlyle*. Critical and Miscellaneous Essays. "Jean Paul Friedrich Richter."

LITTORAL (lit/or-al) *belonging to the shore* L33

. . . the mobile, the marine and fluid temper of the littoral Ionian people.—*Walter Pater*. Plato and Platonism. Ch. viii. (Macmillan).

LORIMER (lor/i-mer) *a maker of bits and spurs* L34

Brummagen is a town maintained chiefly by smiths, nailers, cutlers, edge-tool forgers, lorimers, or bit-makers.—*Holinshed*. Description of Britain. Vol. i, Ch. xxv.

LUCULENT (lu/ku-lent) *clear; lucid; certain* L35

And luculent along
The purer rivers flow.
—*Thomson*. Seasons. "Winter."

They are, against the obstinate incredulity of the Jews, the most luculent testimonies that the Christian religion hath.—*Hooker*. Ecclesiastical Polity.

A luculent oration he made of the miseries of this and happiness of that other life.—*Burton*. Anatomy of Melancholy.

LUSH (lush) *succulent; luxuriant* L36

How lush and lusty the grass looks! how green!
—*Shakespeare*. The Tempest. ii, 1.
And in the warm hedge grew lush eglantine
Green cowbind and the moonlight-coloured may
And cherry-blossoms, and white cups, whose wine
Was the bright dew, yet drained not by the day;
And wild roses, and ivy serpentine
With its dark buds and leaves, wandering astray;
And flowers azure, black and streaked with gold,
Fairer than any wakened eyes behold.
—*Shelley*. The Question.

LUSKISH (lusk/ish) *sluggish; indolent*   L37

>   Nathlesse at length him selfe he did upreare
> In lustlesse wise; as if against his will,
> Ere he had slept his fill, he wakened were,
> And gan to stretch his limbs; which feeling ill
> Of his late fall, awhile he rested still:
> But, when he saw his foe before in vew,
> He shooke off luskishnesse; and courage chill
> Kindling afresh, gan battell to renew,
> To prove if better foote then horsebacke would ensew.
> > > *—Spenser.* The Faerie Queene. Bk. vi, i, 35.

LUSTRATION (lus-tray/shun) *ceremonial purification*   L38

The Sibylline books enjoined ceremonies of a more harmless nature, processions of priests in white robes, attended by a chorus of youths and virgins; lustrations of the city and adjacent country; and sacrifices, whose powerful influence disabled the barbarians from passing the mystic ground on which they had been celebrated.—*Edward Gibbon.* The Decline and Fall of the Roman Empire. Ch. xi.

LUSTRUM (lus/trum) *a period of five years*   L39

>   We push time from us, and we wish him back;
> Lavish of lustrums, and yet fond of life.
> > > > *—Young.* Night Thoughts. ii.

. . . he could not have endured to live in the Caribbean regions but for the prospect of a voyage that he took every fifth year, starting in July. Then he would set out in a boat that had Spitzbergen for its ultimate goal. and, as he sailed further and further towards his strange destination, he would sit longer and longer on deck—wrapped, it is true, in a fur coat—inhale the fresh breath and foam of Arctic seas, lie back and allow the cold mist to dampen his forehead, as though it were a second attending to a boxer after a heated round. Only in those moments, only in that so peculiar culmination to every lustrum, did he feel perfectly content.—*Osbert Sitwell.* Sing High! Sing Low! "Still Life." (2) (Macmillan).

LYCEUM (li-se/um) *a literary association, or the place* L40
    where they meet

LYDIAN (lid/i-an) *denoting soft, slow music; effeminate* L41

>   And ever, against eating cares,
> Lap me in soft Lydian airs.
> > > > *—Milton.* L'Allegro. 135.

>   Softly sweet in Lydian measures,
> Soon he soothed his soul to pleasures.
> > > > *—Dryden.* Alexander's Feast.

LYSAGHT (li/sat)   L42

MACERATE

MADREPORIC

MAGENTA

MAGGIORE

MAGIC

MAGNIFIC

MAHON

MAHONEY

MAINWARING

MALEFIC

MALKIN

MALTWORM

MANCIPLE

MANDARIN

MANDRAKE

MANSARD FLOOR

MARL

MARPLOT

MASQUERADE

MATHESIS

MAUGRE

MAZARINE

MEGALOMANIAC

MEIOSIS

MELHUISH

MENISCUS

MENZIES

MEPHISTOPHELIAN

MEPHITIC

MERIDIONAL

METATHESIS

METEMPSYCHOSIS

METONYMY

MEZZO-RILIEVO

MIASMA

MILLENNIUM

MIRIFIC

MITHRIDATE

MIZZLE

MNEMONIC

MNEMOSYNE

MOLLUSC

MONEGASQUE

MORDANT

MOUJIK

MOUNTEBANK

MUNGE

MYRRH

MYSTAGOGUE

MACERATE (mas/er-ate) *to make lean* M

Sorrow which contracts the heart, macerates the soul, subverts the good estate of the body, hindering all the occupations of it, causing melancholy, and many times death itself.—*Burton*. Anatomy of Melancholy.

It should be a place for nobody but hermits dwelling in prayer and maceration, or mere born-devils drowning care in a perpetual carouse.—*R. L. Stevenson*. " Æs Triplex." (Chatto & Windus).

MADREPORIC (mad-re-por/ik) *made of coral* M2

We went off before dawn. The wind was not yet violent, and after a three hours' tack we reached the edge of the reef of Schab-Ali which runs along the coast of Asia for about twenty miles, eight miles from the shore. This reef was formed of a series of madreporic tables joined together by rocky spikes between which there was no clear passage. Behind this barrier, on which the waves broke, was a little inner sea of calm and limpid blue water, in which ships of small tonnage could come round the most violent head winds. In this sheltered zone other beds of madrepores show their wide yellow patches just under the surface. At this season, when the Red Sea was at its lowest level, there was very little water covering the reefs, and at low tide some of the rocks and tables emerged completely. There were generally sea eagles perched on them, which gave an appearance of lively animation to these strange silhouettes. We went into this inner sea by a narrow opening in the southern extremity of the reef. The wreck of a steamer was spitted on the rocks, so perfectly preserved that for a moment we had the illusion of having arrived just after the disaster had taken place. Two enormous herons had taken up their abode on the deck of the wreck; from a distance we thought they were men. As we came nearer they flew heavily away, followed by a whole flock of screaming birds.—*Henry de Monfreid*. Hashish. Ch. xxii. (Methuen).

MAGENTA (ma-jen/ta) *crimson* M3

From the battle fought during the Austrian and Italian war in 1859, at a place so called. Colour so called, introduced or grown fashionable in that year.

MAGGIORE (ma-jor/a) M4

MAGIC (maj/ik) M5

There is a great deal of confusion in the minds of laymen as to what constitutes magic as practised by the conjuring fraternity. This is in no small measure due to wholly erroneous dictionary definitions of words associated with the subject and popularly considered synonymous terms.

Refer to dictionary definitions of *legerdemain* (sleigh-of-hand); *trick; jugglery*.

Sleight-of-hand is a branch of conjuring only in the sense of its being a " tool " with which certain magical results or effects are achieved. In its highest form, a great degree of digital skill is involved which, even so, is not comparable with that of a first-class juggler. Sleight-of-hand should never, in any circumstances, be paraded as such, but should be used secretly, simply as a means to an end.   The effects one can achieve by pure sleight-of-hand are very limited.   In fact, some of the most baffling effects in existence employ no sleight-of-hand whatever, relying upon far more subtle methods.

The word "trick," as meaning a conjuring effect, is loathed by all who, besides practising magic, have a sound knowledge of its art, theory and principles.   A trick is simply a "dodge," "wheeze," "sleight," or what you will, employed in the presentation of a magical effect, and contrary to popular belief is of relatively small importance in the art of magic as a whole.

Probably the most important feature in the art of magic is misdirection of the senses.   No less authority than the late J. N. Maskelyne gives the following definition in the magical classic "Our Magic" by Maskelyne & Devant (Routledge), page 176, 1st edition, probably 1914:

"Magic consists in creating by misdirection of the senses the mental impression of supernatural agency at work."

The popular catch-phrase as applied to conjuring, "the quickness of the hand deceives the eye" is a fallacy.   Even a highly-skilled hand cannot move so fast as to deceive an attentive eye; in fact, of all movements none is calculated to arouse suspicion or attention more than a quick one.

Jugglery defined as "conjuring" is wholly incorrect.   It is simply highly-skilled manual dexterity, with no attempt at a magical effect or plot.

"Natural magic" is a contradiction in terms, as magic *apparently* defies the laws and forces of nature.

MAGNIFIC (mag-nif/ik) *great*   M6

> Thrones, Dominations, Princedomes, Vertues, Powers!
> If these magnifick Titles yet remain,
> Not meerly titular.
> > —*Milton*. Paradise Lost. v. 772.
>
> O Parent, these are thy magnific deeds,
> Thy Trophies, which thou view'st as not thine own.
> > —*Milton*. Paradise Lost. x, 354.

MAHON (ma-hoon/)   M7

MAHONEY (mar/ni)   M8

MAINWARING (man/er-ing)   M9

MALEFIC (me-lef/ik) *hurtful; noxious*   M10

MALKIN (maw/kin) *a scarecrow; a slattern*   M11

> BRUTUS: . . . the kitchen malkin pins
> Her richest lockram 'bout her reechy neck,
> Clambering the walls to eye him.
> > —*Shakespeare*. Coriolanus. ii, 1.

MALTWORM (malt/worm) *a drunkard*   M12

> Then will she trowl to me the bowl,
> E'en as a maltworm sholde;
> And say, Dear heart I have ta'en my part
> In this jolly good ale and old.
>> *Gammer Gurton's Needle.* i, 1.

GADSHILL: . . . none of these mad, mustachio, purple-hued
           maltworms . . .
>> —*Shakespeare.* Henry IV. Pt. i, ii, 1.

. . . and know not otherwise how to bestow their time but in drinking;
maltworms, men-fishes, or water-snakes, like so many frogs in a puddle.—
Burton. Anatomy of Melancholy.

MANCIPLE (man/sipl) *a steward*   M13

. . . they come furnished with no more experience than they learnt
between the cook and the manciple.—*Milton.* Of Reformation in England.
Bk. ii.

MANDARIN (man/dar-in) *(1) orange; (2) Chinese*   M14
           official; (3) grotesque toy; (4) orange-coloured
           dye; (5) a duck; (6) a liqueur

MANDRAKE (man/drake)   M15

This is a plant about which much superstition gathered in
former times. Its root was fancifully supposed to resemble a
human being and to shriek when it was torn out of the ground.
It was also looked upon as an aphrodisiac, a love-philtre and a
narcotic.

Mandrakes upon known account have lived near an hundred yeares.
—*Sir Thomas Browne.* Garden of Cyrus. Ch. iii.

CLEOPATRA: . . . give me to drink mandragora.
CHARMIAN: Why Madam?
CLEOPATRA: That I might sleep out this great gap of time:
           My Antony is away.
>> —*Shakespeare.* Antony and Cleopatra. i, 5.

> And shrieks like mandrakes, torn out of the earth,
> That living mortals, hearing them, run mad.
>> —*Shakespeare.* Romeo and Juliet. iv, 3.

> Would curses kill, as doth the mandrake's groan,
> I would invent as bitter searching terms,
> As curst, as harsh, and horrible to hear.
>> —*Shakespeare.* Henry VI. Pt. ii, iii, 2.

MANSARD FLOOR *the top floor of a house*   M16

MARL (marl) *a rich soil*   M17
> Over the burning Marle, not like those steps
> On Heavens azure.
>> —*Milton*. Paradise Lost. i, 295.

. . . or afterwards, when he walked in the subterranean shades of Rascaldom, with uneasy steps over the burning marl.˙. . .—*Carlyle*. Critical and Miscellaneous Essays. " Diderot."

MARPLOT (mar/plot) *a conspirator who ruins the joint*   M18
                   undertaking
". . . Had the Prince chosen to remain away, it had been better; but we have gone too far forward to delay."
"What can have brought him?" she cried. " To-day of all days?"
" The marplot, madam, has the instinct of his nature," returned Gondremark. " But you exaggerate the peril . . ."—*R. L. Stevenson*. Prince Otto. Book ii, Ch. v.

With what a world of excellent intentions Otto entered his wife's cabinet! how fatherly, how tender! how morally affecting were the words he had prepared! Nor was Seraphina unamiably inclined. Her usual fear of Otto as a marplot in her great designs was now swallowed up in a passing distrust of the designs themselves.—*Ibid*. Book ii, Ch. vi.

MASQUERADE (mas-ker-ade/) *nocturnal assembly of*   M19
                   persons in disguise
> What guards the purity of melting maids,
> In courtly balls, and midnight masquerades,
> Safe from the treacherous friend, the daring spark,
> The glance by day, the whisper in the dark?
> When kind occasion prompts their warm desires,
> When music softens, and when dancing fires?
>> —*Pope*. The Rape of the Lock. Canto i.

MATHESIS (ma-the/sis) *learning, esp. of mathematics*   M20
> Mad mathesis alone was unconfined,
> Too mad for mere material chains to bind,
> Now to pure space lifts her ecstatic stare,
> Now running round the circle, finds it square.
>> —*Pope*. The Dunciad. iv, 31.

MAUGRE (maw/ger) *in spite of*   M21
> AARON: This, maugre all the world, will I keep safe;
>   Or some of you shall smoke for it in Rome.
>> —*Shakespeare*. Titus Andronicus. iv, 2.
> I through the ample Air in Triumph high
> Shall lead Hell Captive maugre Hell, and show
> The powers of darkness bound. Thou at the sight
> Pleas'd, out of Heaven shalt look down and smile,

While by thee rais'd I ruin all my Foes,
Death last, and with his Carcass glut the Grave:
Then with the multitude of my redeemd
Shall enter Heaven long absent, and returne,
Father, to see thy face, wherein no cloud
Of anger shall remain, but peace assur'd,
And reconcilement; wrauth shall be no more
Thenceforth, but in thy presence Joy entire.
                              —*Milton*. Paradise Lost. iii.

MAZARINE (maz-a-rene/) *deep blue*   M22

MEGALOMANIAC (meg-a-lo-may/ni-ak) *one who*   M23
   insanely exalts himself

Many a morning had he and his staff of assistants spent in the con-
genial task of organisation: for the picnic was to be on the grand scale,
to recall Versailles at its most megalomaniac, while it must also to some
degree, by the smoothness of its running, suggest Detroit.—*Osbert Sitwell*.
Miracle on Sinai. Bk. iii, Ch. i. (Duckworth).

MEIOSIS (mi-o/sis) *understatement*   M24

OF KING GEORGE V.
In fact throughout the years of the war his personality slowly but
ever more surely impressed itself upon the minds of his subjects as that of
one who summed up most perfectly in the thoroughness of his actions and
the modesty of his demeanour the popular conception of the man who,
as the current phrase of that meiosis so dear to the English had it, was
" doing his bit."—*Compton Mackenzie*. The Windsor Tapestry. (Chatto
& Windus).

President Roosevelt's speech . . . named with almost ludicrous meiosis
a " fireside chat."—*Lord Gorell*, in The Quarterly Review. July, 1941.
(John Murray).

" Is it worth it?" cried Daisy, suddenly and shrilly breaking silence.
" Is what worth what?" Raymond was peering through his bird-
glasses, deciphering the wheeling pattern, absent and intent.
" Watching birds. Standing here in this field, freezing to death. Yes,
to death, darling. I shall probably die, quite soon. You won't notice:
you'll be looking at birds, but I shall sink into that frozen sleep from
which people never wake again. I shall be glad. This anguish is too
great."
" Feeling chilly?" Raymond thus, with tranquil meiosis, interpreted
and summarised the eloquence of his betrothed.—*Rose Macaulay*.
Keeping Up Appearances. Ch. xix. (Collins).

MELHUISH (mel/ish)   M25

MENISCUS†   M26

This is a correction to the definition given in D.U.W.(A). The meniscus is the curve which appears plainly at the top of a column of liquid when it is contained in a narrow tube.

MENZIES (ming/is)   M27

MEPHISTOPHELIAN (mef-is-to-fee/li-an) *cunning; cynical*   M28

Reddlemen of the old school are now but seldom seen. Since the introduction of railways Wessex farmers have managed to do without these Mephistophelian visitants, and the bright pigment so largely used by shepherds in preparing sheep for the fair is obtained by other routes.— *Thomas Hardy.* The Return of the Native. Bk. i. (Macmillan).

MEPHITIC (me-fit/ik) *evil-smelling*   M29

He spent hours in the wine-cellar, rocking bits of celluloid and bits of paper in shallow dishes by the light of a mephitic red lantern . . . —*Denis Mackail.* The Square Circle. Ch. viii. (Hodder & Stoughton).

. . . a poisonous book, the atmosphere of which is heavy with mephitic odours of moral and spiritual putrefaction.—*Frank Harris.* Oscar Wilde.

MERIDIONAL (mer-id/i-on-al) *in the manner of a*   M30
                native of the South (of France)

[Queen] Victoria revelled in her holiday; although she took pleasure in the thought of coming fêtes and fine spectacles, she was also half envious of those who were rich and free enough to lead an anonymous life in this delightful Paris. There was not the same freedom for the rich in London. Freedom exists or is suppressed on varying planes. London had political freedom, while Paris was in the grip of dictatorship; but London was exclusive and undemocratic socially and was tied down with many rigid conventions. Here, while Londoners assumed Puritanical Sabbath faces, there was a lightness in the people's manner; they were enjoying Sunday afternoon, and there was an absence of restraint that appealed to Victoria; she responded to it by being very gay and cheerful herself, encouraged by the " dear Empress " at her side who talked in her animated meridional way as they drove along at a leisurely pace.—*Edith Saunders.* A Distant Summer. Ch. v. (Sampson Low, Marston & Co.).

METATHESIS (me-tath/e-sis) *transposition of the letters*   M31
                or sounds in a word

E.g. *Magenta* pronounced as " magneta ". *Cavalcade* as " calvacade."

METEMPSYCHOSIS (me-tem-si-ko/sis) *doctrine of the*   M32
transposition of souls

For as though there were a Metempsuchosis, and the soul of one man passed into another, Opinions do find, after certain Revolutions, men and minds like those that first begat them.—*Sir Thomas Browne.* Religio Medici. First Part.

METONYMY (me-ton/i-mi) *a figure of speech*   M33

The substitution of a concrete and vivid word in place of an abstract conception.

Of metaphors, those generally conduce most to that energy or vivacity of style we are speaking of, which illustrate an intellectual by a sensible object; the latter being always the most early familiar to the mind, and generally giving the most distinct impression to it. Thus we speak of " unbridled rage," " deep-rooted prejudice," " glowing eloquence," a " stony heart," etc. And a similar use may be made of metonymy also: as when we speak of the " throne," or the " crown " for " royalty,"—the " sword " for " military violence."—*Whately.* Elements of Rhetoric.

MEZZO-RILIEVO (med/zo re-lya/vo) *half-relief*   M34

We saw antique figures of men, carved in the natural rock, in mezzo-relievo, and in bigness equal to the life.—*Maundrell.* Travels.

MIASMA (mi-az/ma) *noxious effluvia*   M35

There is scoundrel-life in Beppo Cagliostro; cast him among the mud, tread him out of sight there, the miasmata do but stimulate and refresh him, he rises sneezing, is strong and young again.—*Carlyle.* Critical and Miscellaneous Essays. " Count Cagliostro."

There is one result of the Boer War, however, which has not been noted, and that is the secrecy which ever since it has been allowed to hang like a miasma over much of what should be public affairs. The Unionist politicians attributed their disastrous defeat at the polls in 1906 to the freedom of criticism permitted to the new halfpenny Press during the war, and Liberal politicians when they achieved power showed that they too had learnt the lesson.—*Compton Mackenzie.* The Windsor Tapestry. (Chatto & Windus).

As the tropic sun sank slowly in the west, a thin miasma of mist began to curl upward from the still silent pool around which the mangroves lifted their gnarled trunks on fantastic stilt-like roots from the slime of the swamp.—*W. E. Johns.* Biggles Flies Again. Ch. i. (Hamilton).

In those days . . . the London stretches of the Thames still maintained upon their miasmic surface a life of pleasure as well as of commerce.—*Osbert Sitwell.* Sing High! Sing Low! " Picnics and Pavilions." (Macmillan).

MILLENNIUM (mil-len/i-um) *a period of a thousand*   M36
years; a future time of great rejoicing

> Forerun thy peers, thy time, and let
> Thy feet, millenniums hence, be set
> In midst of knowledge, dreamed not yet.
> —*Tennyson*. The Two Voices.

You come to a milestone on a hill, or some place where deep ways meet under trees; and off goes the knapsack, and down you sit to smoke a pipe in the shade. You sink into yourself, and the birds come round and look at you; and your smoke dissipates upon the afternoon under the blue dome of heaven; and the sun lies warm upon your feet, and the cool air visits your neck and turns aside your open shirt. If you are not happy, you must have an evil conscience. You may dally as long as you like by the roadside. It is almost as if the millennium were arrived, when we shall throw our clocks and watches over the housetop, and remember time and seasons no more.—*R. L. Stevenson.* "Walking Tours." (Chatto & Windus).

MIRIFIC (mir-if/ik) *miraculous*   M37

. . . to help you to picture faintly to yourselves the mirific and horripilant adventure whereby I nearly achieved superhuman success in spite of all the powers of the air, I append a little map . . .—*Hilaire Belloc*. The Path to Rome. (Allen & Unwin).

MITHRIDATE (mith/ri-date) *antidote for poison*   M38

> But you of learning and religion,
> And virtue, and such ingredients, have made
> A mithridate, whose operation
> Keeps off, or cures, what can be done or said.
> —*Donne.* Poems.

MIZZLE (miz/l) *fine rain*   M39

> Now ginnes to mizzle; hye we homeward fast.
> —*Spenser*. Shepherd's Calendar. (November).

MNEMONIC (ne-mon/ik) *assisting the memory;*   M40
of, designed to aid, the memory

MNEMOSYNE (ne-mos/i-ne)   M41

MOLLUSC (mol/usk) *a snail; any similar creature*   M42

Their black figures sank and disappeared from against the sky. They were as two horns which the sluggish heath had put forth from its crown, like a mollusc, and had now drawn in again.—*Thomas Hardy.* The Return of the Native. Bk. i (9). (Macmillan).

MONEGASQUE (mon-e-gask/) *a native of Monaco*   M43

. . . you need have no fear, nor need you think that you are the only foreigner who is working for us. You will probably become acquainted before your work is over with a German, a Monegasque and a Dane. I am not a believer in using one's own countrypeople exclusively.—*E. Phillips Oppenheim*. The Spy Paramount. Ch. ii. (Hodder & Stoughton).

MORDANT (mor/dant) *pungent; caustic*   M44

And the conjurer continued to extract flags and paper ribbons from all sorts of unlikely places, and to cause still more solid objects to vanish and re-appear in the most skilful manner and to tell a number of funny stories at which only the nurses giggled, and to be rather personal and mordant at the expense of the guests who were kind enough to cross the imaginary footlights and assist him.—*Denis Mackail*. The Square Circle. Ch. v. (Hodder & Stoughton).

MOUJIK (moo/zhik) *Russian peasant*   M45

MOUNTEBANK (mount/i-bank) *a charlatan; a quack;   M46 formerly, an itinerant physician*

LAERTES: I will do't;
And for that purpose I'll anoint my sword.
I bought an unction of a mountebank,
So mortal that but dip a knife in it,
Where it draws blood no cataplasm so rare,
Collected from all simples that have virtue
Under the moon, can save the thing from death
That is but scratch'd withal: I'll touch my point
With this contagion, that, if I gall him slightly,
It may be death.
                          —*Shakespeare*. Hamlet. iv. 7.

MUNGE (munge) *seed shaken from a plant?*   M47

A curious grey light hangs over all. It has emerged, dripping and terrible, out of the night. There should be a dead man lying in the yew-trees, dead of starvation, with his mouth gone green from the munge of nettles. There is no sound except the dripping of the leaves.—*Sacheverell Sitwell*. Sacred & Profane Love. Bk. viii. "Evil Dawn." (Faber & Faber).

MYRRH (mir) *gum-resin used in medicine and   M48 perfumery*

The myrrhe sweet-bleeding in the bitter wound.
                          —*Spenser*. The Faerie Queene.

. . . yet at his Birth a Starr
Unseen before in Heav'n proclaims him com,
And guides the Eastern Sages, who enquire

His place, to offer Incense, Myrrh, and Gold;
His place of birth a solemn Angel tells
To simple Shepherds, keeping watch by night;
They gladly thither haste, and by a Quire
Of squadroned Angels hear his Carol sung.
                    —*Milton.*   Paradise Lost.   xii.

MYSTAGOGUE (mis/ta-gog) *an interpreter of divine*   M49
           mysteries
     . . . under the green Paradisiac palms, among the ecstatic mystagogues
and the saints who scream beneath the divine caresses . . .—*Aldous
Huxley.* Antic Hay. Ch. xv. (Chatto & Windus).

NADIR	*NEUMANN*
NAIAD	NEXUS
NARD	NIMBUS
NARGHILE	NONAGE
NEOLOGY	NONPAREIL
NEOPHYTE	NORNS
NEPENTHE	NOSOLOGY
NEPHRITIC	NOSTALGIA
NEREID	NUGATORY

NADIR† N

No human being ever spoke of scenery for above two minutes at a time, which makes me suspect we hear too much of it in literature. The weather is regarded as the very nadir and scoff of conversational topics. And yet the weather, the dramatic element in scenery, is far more tractable in language, and far more human both in import and suggestion than the stable features of the landscape.—*R. L. Stevenson*. Talk & Talkers. (i). (Chatto & Windus).

NAIAD (ni/ad) *a water nymph* N2

IRIS: You nymphs, call'd Naiads, of the wind'ring brooks,
           With your sedg'd crowns, and ever-harmless looks,
           Leave your crisp channels.
                    —*Shakespeare*. The Tempest. iv, 1.

NARD (nard) *an odorous ointment* N3

        Thir glittering Tents he passd, and now is come
Into the blissful field, through Groves of Myrrhe,
And flouring Odours, Cassia, Nard, and Balme;
A Wilderness of sweets.
                —*Milton*. Paradise Lost. v. 291.

NARGHILE (nar/gi-lay) *hookah* N4

In place of tobacco, a substance called *tambac* is used in these pipes. This is moistened to a thick paste. Pieces of red-hot charcoal are laid on the tambac, and the smoke is drawn into the mouth through water.

NEOLOGY† N5

Neology, or the novelty of words and phrases, is an innovation, which, with the opulence of our present language, the English philologer is most jealous to allow; but we have puritans or precisians of English, superstitiously nice! The fantastic coinage of affectation or caprice will cease to circulate from its own alloy; but shall we reject the ore of fine workmanship and solid weight? There is no government mint of words, and it is no statutable offence to invent a felicitous or daring expression unauthorised by Mr. Todd! When a man of genius, in the heat of his pursuits or his feelings, has thrown out a peculiar word, it probably conveyed more precision or energy than any other established word, otherwise he is but an ignorant pretender! . . . Unquestionably, neology opens a wide door to innovation: scarcely has a century passed since our language was patched up with Gallic idioms, as in the preceding century it was piebald with Spanish, and with Italian, and even with Dutch. The political intercourse of islanders with their neighbours has ever influenced their language. In Elizabeth's reign, Italian phrases and Netherland words were imported; in James and Charles the Spanish framed the style of courtesy; in Charles II the nation and the language were equally Frenchified. Yet such are the sources whence we have often derived some of the wealth of our language!—*D'Israeli*. Curiosities of Literature. " History of New Words."

NEOPHYTE†   N6

Now the nuns, in Portugal, have been long dispossessed. They were
abolished after the expulsion of Dom Miguel (the equivalent, in Portugal,
to Don Carlos) by the laws of 1834. Most of them rejoined the world,
since no more neophytes were allowed to take the veil, while the seques-
tration of their property had reduced them all to poverty.—*Sacheverell
Sitwell.* Sacred & Profane Love. Bk. v, Pt. v. (Faber & Faber).

NEPENTHE (ne-pen/thi) *a drug, said to drive away care*   N7

    COMUS: Why are you vext Lady? why do you frown?
                Here dwell no frowns, nor anger, from these gates
                Sorrow flies far: See here be all the pleasures
                That fancy can beget on youthfull thoughts,
                When the fresh blood grows lively, and returns
                Brisk as the *April* buds in Primrose-season.
                And first behold this cordial Julep here
                That flames, and dances in his crystal bounds
                With spirits of balm, and fragrant Syrops mixt.
                Not that *Nepenthes* which the wife of *Thone,*
                In *Egypt* gave to *Jove*-born *Helena*
                Is of such power to stir up joy as this,
                To life so friendly, or so cool to thirst.
                Why should you be so cruel to your self,
                And to those dainty limms which nature lent
                For gentle usage, and soft delicacy?
                            —*Milton.* Comus.

      There where no passion, pride, or shame transport,
    Lull'd with the sweet nepenthe of a court;
    There where no fathers, brothers, friends disgrace,
    Once break their rest, nor stir them from their place.
                    —*Pope.* Epilogue to the Satires. i.

NEPHRITIC (ne-frit/ik) *relating to the kidneys*   N8

A very valuable medicine, and of great account in divers cases,
particularly asthmas, nephritick pains, nervous colicks, and obstructions.
—*Bishop Berkeley.* Siris. s. 62.

NEREID (ner/e-id) *sea nymph*   N9

    ENOBARBUS: Her gentlewomen, like the Nereides,
                So many mermaids, tended her i' the eyes,
                And made their bends adornings: at the helm
                A seeming mermaid steers: the silken tackle
                Swell with the touches of those flower-soft hands,
                That yarely frame the office. From the barge
                A strange invisible perfume hits the sense
                Of the adjacent wharfs.
              —*Shakespeare.* Antony and Cleopatra. ii, 2.

NEUMANN (noi/man)   N10

NEXUS (nek/sus) *a connecting link*   N11

A great life—an entire civilisation—lies just outside the pale of common thought. Cities and countries, inhabitants, intelligences, culture—an entire civilisation. Except by illustrations drawn from familiar things, there is no way of indicating a new idea. I do not mean actual cities, actual civilisation. Such life is different from any yet imagined. A nexus of ideas exists of which nothing is known—a vast system of ideas—a cosmos of thought —*Richard Jefferies*. The Story of My Heart. Ch. iii.

NIMBUS (nim/bus) *a halo*   N12

A nimbus of renown and preternatural astonishment envelopes Cagliostro; enchants the general eye.—*Carlyle*. Critical and Miscellaneous Essays. "Count Cagliostro."

NONAGE (non/age) *under age; immature*   N13

SECOND CITIZEN: In him there is a hope of government,
That in his nonage council under him,
And in his full and ripen'd years himself,
No doubt, shall then and till then govern well.
—*Shakespeare*. Richard III. ii, 3.

NONPAREIL* (non-pa-rel/) *unequalled excellence*   N14

VIOLA: My lord and master loves you: O such love
Could be but recompensed tho' you were crown'd
The nonpareil of beauty.
—*Shakespeare*. Twelfth Night. i, 5.

NORNS (nornz) *the Norse fates*   N15

. . . the palace front was thick with lighted windows, and along the balustrade, the lamp on every twentieth baluster shone clear. A few withered tracks of sunset, amber and glow-worm green, still lingered in the western sky; and she paused once again to watch them fading. "And to think," she said, "that here am I—destiny embodied, a norn, a fate, a providence."—*R. L. Stevenson*. Prince Otto. Bk. ii, Ch. xii.

NOSOLOGY (no-sol/o-ji) *a catalogue of diseases*   N16

So that Society, were it not by nature immortal, and its death ever a new-birth, might appear, as it does in the eyes of some, to be sick to dissolution, and even now writhing in its last agony. Sick enough we must admit it to be, with disease enough, a whole nosology of diseases; . . .—*Carlyle*. Critical and Miscellaneous Essays. "Characteristics."

NOSTALGIA (nos-tal/ji-a) *home-sickness*   N17

   . . . the passion that held Strickland was a passion to create beauty.
It gave him no peace. It urged him hither and thither. He was eternally
a pilgrim, haunted by a divine nostalgia . . .—*W. Somerset Maugham.*
The Moon and Sixpence. liv. (Heinemann).

NUGATORY (nu/ga-tor-i) *trifling, insignificant*   N18

   Lord Lyttelton's Dialogues he deemed a nugatory performance.
" That man (said he) sat down to write a book to tell the world what the
world had all his life been telling him."—*James Boswell.* Life of Johnson.
(Collectanea of Rev. Dr. Maxwell).   A.D. 1770.   Ætat. 61.

OBER-AMMERGAU	OPHICLEIDE
OBFUSCATE	ORDER
OBLIQUITY	OREAD
OBLOQUY	ORISON
OBSIDIAN	ORTHOGRAPHER
OFFICINAL	OSTLER
OLIGARCHY	*OUIDA*
OLIO	OUTRÉ
ONEIROCRITIC	OUZEL
ONTOLOGY	OVERT

OBER-AMMERGAU (o-ber am/er-gow)   O

OBFUSCATE (ob/fus-kate) *to darken; bewilder*   O2

A very obfuscate and obscure sight.—*Burton.* Anatomy of Melancholy.

OBLIQUITY (ob-lik/wit-i) *moral perversity*   O3

        What if the Sun
Be Center to the World, and other Starrs
By his attractive vertue and their own
Incited, dance about him various rounds?
Their wandring course now high, now low, then hid,
Progressive, retrograde, or standing still,
In six thou seest, and what if sev'nth to these
The Planet Earth, so stedfast though she seem,
Insensibly three different Motions move?
Which else to several Sphears thou must ascribe,
Mov'd contrarie with thwart obliquities,
Or save the Sun his labour, and that swift
Nocturnal and Diurnal Rhomb suppos'd
Invisible else above all Starrs, the Wheele
Of Day and Night.
                    —*Milton.* Paradise Lost. viii.

Delude not thyself into iniquities from participation or community, which abate the sense but not the obliquity of them. To conceive sins less or less of sins, because others also transgress, were morally to commit that natural fallacy of man, to take comfort from society, and think adversities less because others also suffer them.—*Sir Thomas Browne.* Christian Morals. s. xviii.

OBLOQUY (ob/lo-kwi) *abuse*   O4

        O argument blasphemous, false and proud!
Words which no eare ever to hear in Heav'n
Expected, least of all from thee, ingrate
In place thy self so high above thy Peeres.
Canst thou with impious obloquie condemne
The just Decree of God, pronounc't and sworn,
That to his only Son by right endu'd
With Regal Scepter, every Soule in Heav'n
Shall bend the knee, and in that honour due
Confess him rightful! King?
                    —*Milton.* Paradise Lost. v.

OBSIDIAN (ob-sid/i-an) *a black vitreous lava*   O5

THE APACHE INDIANS

. . . amongst grass eight or nine inches high, they drop, and in an instant, even as you look, are lost to sight, and if hard pressed sometimes escape attention by standing in a cactus grove and stretching out their arms, looking so exactly like the plant that you may pass close to them and be unaware, till their bow twangs, and an obsidian-headed arrow whistles through the air.—*R. B. Cunninghame Graham.* Thirteen Stories. " A Hegira." (Heinemann).

OFFICINAL (of-fis/in-al) *relating to a shop*   O6

I had always, in my officinal state, been kept in awe by lace and embroideries.—*Dr. Johnson.* Rambler, No. 123.

OLIGARCHY (ol/i-gar-ki) *government of minority*   O7

OLIVER CROMWELL

He never seems to have coveted despotic power. He at first fought sincerely and manfully for the Parliament, and never deserted it, till it had deserted its duty. If he dissolved it by force, it was not till he found that the few members who remained after so many deaths, secessions, and expulsions were desirous to appropriate to themselves a power which they held only in trust, and to inflict upon England the curse of a Venetian oligarchy.—*Macaulay.* " Milton."

WILKES AND LIBERTY

The attack was printed on 23 April, 1763, in Number 45 of the *North Briton,* a number which for a short while became nationally famous. It was far from immoderate in phrasing, but its essential crime was that it attacked the King's Speech, and George III, really or for show, chose to consider this a grave insult. He, or his advisers, decided to make this publication an excuse for a direct blow in the face of the oligarchs who were resisting his influence. A " general warrant " was issued for the apprehension of the printer and author of " Number 45." Forty-eight persons were arrested and questioned on this warrant before Wilkes was detained; when he was seized he declined to answer questions on the pretext of his privilege as an M.P. The case was brought before Chief Justice Pratt, a judge of high probity, who ruled in two successive judgments that Wilkes's privilege should have protected him from arrest, and that general warrants were illegal.—*G. D. H. Cole and Raymond Postgate.* The Common People 1746-1946. Ch. viii. (Methuen).

OLIO (o/li-o) *hotchpotch; miscellany*   O8

I am in a very chaos, to think I should so forget myself: but I have such an olio of affairs, I know not what to do.—*Congreve.* The Way of the World.

" I've got it, Loudon," Pinkerton at last replied. " Got the idea on the Potrero cars. Found I hadn't a pencil, borrowed one from the conductor, and figured on it roughly all the way in town. I saw it was the thing at last; gives you a real show. All your talents and accomplishments come in. Here's a sketch advertisement. Just run your eye over it, *' Sun, Ozone and Music!* PINKERTON'S HEBDOMADARY PICNICS!' (That's a good, catching phrase, ' hebdomadary,' though it's hard to say. I made a note of it when I was looking in the dictionary how to spell *hectagonal.* ' Well, you're a boss word,' I said. ' Before you're very much older, I'll have you in type as long as yourself.' And here it is you see.) *' Five dollars a head, and ladies free.* MONSTER OLIO OF ATTRACTIONS.' (How does that strike you?) *' Free luncheon under the greenwood tree. Dance on the elastic sward. Home again in the Bright Evening Hours. Manager and Honorary Steward, H. Loudon Dodd, Esq., the well-known connoisseur.' "—R. L. Stevenson and Lloyd Osbourne.* The Wrecker. Ch. vii.

ONEIROCRITIC (o-nir-o-krit/ik) *an interpreter of dreams* O9

But why to dream of Lettuce should presage some ensuing disease, why to eat figs should signify foolish Talk, why to eat Eggs great Trouble, and to dream of Blindness should be so highly commended, according to the oneirocritical Verses of Astrampsychus and Nicephorus, I shall leave unto your Divination.—*Sir Thomas Browne.* Letter to a Friend.

ONTOLOGY (on-tol/o-ji) *the theory of pure being;* O10
      metaphysics

For those whose nature demands personality as a source of energy, but who find it impossible to believe that the universe is run by a person in any sense of the word that we can possibly understand—what's the right policy? In most cases, they reject any practice which might be called religious. But this is throwing away the baby with the bath water. The desired relationship with a personality can be historical, not onto-logical. A contact, not with somebody existing at present as manager of the universe, but with somebody known to have existed at some time in the past. The Imitation of Christ (or of any other historical character) is just as effective if the model be regarded as having existed there, then, as it is if the model be conceived as existing here now.—*Aldous Huxley.* Eyeless In Gaza. Ch. 1. (Chatto & Windus).

OPHICLEIDE (of/i-klede) *a large brass wind instrument* O11

The grass under their feet became trodden away, and the hard, beaten surface of the sod, when viewed aslant towards the moonlight, shone like a polished table. The air became quite still; the flag above the waggon which held the musicians clung to the pole, and the players appeared only in outline against the sky; except when the circular mouths of the trom-bone, ophicleide, and French horn gleamed out like huge eyes from the shade of their figures.—*Thomas Hardy.* The Return of the Native. Bk. iv (3). (Macmillan).

ORDER* (or/der) *an architectural style* O12

Posterity admires, and will long admire, the awful remains of the amphitheatre of Titus, which so well deserved the epithet of Colossal. It was a building of an elliptic figure, five hundred and sixty-four feet in length, and four hundred and sixty-seven in breadth, founded on four-score arches, and rising, with four successive orders of architecture, to the height of one hundred and forty feet. The outside of the edifice was encrusted with marble, and decorated with statues. The slopes of the vast concave, which formed the inside, were filled and surrounded with sixty or eighty rows of seats, of marble likewise, covered with cushions, and capable of receiving with ease above fourscore thousand spectators. Sixty-four *vomitories* (for by that name the doors were very apty distinguished) poured forth the immense multitude . . .—*Edward Gibbon.* The Decline and Fall of the Roman Empire. Ch. xii.

OREAD (or/e-ad) *a nymph* O13

    Thus saying, from her husband's hand her hand
  Soft she withdrew, and like a wood-nymph light,
  Oread, or Dryad, or of Delia's train,
  Betook her to the grove. —*Milton.* Paradise Lost. ix, 385.

ORISON (or/i-zon) *prayer*   O14

. . . I could scarce contain my Prayers for a friend at the ringing of
a Bell, or behold his Corps without an Orison for his Soul.—*Sir Thomas
Browne*. Religio Medici. First Part.

> What passing-bells for these who die as cattle
> Only the monstrous anger of the guns.
> Only the stuttering rifles' rapid rattle
> Can patter out their hasty orisons.
> No mockeries for them from prayers or bells,
> Nor any voice of mourning save the choirs,—
> The shrill, demented choirs of wailing shells;
> And bugles calling for them from sad shires.
> —*Michael Roberts*. " Anthem for Doomed Youth."
>   (Faber & Faber).

ORTHOGRAPHER (awr-thog/ra-fer) *an expert at spelling*   O15

He was wont to speak plain, like an honest man and a soldier; and
now he is turn'd orthographer; his words are just so many strange dishes.
—*Shakespeare*. Much Ado about Nothing. ii, 3.

OSTLER (os/ler) *stableman*   O16

JOHNSON: ". . . Richardson used to say, that had he not
              known who Fielding was, he should have believed he
              was an ostler."—*James Boswell*. Life of Johnson.
              A.D. 1772. Ætat. 63.

OUIDA (we/da)   O17

OUTRÉ (oo-tray/) *eccentric*   O18

OUZEL (oo/zel) *the blackbird; possibly other species*   O19
> The merry lark her matins sings aloft,
> The thrush replies, the mavis descant plays,
> The ousel shrills, the ruddock warbles soft;
> So goodly all agree, with sweet consent,
> To this day's merriment.
>   —*Spenser*. Epithalamium.
>   The ousel cock so black of hue,
> With orange-tawny bill.
> —*Shakespeare*. A Midsummer-Night's Dream. iii, 1.

OVERT†   O20

DUKE: To vouch this is no proof,
            Without more certain and more overt test,
            Than these thin habits and poor likelihoods.
                        —*Shakespeare*. Othello. i, 3.

PACHYDERM
PAGURIAN
PALADIN
PALIMPSEST
PALINDROME
PALINGENESIA
PALINODE
PALMER
PANACEA
PAN-AMERICAN
PANDICULATION
PANEGYRIC
PANURGIC
PAOLI
PARABOLICAL
PAPERASSERIE
PARGET
PARIAN ,
PARONOMASIA
PARONYM
PARTHENOGENESIS
PARVENU
PARVIS
PASQUINADE
PATINA
PAVANE
PAVONINE
PEA-JACKET
PEASECOD
PEJORATIVE
PELLUCID
PENMAENMAWR
PENTASTICH
PENTHOUSE
PEPYS
PERIAPT
PERIPHERY
PERIPHRASIS
PERISTYLE
PERNOCTATION
PERPEND
PERSPICUITY
PHAETON
PHILOSOPHE
PHYLACTERY
PINFOLD
PISHOGUE
PLEDGET
PLENARY

PLENILUNE
PLETHORIC
PLURIPRESENCE
POETASTER
POLEMIC
POLITIC
POLYGRAPHY
POMACE
POMEGRANATE
PONDERABLE
PONTIFICAL
PORTICO
POSSET
POTABLE
PRAGMATIC
PRECATORY
PREDATORY
PREFIGURE
PRELAPSARIAN
PRELIBATION
PRELUSIVE
PRESAGE
PRESBYOPIA
PRESCIENT
PRESCIND
PRETERNATURAL
PREVENIENT
PROCELEUSMATIC
PROLATE
PROLEGOMENON
PROLIFERATION
PROPHYLACTIC
PROSCENIUM
PROSCRIBE
PROTAGONIST
PROTEAN
PROTOTYPE
PRURIENT
PSEUDONYM
PSYCHE
PUDENCY
PUISSANT
PURBLIND
PURLIEUS
PURULENT
PUSILLANIMOUS
PYROMANCY
PYRRHONISM

PACHYDERM (pak/i-derm) *thick-skinned quadruped*   P

Ominous, revengeful zodiacal host! They moan, passing upon the clouds, horned and capricorned, the trumpeted with the tusked, the lion-maned the giantantlered, snouter and crawler, rodent, ruminant and pachyderm, all their moving moaning multitude, murderers of the sun.— *James Joyce*. Ulysses (ii). (John Lane).

PAGURIAN (pa-gure/i-an) *a hermit crab*   P2

He owned a castle in the Highlands, and the temperament of the old pagurian often led him to identify his ancestry with that of the romantic but vigorous race which inhabited those hills, moors and valleys.—*Osbert Sitwell*. Miracle on Sinai Bk. i, Ch. iii. (Duckworth).

PALADIN (pal/a-din) *outstanding personality*   P3

Amadis de Gaul himself never surpassed the chivalrous achievement of the Earl of Essex; his life, indeed, would form the finest of romances, could it be written. He challenged the Governor of Corunna to single combat for the honour of the nation, and proposed to encounter Villars, Governor of Rouen, on foot or on horseback. And thus ran his challenge:— " I will maintain the justice of the cause of Henry the Fourth of France against the League and that I am a better man than thou; and that my mistress is more beautiful than thine." This was the very language and deed of one of the Paladins.—*D'Israeli*. Amenities of Literature. " Sir Philip Sydney."

. . . by far the most remarkable figure among them was H. W. Nevinson, who had been sent out to represent the Provincial Press. He looked and was a paladin.—*Compton Mackenzie*. Gallipoli Memories. Ch. xiii.

PALIMPSEST (pal/imp-sest)   P4

A manuscript or paper written over more than once and therefore difficult to decipher.

For though the whole meaning [of the present and future in history] lies far beyond our ken, yet in that complex manuscript, covered over with formless inextricably-entangled characters,—nay, which is a palimpsest, and had once prophetic writing, still dimly legible there—some letters, some words may be deciphered.—*Carlyle*. Critical and Miscellaneous Essays. " History."

PALINDROME†   P5

Roma, tibi subito motibus ibit amor.
This palindrome is said to date from the 15th century.

PALINGENESIA (pal-in-je-nee/si-a) *regeneration*   P6

All work is as seed sown; it grows and spreads, and sows itself anew, and so, in endless palingenesia, lives and works.—*Carlyle*. Critical and Miscellaneous Essays. " Boswell's Life of Johnson."

PALINODE (pal/i-node) *a recantation*   P7

PALMER (parma) *a pilgrim*   P8
> Behold yon isle, by palmers, pilgrims trod,
> Men bearded, bald, cow'ld, uncowl'd, shod, unshod.
> —*Pope*. The Dunciad.   iii, 113.

PANACEA (pan-a-se/a) *universal remedy*   P9
> Into the woods thenceforth in haste shee went,
> To seeke for hearbes that mote him remedy;
> For she of herbes had great intendiment,
> Taught of the Nymphe which from her infancy
> Her nourced had in trew Nobility:
> There, whether yt divine Tobacco were,
> Or Panachæa, or Polygony,
> Shee fownd, and brought it to her patient deare,
> Who al this while lay bleeding out his hartblood neare.
>
> The soveraine weede betwixt two marbles plaine
> Shee pownded small, and did in peeces bruze;
> And then atweene her lilly handes twaine
> Into his wound the juice thereof did scruze;
> And round about, as she could well it uze,
> The flesh therewith shee suppled and did steepe,
> T' abate all spasme, and soke the swelling bruze;
> And, after having searcht the intuse deepe,
> She with her scarf did bind the wound from cold to keepe.
> —*Spenser*. The Faerie Queene.   iii, 5, 32/3.

PAN-AMERICAN (pan-a-mer/i-kan) *relating to the whole*   P10
     or North and South America

PANDICULATION (pan-dik-u-lay/shun) *yawning and/or*   P11
          stretching
Believe all that I ask of you, viz., that I could resist no longer; believe it liberally, and as an act of grace: or else in mere prudence; for, if not, then in the next edition of my Opium Confessions revised and enlarged, I will make you believe and tremble: and à force d'ennuyer, by mere dint of pandiculation I will terrify all readers of mine from ever again questioning any postulate that I shall think fit to make.—*De Quincey.* Confessions of an English Opium-eater.

PANEGYRIC†   P12
It is not difficult to trace the process by which the old songs were transmuted into the form which they now wear. Funeral panegyric and chronicle appear to have been the intermediate links which connected the lost ballads with the histories now extant. From a very early period it was the usage that an oration should be pronounced over the remains of a noble Roman.—*Macaulay*. Lays of Ancient Rome. (Preface).

PANURGIC (pan-er/jik) *able to do any kind of work*   P13

PAOLI (pay/o-le)   P14

PAPERASSERIE (pa-pras/er-e) *old waste paper*   P16

Thus the State at length took over the major part of the responsibility for the elementary education of the poor. There is no doubt that this would have taken place much earlier, and much more completely when it did take place, but for the religious controversy. Long before Robert Lowe proclaimed, on the morrow of the second Reform Act, the need for the governing classes to "educate their masters," the necessity at the very least for the general diffusion of the three R's existed by virtue of the very character of the new civilization of the machine age. Industry needed operatives who were able to read its rules and regulations, and an increasing supply of skilled workers able to work to drawings and to write at any rate a simple sentence. Commerce needed a rapidly growing army of clerks, book-keepers, shop assistants, touts and commercial travellers. The State needed more Civil Servants and local government employees for the developing tasks of public administration. The growing professions needed more skilled helpers. And, apart from all this, the *paperasserie* of the new world of machine production and parliamentary government made illiteracy more and more a nuisance which had to be put down.—*Cole & Postgate*. The Common People 1746-1946. Ch. xxix. (Methuen).

PARABOLICAL (par-a-bol/ik-al) *figurative; allegorical*   P15

Thus Thoreau was an exaggerative and a parabolical writer, not because he loved the literature of the East, but from a desire that people should understand and realise what he was writing. He was near the truth upon the general question; but in his own particular method, it appears to me he wandered. Literature is not less a conventional art than painting or sculpture; and it is the least striking as it is the most comprehensive of the three. To hear a strain of music, to see a beautiful woman, a river, a great city, or a starry night, is to make man despair of his Lilliputian arts in language. Now, to gain that emphasis which seems denied to us by the very nature of the medium, the proper method of literature is by selection, which is a kind of negative exaggeration. It is the right of the literary artist, as Thoreau was on the point of seeing, to leave out whatever does not suit his purpose. Thus we extract the pure gold; and thus the well-written story of a noble life becomes by its very omissions, more thrilling to the reader. But to go beyond this, like Thoreau, and to exaggerate directly is to leave the saner classical tradition, and to put the reader on his guard. And when you write the whole for the half, you do not express your thought more forcibly, but only express a different thought which is not yours.—*R. L. Stevenson*. Familiar Studies of Men and Books. "Henry David Thoreau." (Chatto & Windus).

PARGET (par/jet) *rough-cast; plaster*   P17

> Gold was the parget; and the ceiling bright
> Did shine all scaly with great plates of gold;
> The floor of jasp and emerald was dight.
>   —*Spenser.* Translation of the Visions of Bellay.

PARIAN (par/i-an) *a white porcelain*   P18

. . . his teeth, which were quite unimpaired, showed like parian from his parted lips.—*Thomas Hardy.* The Return of the Native. Bk. i (6). (Macmillan).

PARONOMASIA (par-o-no-ma/zi-a) *play on words*   P19

It was between Whitefield Street and the Tottenham Court Road, in a "heavenly Mews," as he liked to call it (for he had a characteristic weakness for philosophical paronomasia), that Casimir Lypiatt lived and worked.—*Aldous Huxley.* Antic Hay. Ch. vi. (Chatto & Windus).

PARONYM (par/o-nim) *a word similar in sound but*   P20
differing in other respects

In the mountains north of Florence men had given their orders to advance, and others had cursed them, in the accents of New England and the Middle West, in voices from the cornfields of Kansas and the cold plains of Nebraska, from the black soil of the deep South and the arrogant immensity of Texas. Voices from the Transvaal and the Cape had answered them, and to the eastward came a clamour of tongues from Hindustan. Soldiers had died with a sentence, half-spoken, of Urdu on their lips. They had called gently to each other in the night in Gurkhali and Mahratti, and heard the debate of comrades in the broad accent of Yorkshire, the lazy flow of Cotswold villages, the quick traffic of a London borough, and here and there the softness of Gaelic. Christchurch and Dunedin had spoken to Glasgow and Liverpool, Manitoba and Quebec to Warsaw and Athens. Pietermaritzburg had conversed with Little Rock, the Grampians with the Punjab, and tied each other's wounds. Hardly since the confounding of the people at Babel had such a diversity of tongues been heard, and month by month their weary or their hopeful speech had sounded a little farther to the north, till now, in the cold bright air of spring, the languages and lingos, the argots and parley and paronyms of half the world, to the orchestration of their innumerable artillery, were shouting for the kill.—*Eric Linklater.* Private Angelo. Ch. xix. (Jonathan Cape).

PARTHENOGENESIS (par-the-no-jen/e-sis) *reproduction*   P21
without sexual union

Arriving safely at Horsham, Mr. Clifford had discovered his friend's address by means of the telephone-book, but on calling was disappointed to find that he was out on a case. He and Peter had consequently made for the nearest pub, in the saloon-bar of which Mr. Clifford found his friend, surrounded by a body of local sportsmen to whom he was expounding his theory of a case of apparent parthenogenesis in pigs.

It was from this point that Peter's recollection became hazy. Mr. Clifford's friend had been delighted to see them. He bought them beer. They bought him beer. His friends bought beer; beer was bought for his friends. The Horsham beer impacted heavily on a system already rendered indignant by the mixed fluids of Worthing and Peter took to gin instead.—*Hugh McGraw.* Rude Society. Ch. xix. (Heinemann).

PARVENU (par/ve-nu) *newcomer, in a pejorative sense*   P22

Take, for example, *The Possessed.* In the whole of that extraordinary and horrible novel (and the same is true of all Dostoevsky's books) there is not one single character who has a decent physical relationship with any one or any thing whatsoever. Dostoevsky's people do not even eat normally, much less make love, or work, or enjoy nature. That would be much too easy and obvious for such parvenus of intelligence and consciousness as the Russians.—*Aldous Huxley.* "Baudelaire." (Chatto & Windus).

It was the same lack of confidence that made him almost as chary of fixing his eyeglass in the presence of the rich. With them, he never felt quite sure that he had a right to his monocle. He felt himself a parvenu to monocularity.—*Aldous Huxley.* "The Monocle." (Chatto & Windus).

PARVIS (par/vis) *enclosed area in front of a large building*   P23

Through boulevards, parvis, cités, along the quays, in the vast open spaces which, like Saharas of grey stone, make the town desolate, in cafés, brothels, theatres, in church and studio, and wherever men most congregate.—*R. B. Cunninghame Graham.* Thirteen Stories. "Victory." (Heinemann).

PASQUINADE (pas-kwi-nade/) *scurrilous personal attack;*   P24
abuse

Could a historiographer drive on his history, as a muleteer drives on his mule,—straight forward;—for instance from *Rome* all the way to *Loretto,* without ever once turning his head aside either to the right hand or to the left,—he might venture to foretell you to an hour when he should get to his journey's end;—but the thing is, morally speaking, impossible: For, if he is a man of the least spirit, he will have fifty deviations from a straight line to make with this or that party as he goes along, which he can no ways avoid. He will have views and prospects to himself perpetually soliciting his eye, which he can no more help standing still to look at than he can fly; he will moreover have various

> Accounts to reconcile:
> Anecdotes to pick up:
> Inscriptions to make out:
> Stories to weave in:
> Traditions to sift:
> Personages to call upon:
> Panegyrics to paste up at this door;

Pasquinades at that:—All which both the man and his mule are quite exempt from. To sum up all; there are archives at every stage to be look'd into, and rolls, records, documents, and endless genealogies, which justice ever and anon calls him back to stay the reading of:— In short, there is no end of it;—for my own part, I declare I had been at it these six weeks, making all the speed I possibly could,—and am not yet born:—I have just been able, and that's all, to tell you *when* it happen'd, but not *how;*—so that you see the thing is yet far from being accomplished.—*Sterne.* Tristram Shandy. Bk. i, Ch. xiv.

PATINA (pat/i-na)   P25

Patina [is] the fine rust with which coins become covered by lying in peculiar soils, and which, like varnish, is at once preservative and orna- mental. It is . . . a natural varnish, not imitable by any effort of human art; sometimes of delicate blue, like that of a turquoise: sometimes of a bronze brown, equal to that observable in ancient statues of bronze; sometimes of an exquisite green, verging on the azure hue, which last is the most beautiful of all. It is also found of a fine purple, of olive, and of a cream colour, or pale yellow. The Neapolitan patina is of a light green; and when free from excrescence or blemish, is very beautiful. Sometimes the purple patina gleams through an upper coat of another colour, with as fine effect as a variegated silk or gem. In a few instances a rust of deeper green is found, and it is sometimes spotted with the red or bronze shade, which gives it the appearance of the East Indian stone called bloodstone. These rusts are all, when the real product of time, as hard as the metal itself, and preserve it much better than any artificial varnish could have done; concealing, at the same time, not the most minute particle of the impression of the coin. Gold admits no rust but iron-mould, when lying in a soil impregnated with iron. Silver takes many kinds, but chiefly green and red, which yield to vinegar; for in this metal the rust is prejudicial. The term patina is applied to the coat of dirt and varnish which, through time, covers the surfaces of pictures. The patina or dirty varnish of an old picture often gives the work an adventitious harmony and effect which does not belong to it; and when this extraneous coating has been removed by the cleaner, the picture has lost these borrowed qualities, and is by the inexperienced supposed to have been injured. Hence, skilful cleaners, after cleaning and repairing a picture, cover it with an artificial patina or glazing, and restore the effect of dirt and age.—*Brande and Cox.* Dictionary of Science, Literature, and Art.

Forgers give patina to their mediæval ivories by lending them to stout young Jewesses to wear for a few months hanging, like an amulet, between their breasts.—*Aldous Huxley.* Antic Hay. Ch. xxi. (Chatto & Windus).

PAVANE (pav/an) *a stately dance*   P26

That gracious Eighteenth Century world, so cruel to the unfortunate, so delightful to its favourites, was no doubt all Thackeray called it, shrinking aghast from the revelations in Harvey's memoirs; it was rouged and fawning and lying and pushing and struggling and heartless and god- less, and it lacked most of the virtues which have since come in with industrial capitalism and the late Liberal Party. Yet to hear some twit- tering pedant of the Twentieth Century patronising it gives one a grue. For if the Eighteenth Century lacked a great many things, including that mass-produced brilliance of thought and expression which is the glory of its present heirs, it did not lack a certain distinction of its own. Its privileged classes defended themselves against the poor with laws of devilish savagery, but its most odious politicians quoted Homer and Virgil in the House of Commons as a matter of course. To be rich under the Georges was to be disliked, as in every other age, yet what delicious compensations the Georgian rich enjoyed in their brief uneasy passage through this world! Their dignified pavane to that paradise reserved for them, despite themselves, by their State clergy, who, like Pope's Dean, never mentioned Hell to ears polite, was chimed away in Palladian mansions by the mellow comely clocks of Tompion and Rimbault. Their delicate "chaney" lived in cabinets by Chippendale and their soberly elegant, apricot-calf-bound books in tall cases carved and gilded by the school of Kent. Their wine was sipped from the glass of Venice and Bristol, their tea poured, sugared, and creamed by silverware signed by Paul Lamerie. Their ceilings and coaches were painted by Angelica Kauffmann and Cipriani.—*D. B. Wyndham Lewis.* The Hooded Hawk. (Eyre & Spottiswoode).

PAVONINE (pav/o-nine) *like a peacock*   P27

The jays with the peacock's feathers are the snobs of the world . . . The imitation of the great is universal in this city . . . Peacock's feathers are stuck in the tails of most families. Scarce one of us domestic birds but imitates the lanky, pavonine strut, and shrill genteel scream.— *Thackeray.* Book of Snobs. Ch. xx.

PEA-JACKET (pe/jak-et) *a coarse loose-fitting overcoat*   P28
worn by seamen; a duffel-coat

Standing at the bar was a burly, black-bearded man in sea-boots, pea-jacket and peaked cap, pipe in mouth and a blue-china quart pot at his elbow.—*Neil Bell.* The Skarhaven Tercentenary. (Collins).

PEASCOD (peze/cod) *a pea pod*   P29

I saw a green caterpillar as big as a small peascod.—*Izaac Walton.* The Compleat Angler.

PEJORATIVE (pe/jo-ra-tiv) *depreciatory*   P30

"You are Nigel's woman, aren't you?" said the Duchess, still busy with the dandelion. "Yes." Myrtle was accustomed to this phrase from her contemporaries, but it seemed a little pejorative from the lips of the old lady.—*Barbara Worsley-Gough.* Public Affaires. Ch. vi. (Gollancz).

No game licences are issued in the Reserve where the great pachyderms of the film trade bask and browse complacently. They have no suspicion that in most of America and in the whole of Europe the word "Hollywood" is pejorative.—*Evelyn Waugh.* Why Hollywood is a Term of Disparagement. "Daily Telegraph," 30th April, 1947.

PELLUCID†   P31

   Of all that is most beauteous-imaged there
  In happier beauty; more pellucid streams,
  An ampler ether, a diviner air,
  And fields invested with purpureal gleams;
  Climes which the sun, who sheds the brightest day
  Earth knows, is all unworthy to survey.
         —Wordsworth. Laodamia.

PENMAENMAWR (pen-may/en-mour)   P32

PENTASTICH (pen/ta-stik) *a stanza; five lines of verse*   P33

   Hail to thee, blythe spirit!
    Bird thou never wert;
  That from Heaven or near it
    Pourest thy full heart,
  In profuse strains of unpremeditated art.
        —Shelley. Ode to a Skylark.

PENTHOUSE (pent/hous) *a shed standing aslope from the*   P34
    main building

    This is the penthouse under which Lorenzo
  Desired us to make stand.
      —Shakespeare. The Merchant of Venice. ii, 6.
   The chill rain
  Drops from some penthouse on her wretched head.
      —Rowe. Jane Shore. v, 1.

PEPYS (pep/is; peps; peeps)   P35

PERIAPT (per/i-apt) *a charm worn as a preservative*   P36
    against diseases or mischief

  LA PUCELLE: The regent conquers, and the Frenchmen fly;
     Now help, ye charming spells and periapts!
      —Shakespeare. Henry VI. Pt. i, v, 3.

PERIPHERY (per-if/er-i) *boundary line or surface*   P37

  . . . beside me, a point of civilization in a radius of several hundred
miles, were grouped a Cadillac, an English driver, a behaviourist, a
colonel, a smashed aeroplane, a Polish neuropath, some sausages, tea,
cardboard plates, marmalade, Lea and Perrin's sauce. These facts grouped
themselves in the peripheral focus.—*Harold Nicolson.* Some People.
" Miriam Codd." (Constable).

THE WENTWORTH-BRABAZON ROTO-KINETIC GUN

The principle, as described in the brochure, seemed simple almost to the point of absurdity. The flat drum contained two radial tubes rotated at a high speed by an electric motor. Steel balls, about half an inch diameter, were fed into it through the short tube at the top and were in due course slung out by centrifugal force through a slot in the periphery of the drum, to the grave discomfiture of the enemy.—*Hugh McGraw*. The Boon Companions. Ch. x. (Heinemann).

PERIPHRASIS (per-if/ra-sis) *circumlocution*   P38

Where there is an obscurity too deep for our Reason, 'tis good to sit down with a description, periphrasis or adumbration; for by acquainting our Reason how unable it is to display the visible and obvious effects of Nature, it becomes more humble and submissive unto the subtleties of Faith.—*Sir Thomas Browne*. Religio Medici. First Part.

> First, a piece of glass he coated
> With Collodion and plunged it
> In a bath of Lunar Caustic
> Carefully dissolved in water,
> There he left it certain minutes.
>
> Secondly, my Hiawatha
> Made with cunning hand a mixture
> Of the acid Pyro-gallic,
> And of Glacial Acetic
> And of Alcohol and water;
> This developed all the picture.
>
> Finally, he fixed each picture
> With a saturate solution
> Of a certain salt of Soda—
> Chemists call it Hyposulphite.
> Very difficult the name is
> For a metre like the present,
> But periphrasis has done it.
>   —*Lewis Carroll*. Phantasmagoria and Other Poems.

PERISTYLE (per/i-stile) (1) *a row of columns;* (2) *a colonnaded court*   P39

. . . there still remains a considerable claim for privacy in Utopia. The room, or apartments, or home, or mansion, whatever it may be a man or woman maintains, must be private, and under his or her complete dominion; it seems harsh and intrusive to forbid a central garden plot or peristyle, such as one sees in Pompeii, within the house walls, and it is almost as difficult to deny a little private territory beyond the house.—*H. G. Wells*. A Modern Utopia. Ch. ii. (Collins).

PERNOCTATION (per-nok-tay/shun) *staying up/out all night*   P40

Whether we have paid for the pleasure of our sin by smart or sorrow, by the effusion of alms, or pernoctations or abodes in prayers.—*Jeremy Taylor*. Rule and Exercises of Holy Dying. Ch. iv. s. 6.

PERPEND (per-pend/) *to consider*   P41

POLONIUS: Madam, I swear I use no art at all.
That he is mad, 'tis true: 'tis true, 'tis pity,
And pity 'tis 'tis true: a foolish figure;
But farewell it, for I will use no art.
Mad let us grant him then: and now remains
That we find out the cause of this effect,
Or rather say, the cause of this defect,
For this effect defective comes by cause:
Thus it remains and the remainder thus.
Perpend.
I have a daughter,—have while she is mine,—
Who in her duty and obedience, mark,
Hath given me this: now gather and surmise.
                          —*Shakespeare*. Hamlet. ii, 2.

PERSPICUITY†   P42

Perspicuity.—I shall waste no words on the need of this: since the
first aim of speech is to be understood. The more clearly you write the
more easily and surely you will be understood. I propose to demonstrate
to you further, in a minute or so, that the more clearly you write the
more clearly you will understand yourself. But a sufficient reason has
been given in ten words why you should desire perspicuity.—*Sir Arthur
Quiller-Couch*. On the Art of Writing. Lecture ii.

PHÆTON (fay/e-ton) *a light four-wheeled open carriage,*   P43
usually drawn by two horses

In summer . . . he drove in his pony phaeton after luncheon to
Virginia Water, members of the household following in landaus.—*Roger
Fulford*. George the Fourth. Bk. iii. (iv). (Duckworth).

PHILOSOPHE (fil/o-sof) *fake philosopher*   P44

Their [the Germans'] philosophy too must be regarded as uncertain;
at best only the beginning of better things. But surely even this is not
to be neglected. A little light is precious in great darkness: nor amid
myriads of poetasters and philosophes, are poets and philosophers so
numerous that we should reject such, when they speak to us in the hard,
but manly, deep, and expressive tones of that old Saxon speech, which is
also our mother-tongue.—*Carlyle*. Critical and Miscellaneous Essays.
" State of German Literature."

PHYLACTERY (fi-lak/ter-i) *a periapt*   P45

Her front erect with majesty she bore,
The crosier wielded, and the mitre wore.
Her upper part of decent discipline
Showed affectation of an ancient line;
And fathers, councils, Church and Church's head,
Were on her reverend phylacteries read.
                          —*Dryden*. The Hind and the Panther. i, 394.

PINFOLD (pin/fold) *a cattle pound* P46

    . . . this dim spot,
Which men call Earth, and with low-thoughted care
Confin'd, and pester'd in this pin-fold here,
Strive to keep up a frail, and Feaverish being
Unmindfull of the crown that Vertue gives
After this mortal change, to her true Servants
Amongst the enthron'd gods on Sainted seats.
        —*Milton.* Comus.

PISHOGUE (pi-shogue/) *a sorcerer; sorcery* P47

    —Pity about her, says the citizen. Or any other woman marries a half and half.
    —How half and half? says Bloom. Do you mean he . . .
    —Half and half I mean, says the citizen. A fellow that's neither fish nor flesh.
    —Nor good red herring, says Joe.
    —That's what I mean, says the citizen. A pishogue, if you know what that is.—*James Joyce.* Ulysses (ii). (John Lane).

PLEDGET (plej/et) *a wound dressing; piece of lint or rag* P48

    Saul Deth recognised between a hat once smartly cocked, now a mere limp pledget of felt, and a once spruce blue camlet coat, now drenched to irretrievable ruin by the rain, the tallowy features of his quondam apprentice and now junior book-keeper, Simnel Coxworthy.—*Sala.* Dutch Pictures. " The Ship-Chandler."

PLENARY (plen/na-ri) *complete; absolute* P49

    . . . high breeding then was of more difficult attainment than that which is now so called; and, consequently, entitled the successful professor to a proportionable degree of plenary indulgences and privileges. —*Sir Walter Scott.* " The Mirror." Ch. i.

PLENILUNE (plen/i-loon) *full moon* P50

    Whose glory (like a lasting plenilune)
Seems ignorant of what it is to wane.
        —*Ben Jonson.* Cynthia's Revels.

PLETHORIC† P51

    At last the nation found, with fruitless skill,
Its former strength was but plethorick ill.
        —*Oliver Goldsmith.* The Traveller.

PLURIPRESENCE (plu-ri-prez/ens) *presence in more*   P52
        than one place

    Cf. *omnipresence* which is a synonym for ubiquity.

    I here suggested something favourable of the Roman Catholicks.
TOPLADY: " Does not their invocation of saints suppose omnipresence
of the saints?"   JOHNSON: " No, Sir, it supposes only pluripresence."
—*James Boswell.* Life of Johnson.   A.D. 1773.   Ætat. 64.

POETASTER (po/et-as-ter) *an inferior poet*   P53

    We have already, as occasion served, borne testimony to the merits
of various German poets; and must now say a word on certain German
poetasters, hoping that it may be chiefly a regard to the former which has
made us take even this slight notice of the latter; for the bad is in itself
of no value, and only worth describing lest it be mistaken for the good
. . . To exhaust [this subject] or attempt discussing it with scientific
precision, would be an impossible enterprise.   What man is there that
could assort the whole furniture of Milton's Limbo of Vanity; or where
is the Hallam that would undertake to write the Constitutional History of
a Rookery?—*Carlyle.*   Critical and Miscellaneous Essays.   " German
Playwrights."

    Mulgrave wrote verses which scarcely ever rose above absolute
mediocrity; but, as he was a man of high note in the political and
fashionable world, these verses found admirers.   Time dissolved the charm,
but unfortunately for him, not until his lines had acquired a prescriptive
right to a place in all collections of the works of English poets.   To this
day accordingly his insipid essays in rhyme and his paltry songs to
Amoretta and Gloriana are reprinted in company with Comus and
Alexander's Feast.   The consequence is that our generation knows Mul-
grave chiefly as a poetaster, and despises him as such.—*Macaulay.*
History of England.

POLEMIC (po-lem/ik) *controversial*   P54

    Used as a noun the word means a controversialist.

        Each staunch polemick, stubborn as a rock,
                —*Pope.* The Dunciad. iv., 195.

POLITIC (pol/i-tik) *prudent; artful*   P55

        No less alike the politick and wise,
        All sly slow things, with circumspective eyes;
        Men in their loose unguarded hours they take,
        Not that themselves are wise, but others weak.
                —*Pope.* Essay on Man. iv., 225.

POLYGRAPHY (pol-ig/ra-fi) *the art of writing in cipher*   P56

    Such occult notes, steganography, polygraphy, or magnetical telling
of their minds.—*Burton.* Anatomy of Melancholy.

POMACE (pum/as) *apple-pulp*   P57

". . . Now this remarkable large piece" (pointing to a patch nailed
to the side), "shows a' accident he received by the tread of a horse, that
squashed his foot almost to a pomace. The horse-show came full-butt
on this point, you see."—*Thomas Hardy.* Under the Greenwood Tree.
Pt. i, Ch. iii. (Macmillan).

POMEGRANATE (pome/gran-at) *a tropical fruit*   P58

CAPULET'S ORCHARD

JULIET: Wilt thou be gone? It is not yet near day:
It was the nightingale, and not the lark,
That pierced the fearful hollow of thine ear;
Nightly she sings on yond pomegranate-tree:
Believe me, love, it was the nightingale.

ROMEO: It was the lark, the herald of the morn,
No nightingale: look, love, what envious streaks
Do lace the severing clouds in yonder east:
Night's candles are burnt out, and jocund day
Stands tiptoe on the misty mountain tops:
I must be gone and live, or stay and die.
—*Shakespeare.* Romeo and Juliet. iii. v.

PONDERABLE (pon/der-abl) *measurable; capable of*   P59
being weighed

The bite of an asp will kill within an hour, yet the impression is
scarce visible, and the poison communicated not ponderable.—*Sir Thomas
Browne.* Vulgar Errors.

PONTIFICAL (pon-tif/ik-al) *excessively dignified*   P60

KING: Thus did I keep my person fresh and new,
My presence like a robe pontifical,
Ne'er seen, but wonder'd at.
—*Shakespeare.* Henry IV. Pt. i, iii, 2.

PORTICO (por/ti-ko) *architectural equivalent of the*   P61
pergola

" Imagine every entertainment for mind and body—enumerate all the
gymnastic games our fathers invented . . . intersperse the whole with
gardens, with theatres, with porticos, with schools—suppose in one word,
a city of the gods, composed but of palaces and public edifices, and you
may form some faint idea of the glories of the great baths of Rome!"
" By Hercules!" said Diomed, opening his eyes, " why it would take a
man's whole life to bathe!" "At Rome . . . there are many who live
only at the baths. . . They seem as if they knew nothing of the rest of
Rome, as if they despised all other existence." " By Pollux! you amaze
me." " Even those who bathe only thrice a day contrive to consume
their lives in this occupation. They take their exercise in the tennis-
court or the porticos, to prepare them for the first bath; they lounge into
the theatre, to refresh themselves after it!"—*Bulwer Lytton.* The Last
Days of Pompeii. Bk. i, Ch. viii.

POSSET (pos/et) *to curdle; to thicken*   P62

A posset (noun) is a drink made of milk curdled with wine
or other liquor.

GHOST: Sleeping within my orchard,
                My custom always of the afternoon,
                Upon my secure hour thy uncle stole,
                With juice of cursed hebenon in a vial,
                And in the porches of my ears did pour
                The leperous distilment; whose effect
                Holds such an enmity with blood of man
                That swift as quick-silver it courses through
                The natural gates and alleys of the body;
                And with a sudden vigour it doth posset
                And curd, like eager droppings into milk,
                The thin and wholesome blood:
                                —*Shakespeare*. Hamlet. i, 5.

POTABLE†   P63

PRINCE: Thou best of gold art worst of gold,
                Other less fine in carat, is more precious,
                Preserving life in med'cine potable.
                        —*Shakespeare*. Henry IV. Pt. ii, iv, 5.

PRAGMATIC†   P64

There is not so impudent a thing in nature as the saucy look of an
assured man, confident of success. The pedantic arrogance of a very
husband has not so pragmatical an air. Ah! I'll never marry, unless I
am first made sure of my will and pleasure.—*Congreve*. The Way of the
World.

PRECATORY (prek/a-tor-i) *entreating; praying*   P65

"I do pray you, sir—Sir Knight—good now, Sir Piercie—Be quiet,
Benedict, there is a good steed—soh, poor fellow!" uttering all the other
precatory and soothing exclamations by which a timid horseman usually
bespeaks the favour of a frisky companion, or of his own unquiet nag.
—*Sir Walter Scott*. The Monastery. Ch. v.

Literature, except in the way of Sermons for the Portuguese Colonies,
or other the like small private dealings, had not yet opened her hospitable
bosom to him. Epistles, precatory and amatory, for such as had more
cash than grammar, he may have written; . . .—*Carlyle*. Critical and
Miscellaneous Essays. " Diderot."

PREDATORY (pred/a-tor-i) *plundering*   P66

The principle which directed all his dealings with his neighbours is
fully expressed by the old motto of "one of the great predatory families
of Teviotdale, " Thou shalt want ere I want." He seems to have laid it
down, as a fundamental proposition which could not be disputed, that,
when he had not as many lacs of rupees as the public service required, he
was to take them from anybody who had.—*Macaulay*. Critical and
Historical Essays. " Warren Hastings."

PREFIGURE (pre-fig/ur) *to imagine antecedently* P67

What the Old Testament hath, the very same the New containeth; but that which lieth there, as under a shadow, is here brought forth into the open sun; things there prefigured are here performed.—*Hooker.* Ecclesiastical Polity.

PRELAPSARIAN (pre-lap-sáre/i-an) P68

Literally, before the Fall. Compare *sublapsarian,* in D.U.W.(A).

. . . prelapsarian ingenuousness.—*Aldous Huxley.* Those Barren Leaves. Pt. iii, Ch. v. (Chatto & Windus).

PRELIBATION (pre-li-bay/shun) *a foretaste* P69

Rich prelibation of consummate Joy.—*Young.* Night Thoughts. ix.

PRELUSIVE (pre-lu/siv) *introductory* P70

The clouds
Softly shaking on the dimpled pool
Prelusive drops, let all their moisture flow.
　　　　　　　　—*Thomson.* Seasons. " Spring."

PRESAGE (pres/aj) *to foretell; anything that foretells* P71

Amazement seis'd
The Rebel Thrones, but greater rage to see
Thus foil'd thir mightiest, ours joy fill'd, and shout
Presage of Victorie and fierce desire
Of Battel: whereat *Michael* bid sound
Th' Arch-angel trumpet; through the vast of Heav'n
It sounded, and the faithful Armies rung
Hosanna to the Highest: nor stood at gaze
Th' adverse Legions, nor less hideous joyn'd
The horrid shock: now storming furie rose,
And clamour such as heard in Heav'n till now
Was never, Arms on Armour clashing bray'd
Horrible discord, and the madding Wheeles
Of brazen Chariots rag'd; dire was the noise
Of conflict; over head the dismal hiss
Of fiery Darts in flaming volies flew,
And flying vaulted either Host with fire.
So under fierie Cope together rush'd
Both Battels maine. with ruinous assault.
　　　　　　　　—*Milton.* Paradise Lost. vi.

PRESBYOPIA (prez-bi-o/pi-a) *long-sightedness*   P72

VELASQUEZ

. . . he enriched his palette with several new colours, especially carmine, which he found in Greco, and silvery tones succeeded the dryer and harder burnt tones of his earlier work. And at length also (after his second Italian visit) his figures became bathed in atmosphere. Later, as he approached his fiftieth year, he acquired his breadth of touch, aided in this, no doubt by the normal presbyopia of advancing age, which made it necessary to stand farther from the pictures.—*Havelock Ellis.* The Soul of Spain. (Constable).

PRESCIENT (pre/shyent) *foreknowledge; foresight*   P73

Who taught the nations of the field and wood
To shun their poison and to choose their food?
Prescient the tides or tempests to withstand,
Build on the wave, or arch beneath the sand?
          —*Pope.* Essay on Man. iii, 99.

BOSWELL: " It appears to me, Sir, that predestination, or what is equivalent to it, cannot be avoided, if we hold an universal prescience in the Deity." JOHNSON: " Why, Sir, does not GOD every day see things going on without preventing them?"—*James Boswell.* Life of Johnson. A.D. 1769. Ætat. 60.

PRESCIND (pre-sind/) *to cut off; isolate*   P74

. . . not an abstract idea compounded of inconsistencies, and prescinded from all real things.—*Bishop Berkeley.* Siris. s. 323.

PRETERNATURAL (pre-ter-nat/ur-al) *beyond what is*   P75
     natural

The world has nothing to show of the preternatural in painting, transcending the figure of Lazarus bursting his grave-clothes, in the great picture at Angerstein's. It seems a thing between two beings. A ghastly horror at itself struggles with newly-apprehending gratitude at second life bestowed. It cannot forget that it was a ghost. It has hardly felt that it is a body.—*Charles Lamb.* Essays of Elia. " On the Productions of Modern Art."

When the disguised Queen of Love appeared before Æneas a preternatural perfume accompanied her presence and betrayed her quality.—*Thomas Hardy.* The Return of the Native. Bk. ii (6). (Macmillan).

PREVENIENT (pre-ven/i-ent) *going before*   P76

Thus they in lowliest plight repentant stood
Praying, for from the Mercie-seat above
Prevenient Grace descending had remov'd
The stonie from thir hearts, and made new flesh
Regenerate grow instead, that sighs now breath'd
Unutterable, which the Spirit of prayer
Inspir'd, and wing'd for Heav'n with speedier flight
Then loudest Oratorie.
          —*Milton.* Paradise Lost. xi, 2.

PROCELEUSMATIC (pros-e-luse-mat/ik) *metrical foot* P77
of four short syllables

The ancient proceleusmatick song, by which the rowers of galleys were animated, may be supposed to have been of this kind. There is now an oar-song used by the Hebridians.—*Dr. Johnson*. Journey to the Western Islands of Scotland.

PROLATE† P78

The meaning of this word was unintentionally omitted from D.U.W.(A). It means lengthened, elongated as applied to a curved or rounded object—roughly, the shape of a Rugby football as compared with an ordinary football. The word may also be used for extension of other kinds. It may be applied, for example, to the lengthening of pronunciation; or perhaps even the mere lateral extension of a straight object.

PROLEGOMENON (pro-le-gom/e-non) *introduction* P79

KEATS' ENDYMION

. . . with all its faults it is a work full of passages of great beauty into which Keats precociously poured some of his most vital intuitions. For that very reason, it is repellent to a "consequitive man" or logical mind, and those intuitions have not yet been fully understood, for Keats, poet that he was, often wrote elliptically and clothed his perceptions in a symbolism the key to which has not yet been fully grasped. Yet there was an actual key to Keats' maturing conceptions of life, nature, and art, love and beauty and truth. In *Endymion,* moreover, he merely uttered those conceptions in what proved to be a sort of prolegomenon to his riper masterpieces. This fact and the fascinating process involved in the creation of *Endymion* make it a poem which warrants and repays the minute study devoted to it in the following pages.—*Werner W. Beyer*. Keats and the Daemon King. Ch. iii. (Oxford University Press).

PROLIFERATION (pro-lif-er-ay/shun) *a growth; a* P80
multiplication

This collection of papers was not a story, not an essay, not a confession, not a diary. It was—nothing definable. It went into no conceivable covers. It was just, White decided, a proliferation. A vast proliferation. It wanted even a title.—*H. G. Wells*. The Research Magnificent. (Collins).

PROPHYLACTIC (pro-fi-lak/tik) *preventing disease*   P81

A prophylactic (noun) is a cure, or (more strictly) a preventive.

Suddenly, for no reason, in the middle of the night, or even in the middle of the jolliest party, she would remember an ancient floater—just like that, *à propos de bottes*—would remember and be overcome by a feeling of self-reproach and retrospective shame. And there was no remedy, no spiritual prophylaxis.—*Aldous Huxley.* Those Barren Leaves. (Chatto & Windus).

PROSCENIUM (pro-see/ni-um) *the narrow edge of the*   P82
                            stage in front of the curtain

Over the sideboard hung one of John Bidlake's paintings of the theatre. A curve of the gallery, a slope of faces, a corner of the bright proscenium.

"How good that is!" said Spandrell, shading his eyes to see it more clearly.—*Aldous Huxley.* Point Counter Point. Ch. xii. (Chatto & Windus).

PROSCRIBE (pro-skribe/) *to denounce; to forbid*   P83

Thy murder of thy brother, (being so bribed),
And writ him in the list of my proscribed
After thy fact.
                    —*Ben Jonson.* Catiline's Conspiracy. i, 1.

PURITAN ENGLAND
The fine arts were all but proscribed. The solemn peal of the organ was superstitious, the light music of Ben Jonson's masques was dissolute. Half the fine paintings in England were idolatrous, and the other half indecent.—*Macaulay.* History of England. Ch. i.

MILTON
Neither blindness, nor gout, nor age, nor penury, nor domestic afflictions, nor political disappointments, nor abuse, nor proscription, nor neglect, had power to disturb his sedate and majestic patience.—*Macaulay.* "Milton."

PROTAGONIST (pro-tag/on-ist) *leader; principal character*   P84

I have called his Diary a work of art. Now when the artist has found something, word or deed, exactly proper to a favourite character in play or novel, he will neither suppress nor diminish it, though the remark be silly or the act mean. The hesitation of Hamlet, the credulity of Othello, the baseness of Emma Bovary, or the irregularities of Mr. Swiveller, caused neither disappointment nor disgust to their creators. And so with Pepys and his adored protagonist: adored not blindly, but with trenchant insight and enduring human toleration.—*R. L. Stevenson.* Familiar Studies of Men and Books. "Samuel Pepys."

PROTEAN (pro-tee/an) *variable; changeable* P85

We are merry with one, grave with another, as befits the nature and demands of the relation. Pepys's letter to Evelyn would have little in common with that other one to Mrs. Knipp which he signed by the pseudonym of *Dapper Dicky;* yet each would be suitable to the character of his correspondent. There is no untruth in this, for man, being a Protean animal, swiftly shares and changes with his company and surroundings; and these changes are the better part of his education in the world. To strike a posture once for all, and to march through life like a drum-major, is to be highly disagreeable to others and a fool for oneself into the bargain.—*R. L. Stevenson.* Familiar Studies of Men and Books. " Samuel Pepys."

PROTOTYPE (pro/to-type) *an original model* P86

Jean des Esseintes and Dorian Gray are the authentic decadent types. Extreme they are, as a matter of course, but their prototypes did exist in real life, and minus those incidents wherein extreme decadence expresses itself in serious crime, such as murder or incitement to murder, those prototypes had recognisable corporeal being.—*Holbrook Jackson.* The Eighteen Nineties. Ch. iii. (Jonathan Cape).

The first, largest and not the most pleasant of these was that upon which Noah and his wife, his family and the strange procession of animals which followed them—that stiff-necked company familiar from nursery days to every English child—embarked: but this is by no means the prototype of what I strive to indicate: for Noah and company were refugees, whereas the description *water-party* should evoke pictures of indolence and music, of gay comrades seeking a day of ease and coolness.—*Osbert Sitwell.* Sing High! Sing Low! " Picnics & Pavilions." (Macmillan).

PRURIENT† P87

> O godlike isolation, which art mine,
> I can but count thee perfect gain,
> What time I watch the darkening droves of swine
> That range on yonder plain.
> In filthy sloughs they roll a prurient skin,
> They graze and wallow, breed and sleep;
> And oft some brainless devil enters in,
> And drives them to the deep.
> —*Tennyson.* The Palace of Art.

Charity is the most michievous sort of pruriency.—*Bernard Shaw.* Man and Superman. " Maxims for Revolutionists."

PSEUDONYM (su/do-nim) *a nickname* P88

In the year 1890 Bernard Shaw was hardly a name to those who were outside of convinced Socialist and revolutionary circles, although his articles on music, over the pseudonym *Corno di Bassetto,* in *The Star* (1888-1890), afterwards continued in *The World* from 1890-1894, made him the subject of discussion in musical circles.—*Holbrook Jackson.* The Eighteen Nineties. Ch. xiv. (Jonathan Cape).

PSYCHE (si/ke)   P89

PUDENCY (pu/den-si) *modesty*   P90
POSTHUMUS: A pudency so rosy, the sweet view on't
                Might well have warm'd old Saturn.
                                —*Shakespeare*. Cymbeline. ii, 5.

PUISSANT (pwis/ant) *potent; great; powerful*   P91
          The queen is coming with a puissant host.
                            —*Shakespeare*. Henry VI. Pt. iii, ii, 1.
          For piety renow'nd and puissant deeds.
                            —*Milton*. Paradise Lost. xii. 322.

PURBLIND (pur/blind) *near sighted*   P92
          A wondrous phantom, from the dreams
          Of human errors dense and purblind faith,
          I will evoke, to meet thy questioning.
                                —*Shelley*. Queen Mab.

    BLOOM: (Impassionedly): These flying Dutchmen or lying Dutch-
men as they recline in their upholstered poop, casting dice, what reck
they? Machines is their cry, their chimera, their panacea. Labour-saving
apparatuses, supplanters, bugbears, manufactured monsters for mutual
murder, hideous hobgoblins produced by a horde of capitalistic lusts upon
our prostituted labour. The poor man starves while they are grassing
their royal mountain stags or shooting pheasants and partridges in their
purblind pomp of pelf and power. But their reign is rover for rever and
ever and ev . . .—*James Joyce.*. Ulysses. (John Lane).

PURLIEUS (pur/luz) *environs*   P93
          In the purlieus of this forest stands
          A sheepcote, fenced about with olive trees.
                                —*Shakespeare*. As You Like It. iv, 3.

OF CHARLES II.
    He wished merely to be a King such as Louis the Fifteenth of France
afterwards was; a King who could draw without limit on the treasury for
the gratification of his private tastes, who could hire with wealth and
honours persons capable of assisting him to kill time, and who, even when
the state was brought by maladministration to the depths of humiliation
and to the brink of ruin, could still exclude unwelcome truth from the
purlieus of his own seraglio, and refuse to see and hear whatever might
disturb his luxurious repose.—*Macaulay*. History of England. Ch. ii.

    . . . though we place Hell under Earth, the Devil's walk and purlue is
about it: men speak too popularly who place it in those flaming mountains,
,which to grosser apprehensions represent Hell. The heart of men is the
place Devils dwell in.—*Sir Thomas Browne*. Religio Medici. First Part.

    In the interim Orianda had resigned her appointment and several
times Gerald had met her secretly in the purlieus of Tillington Park. The
girl's cool casual nature fascinated him not less than her appearance.—
A. E. Coppard. The Black Dog. ii. (Jonathan Cape).

PURULENT (pur/u-lent) *consisting of pus or the*   P94
         running of wounds

>It spews a filthy froth
>Of matter purulent and white,
>Which happen'd on the skin to light,
>And there corrupting on a wound.
>Spreads leprosy.
>   *—Swift.* Miscellanies.

PUSILLANIMOUS (pu-si-lan/i-mus) *weak; shifty*   P95

An argument fit for great and mighty princes . . . that neither by overmeasuring their forces they lose themselves in vain enterprizes; nor, on the other side, by undervaluing them, descend to fearful and pusillanimous counsels.—*Bacon.* Essays. "Of the True Greatness of Kingdoms and Estates."

PYROMANCY (pire/o-man-si) *divination by fire*   P96

Divination was invented by the Persians, and is seldom or never taken in a good sense: there are four kinds of divination, hydromancy, pyromancy, aeromancy, geomancy.—*Ayliffe.* Parergon Juris Canonici.

The ancients imagined they could foretell futurity by inspecting fire and flame; for this purpose they considered its direction, or which way it turned. Sometimes they threw pitch into it, and if it took fire instantly they considered it a favourable omen.—*Joseph Ennemoser.* The History of Magic. "Divination."

PYRRHONISM (pir/o-nizm) *universal scepticism*   P97

If there was any single way of life he could lastingly believe in, it was that mixture of pyrrhonism and stoicism which had struck him, an enquiring schoolboy among the philosophers, as the height of human wisdom, and into whose mould of sceptical indifference he had poured his unimpassioned adolescence. Against the pyrrhonian suspense of judgment and the stoical imperturbability he had often rebelled . . .—*Aldous Huxley.* Point Counter Point. Ch. xiv. (Chatto & Windus).

QUADRATURE

QUADRILLE

QUAG

QUALM

QUALMISH

QUARTO

QUATERNION

QUEASY

QUIDNUNC

QUIETUS

QUILLER-COUCH

QUINCUNX

QUITO

QUIXOTIC

QUOIN

QUADRATURE (kwod/ra-ture) *a square; the act of squaring*   Q

On the quadrature of the circle, he says he [Maupertuis] cannot decide if this problem be resolvable or not; but he observes, that it is very useless to search for it any more; since we have arrived by approximation to such a point of accuracy, that on a large circle, such as the orbit which the earth describes round the sun, the geometrician will not mistake by the thickness of a hair. The quadrature of the circle is still, however a favourite game of some visionaries, and several are still imagining that they have discovered the perpetual motion; the Italians nickname them " matto perpetuo "; and Bekker tells us of the fate of one Hartmann of Leipsic, who was in such despair at having passed his life so vainly, in studying the perpetual motion, that at length he hanged himself!— *D'Israeli.* Curiosities of Literature.

QUADRILLE (ka-dril/) (1) *a card game;* (2) *a dance in sets of four couples; the music for this dance*   Q2

O filthy check on all industrious skill
To spoil the nation's last great trade—quadrille!
> —*Pope.* Moral Essays. iii, 75.

QUAG†   Q3

Behold, on the left hand, there was a very dangerous quag, into which, if even a good man falls, he can find no bottom for his foot to stand on. Into that quag king David once did fall, and had no doubt therein been smothered, had not He that is able plucked him out.—*Bunyan.* The Pilgrim's Progress.

QUALM (kwawm) *spasm of sickness*   Q4

Compared to these storms, death is but a qualm,
Hell somewhat lightsome, the Bermudas calm.
> —*Donne.*

QUALMISH (kwam/ish) *affected with sickness at the stomach*   Q5

. . . my dear angel has been qualmish of late, and begins to grow remarkable round in the waist; so that I cannot leave her in such an interesting condition, which I hope will produce something to crown my felicity.—*Smollett.* The Adventures of Roderick Random. Ch. lxix.

QUARTO (kwar/to)   Q6

A sheet of paper measuring approximately 10 x 8 inches (the size varies). Hence, a book of such a size.

The form and magnitude of a quarto imposes upon the mind; and men, who are unequal to the labour of discussing an intricate argument, or wish to avoid it, are willing enough to suppose, that much has been proved, because much has been said.—*The Letters of Junius.* Letter xxx.

QUATERNION (kwa-ter/ni-on) *a set or file of four*   Q7

> Aire, and ye Elements the eldest birth
> Of Natures Womb, that in quaternion run
> Perpetual Circle, multiform; and mix
> And nourish all things, let your ceasless change
> Varie to our great Maker still new praise.
> Ye Mists and Exhalations that now rise
> From Hill or steaming Lake, duskie or grey,
> Till the Sun paint your fleecie skirts with Gold,
> In honour to the Worlds great Author rise,
> Whether to deck with Clouds the uncolourd skie,
> Or wet the thirstie Earth with falling showers,
> Rising or falling still advance his praise.
> —*Milton.* Paradise Lost. v.

QUEASY (kwe/zi) (1) *sick; nauseated;* (2) *squeamish*   Q8

In this connection I remember my father's partner, a crack shot, gaunt, humourless and irreproachable, vaguely possessed of county connections, under whose cheerful wing I began life. I remember a Saturday morning when Sarah Bernhardt, on her way from Buenos Aires to Timbuctoo, proposed to give Manchester an afternoon taste of the Lady of the Camellias. Recognizing the necessity for posting the letters early, " I suppose, Sir," I said, " you are going to see Sarah Bernhardt?" "You suppose wrong, young man," the graven image replied, " I do not approve of that sort of acting, and should be glad to see it discouraged." I have never forgotten the queasy piety with which, as the poor, dignified fool said this, the whole Nonconformist Conscience overflowed his narrow eyes and dribbled down his thin beard.—*James Agate.* Playgoing. (i). (Jarrolds).

QUIDNUNC (kwid/nunk) *a person who is curious to know*   Q9
              everything; a gossip

Our quidnuncs between whiles go to a coffee-house, where they have several warm liquors made of the waters of Lethe, with very good poppy-tea.—*Tatler.* No. 118.

Round the portico of the Green Dragon hotel and commercial inn, a knot of principal personages, the chief lawyer, the brewer, the vicar himself, and several of those easy quidnuncs who abound in country towns, and who rank under the designation of retired gentlemen, were in close and very earnest converse.—*Disraeli.* Sybil. Bk. ii, Ch. iii.

QUIETUS (kwi-e/tus) *discharge; final settlement*   Q10

> O thou, my lovely boy, who in thy power
> Dost hold Time's fickle glass, his sickle, hour
> Who hast by waning grown, and therein show'st
> Thy lovers withering as thy sweet self growest;
> If Nature, sovereign mistress over wrack,
> As thou goest onwards, still will pluck thee back,
> She keeps thee to this purpose, that her skill

May time disgrace and wretched minutes kill.
Yet fear her, O thou minion of her pleasure!
She may detain, but not still keep, her treasure:
Her audit, though delay'd, answer'd must be,
And her quietus is to render thee.
                    —*Shakespeare*. Sonnets. cxxvi.

QUILLER-COUCH (kwil/er kooch)   Q11

QUINCUNX (kwin/kunks) *an arrangement of five points,*   Q12
four of which form a square with the fifth in the centre

. . . the single Quincunx of the Hyades . . .—*Sir Thomas Browne.*
The Garden of Cyrus. Ch. iii.

. . . the Quincunciall Specks on the top of the Miscle-berry, especially
that which grows upon the *Tibia* or Lime Tree.—*Sir Thomas Browne.*
The Garden of Cyrus. Ch. iii.

QUITO (key/to)   Q13

QUIXOTIC (kwik-sot/ik) *chivalrous but unpractical*   Q14
I was criticised in early days for quixotry and priggishness in pro-
tecting Jews.—*G. K. Chesterton.* Autobiography. Ch. iii. (Hutchinson).

QUOIN (koin) *a corner*   Q15
Also spelt *coign.*

RABELAISIAN	RHETORICIAN
RACONTEUR	RHOMB
RADDLE	RHOMBOID
RAILWAY NOVEL	RIANT
RAKE-HELL	*RIO GRANDE*
RAMADAN	RISORGIMENTO
RAMPANT	ROAN
RATHE	ROC
RATIOCINATION	ROCHET
RATIONALE	RODOMONTADE
REAVE	*ROMFORD*
REBECK	*ROMOLA*
RÉCHERCHÉ	ROSICRUCIAN
RECUSANT	ROTUNDA
REDDITION	ROULADE
REDINTEGRATE	ROULEAU
REDOLENT	ROUNDEL
RE-EDIFY	ROUNDELAY
REGIMEN	ROUTINEER
REMBRANDTESQUE	*ROWTON*
REQUIEM	RUG-HEADED
RESTAURATEUR	RUM BLOSSOM
RESUSCITATE	*RUTHVEN*
RETICULAR	*RUY BLAS*
RHABDOMANCY	

RABELAISIAN (rab-e-lay/zi-an) *coarsely humorous*   R

RACONTEUR (ra-kon-ter/)   R2

One addicted to relating anecdotes and stories in conversation. The term implies that there is some skill or art in the telling. The raconteur is by nature sociable; a diner-out; a clubman and a host. He is a person of means, well-spoken, properly educated. He is perhaps a company director. That is as far as he goes in the way of business. It is more likely that he specialises in horse-racing, the arts, game hunting, chemistry, first editions, food, clothes, intoxicating liquor, foreign travel, speedway racing, amateur detection, light poetry or some combination of two or more of these.

RADDLE (rad/l) *to make up the face with red ochre*   R3

. . . Leopold, who even on his deathbed was rouged and raddled to the eyes . . .—*Roger Fulford*. George the Fourth.   Bk. iii (iv). (Duckworth).

RAILWAY NOVEL (rail/way nov/l) *a novel of the type   R4
        sold on railway bookstalls*

RAKE-HELL†   R5

. . . amid their rake-hell bands,
They spy'd a lady left all succourlesse.
        —*Spenser*. The Faerie Queene.

RAMADAN (ram/a-dan)   R6

The ninth month of the Mohammedan year, which moves round the calendar. Throughout this month fasting is observed by those of the Mohammedan faith each day between dawn and sunset.

RAMPANT (ram/pant) *exuberant; violent; spreading   R7
        or growing profusely*

The seeds of death grow up, till like rampant weeds, they choke the tender flower of life.—*Richardson*. Clarissa.

RATHE (rarth) *coming or blooming early* R8

> Throw hither all your quaint enameld eyes,
> That on the green turf suck the honied showres,
> And purple all the ground with vernal flowres.
> Bring the rathe Primrose that forsaken dies,
> The tufted Crow-toe, and pale Gessamine,
> The white Pink, and the Pansie freakt with jeat,
> The glowing Violet.
> The Musk-rose and the well attir'd Woodbine,
> With Cowslips wan that hang the pensive head
> And every flower that sad embroidery wears.
>
> —*Milton.* Lycidas.

RATIOCINATION† R9

I come of Nonconformist stock, and every Sunday morning was forced to attend ratiocination in the ugliest building ever put up to the glory of God and the shame of an architect. There was a barber's shop next door, where pale and clammy little boys destroyed their thin hands on the stubble of navvies recovering from Saturday night's debauch.—*James Agate.* Playgoing. (i). (Jarrolds).

RATIONALE (ra-shun-ay/le) *detailed explanation of* R10
  reasons

REAVE (reve) *to take away violently* R11

> Ah! who hath reft, quoth he, my dearest pledge.
>
> —*Milton.* Lycidas. 107.

REBECK (re/bek) *primitive violin* R12

> When the merry bells ring round,
> And the jocund rebecks sound,
> To many a youth and many a maid,
> Dancing in the checker'd shade.
>
> —*Milton.* L'Allegro. 93.

RÉCHERCHÉ (ray-share/shay) *choice; rare* R13

May also be used in a pejorative sense to mean *far-fetched; abstruse.*

RECUSANT (rek/u-zant) *one who refuses to conform* R14

The catholics were disappointed by an act inflicting new penalties on recusants, and especially debarring them from educating their children according to their consciences.—*Hallam.* Constitutional History of England. Ch. vii.

REDDITION* (red-dish/un) *explanation*   R15

Also means restitution, or surrender.

This hipshot grammarian cannot set it into right frame of construction, neither here in the similitude, nor in the following reddition thereof.
—*Milton*. Apology for Smectymnuus.   s. 4.

REDINTEGRATE†   R16

Charles VIII, received the kingdom of France in flourishing estate,
being redintegrate in those principal members, which anciently had been
portions of the crown, and were after disserved: so as they remained
only in homage, and not in sovereignty.—*Bacon*. History of the Reign of
Henry VII.

REDOLENT (red/o-lent) *giving out a sweet scent*   R17

RE-EDIFY (re-ed/i-fi) *to rebuild*   R18

TITUS: Traitors, away! he rests not in this tomb:
            This monument five hundred years hath stood,
            Which I have sumptuously re-edified:
            Here none but soldiers and Rome's servitors
            Repose in fame: none basely slain in brawls:
            Bury him where you can, he comes not here.
                        —*Shakespeare*. Titus Andronicus. i, 1.

REGIMEN (rej/i-men) *a strict diet or discipline*   R19

Sydenham first discovered that the cool regimen succeeded best in
cases of small-pox.—*Macaulay*. Critical and Historical Essays.   " Sir J.
Macintosh's History of the Revolution."

REMBRANDTESQUE (rem-brant-esk/) *like a Rembrandt*   R20

Compare *Zolaesque; Düreresque; Raffaelesque, etc.*

. . . the Rembrandtesque effect of his great head, with .its white
hair, against the cushion of his high-backed chair . . .—*John Galsworthy*.
The Man of Property. Ch. ii. (Heinemann).

REQUIEM (rek/wi-em) *a mass; a dirge*   R21

From the first word of the introit *Requiem æternam dona
eis, Domine.* See INTROIT.

            We should profane the service of the dead
            To sing a requiem and such peace to her,
            As to peace-parted souls.
                        —*Shakespeare*. Hamlet, v, 1.

RESTAURATEUR†   R22

Impossible to recapture the Mitre atmosphere in modern London.
It evaporated with the Mitre itself, on whose site Hoare's Bank now
stands. In a London tavern of this quality, we may reflect again, fire-
light and candle-light, sanded floor and red-curtained windows, mellow
oaken furniture and panelling, white-aproned waiters and good fare
blended in an aura of solid cheer which did not vanish completely,
according to Disraeli, till the 1850's. At the Mitre there was no haste.
Boswell and Johnson got there at 9 p.m. and sat till between one and two
in the morning, eating a leisurely supper, finishing a couple of bottles of
port, stretching their legs and having their talk out, like civilised beings.
Nearly five hours of pure rational pleasure. No modern London
restaurateur would endure it, even if the police allowed him.—*D. B.
Wyndham Lewis.* The Hooded Hawk. Ch. ii. (Eyre & Spottiswoode).

RESUSCITATE (re-sus/i-tate) *to revive*   R23

These things, I have resuscitated from the oblivion in which they
had long been buried.—*Buckle.* History of Civilization in England.
Vol. ii, Ch. v.

RETICULAR (re-tik/u-lar) *in the form or pattern of a net*   R24

THE TIDE COMING IN
. . . what looked like boiling milk would thrust out over the brown
sleek sands; and as the mess spread it would thin to a reticulated white-
ness, like lace, and then to the appearance of smoke sprays clinging to
the sands.—*James Branch Cabell.* Jurgen. Ch. xxix. (John Lane).

Such great tramways as this will be used when the Utopians wish to
travel fast and far; thereby you will glide over the land surface of the
planet; and feeding to them and distributing from them, innumerable
minor systems, clean little electric tramways I picture them, will spread
out over the land in finer reticulations, growing close and dense in the
urban regions and thinning as the population thins.—*H. G. Wells.* A
Modern Utopia. Ch. ii. (Collins).

RHABDOMANCY (rab/do-man-si) *dowsing*   R25

Of peculiar rhabdomancy is that which is used in mineral discoveries
with a forked hazel, commonly called Moses's rod, which, freely held
forth, will stir and play if any mine be under it.—*Sir Thomas Browne.*
Vulgar Errors.

RHETORICIAN (ret-or-ish/an) *an orator*   R26

RHOMB (rom) *a figure of four equal sides with unequal*   R27
       angles

> See how in warlike muster they appear,
> In rhombs and wedges, and half moons and wings.
>   —*Milton*   Paradise Regained. iii, 309.

RHOMBOID (rom/boid) *a figure like a rhomb but having*   R28
       only the opposite sides equal

The floor is covered with an oilcloth mosaic of jade and azure and cinnabar rhomboids.—*James Joyce.* Ulysses. (John Lane).

RIANT (ri/ant) *gay; laughing*   R29

In such cases the sublimity must be drawn from the other sources; with a strict caution however against anything light and riant.—*Burke.* On the Sublime and Beautiful. Pt. ii, s. 16.

RIO GRANDE (re/o gran/day)   R30

RISORGIMENTO (re-zor-ji-men/to)   R31

The Italian rising against Austrian domination which led to the unification of Italy in 1870.

ROAN (rone)   R32

A horse of a bay, sorrel or black colour, with grey or white spots thickly interspersed.

ROC (roc) *a fabulous bird mentioned in the story of*   R33
       Sinbad the Sailor

In ancient Indian mythology, the delicate white cirrus cloud drifting overhead was a fleeting swan; and so it was as well in the creed of the Scandinavian . . . The rushing vapour is the roc of the Arabian Nights, which broods over its great luminous egg, the sun, and which haunts the sparkling valley of diamonds.—*Baring-Gould.* Curious Myths of the Middle Ages.

ROCHET (roch/et) *a kind of surplice*   R34

Hail to thy returning festival, old Bishop Valentine! . . . or wert thou indeed a mortal prelate, with thy tippet and thy rochet, thy apron on, and decent lawn sleeves? Mysterious personage! like unto thee, assuredly, there is no other mitred father in the calendar.—*Charles Lamb.* Essays of Elia. " Valentine's Day."

RODOMONTADE (rod-o-mon-tarde/) *empty bluster;*   R35
  boasting

ROMFORD (rum/ford)   R36

ROMOLA (rom/o-la)   R37

ROSICRUCIAN (ro-zi-kroo/shun) *occult; mysterious*   R38
  From the name of a secret society founded in the 15th
century.

  Among other odd notions she professes the principles of Rosicrutius:
and believes the earth, air, and sea are inhabited by invisible beings, with
whom it is possible for the human species to entertain correspondence and
intimacy, on the easy condition of living chaste.—*Smollett*. Roderick
Random. Ch. 38.

ROTUNDA (ro-tun/da) *a building circular within and*   R39
    without

  Could tumult awaken the old dead, Burgundian Charles the Bold
might stir from under that Rotunda of his; never since he, raging, sank
in the ditches, and lost Life and Diamond, was such a noise heard here.—
Carlyle. The French Revolution. Pt. ii, Bk. ii, Ch. v.

ROULADE (roo-lard/) *a quick run of notes in music*   R40

ROULEAU (roo/low) *cylindrical packet of coins*   R41
   Exposed in glorious heaps the tempting bank,
   Guineas, half-guineas, all the shining train,
   The winner's pleasure, and the loser's pain:
   In bright confusion open rouleaus lie,
   They strike the soul, and glitter in the eye.
        —*Pope*. The Basset-Table.

ROUNDEL (round/l) (1) *a small disc;* (2) *a roundelay*   R42
  TITANIA: Come, now a roundel and a fairy song;
    Then, for the third part of a minute, hence;
    Some to kill cankers in the musk-rose buds;
    Some war with rere-mice for their leathern wings,
    To make my small elves coats; and some keep back
    The clamorous owl, that nightly hoots and wonders
    At our quaint spirits. Sing me now asleep;
     Then to your offices, and let me rest.
    —*Shakespeare*. A Midsummer-Night's Dream. ii, 2.

ROUNDELAY (roun/de-lay) *short song with refrain*   R43

Twice and thrice his roundelay,
Alone and warming his five wits,
The white owl in the belfrey sits.

—Tennyson.

ROUTINEER (rou-tee-neer/) *a person whose life is a*   R44
matter of routine

The difference between the shallowest routineer and the deepest thinker appears, to the latter, trifling; to the former, infinite.—*Bernard Shaw*. Man and Superman. " Maxims for Revolutionists." (Constable).

ROWTON (ro/ton)   R45

RUG-HEADED *with untidy, uncut hair*   R46

KING RICHARD: We must supplant those rough, rug-headed kerns,
Which live like venom, where no venom else,
But only they, hath privilege to live.
—Shakespeare. Richard II. ii, 1.

RUM BLOSSOM   R47

An eruption on the skin caused by heavy drinking.

RUTHVEN (riv/en or ruth/ven)   R48

RUY BLAS (roo/e blas)   R49

SABBATIC YEAR
SABLE
SABLE-VESTED
SACCHARINE
SACKBUT
SACRARIUM
SAFFRON
SAGA
SALOME
SALONIKA
SALTATION
SALT MARSH
SALUBRIOUS
SAMITE
SANCTIMONY
SANS SOUCI
SAPID
SAPIENT
SAPPHIRE
SAPPHIRINE
SARCENET
SATRAP
SATURNINE
SA'UDI ARABIA
SAUTÉ
SAVANNAH
SAVOIR FAIRE
SCÆVOLA
SCHERZO
SCIOLISM
SCION
SCONCE
SCOW
SCRANNEL

SCREE
SCRIPTORIUM
SCRYMGEOUR
SCUD
SEBACEOUS
SEMPITERNAL
SENNIGHT
SENTENTIOUS
SEPULCHRAL
SEQUACIOUS
SEQUELÆ
SEQUENTIAL
SERAI
SERBONIAN
SEVEN WONDERS OF
THE WORLD
SFORZANDO
SHAWM
SHEET ANCHOR
SHELDRAKE
SHIPWRIGHT
SHIRAZ
SILLABUB
SIMONY
SIMULACRUM
SOLECISM
SOMNIFEROUS
SOPHISM
SOPHISTRY
SOPORIFEROUS
SPAGYRIC
SPOLIATION
SQUIREEN
STANZA

STRAMINEOUS
STRATOPHOBIA
STRIDULOUS
STROPHE
STUPEFACIENT
STUPENT
SUBAUDITION
SUBLUNAR
SUBEQUAL
SUBORN
SUCCEDANEUM
SUMPTUARY
SUPERABLE
SUPEREMINENT
SUPERFICIES
SUPERNACULUM
SUPERNAL
SUPERVENIENT
SUPPURATE
SUPRALAPSARIAN
SURQUEDRY
SURTOUT
SWAG-BELLIED
SWIM
SWINK
SYBARITE
SYCOPHANT
SYLLOGISM
SYLPH
SYMBIOSIS
SYNDERESIS
SYNERGIC
SYRTIS
SYSTOLE

SABBATIC YEAR (sa-bat/ik yer)   S

A free year—usually one in seven—sometimes allowed by universities and similar institutions to their teachers to enable them to give their undivided attention, during this period, to authorship or research.

SABLE (sable) *a brown fur; in heraldry, the word denotes*   S2
the colour black

> By this the drooping daylight gan to fade,
> And yield his room to sad succeeding night,
> Who with her sable mantle gan to shade
> The face of earth, and ways of living wight.
>   —*Spenser.* The Faerie Queene.

The masses of furze and heath to the right and left were dark as ever; a mere half-moon was powerless to silver such sable features as theirs.— *Thomas Hardy.* The Return of the Native. Bk. ii (5). (Macmillan).

SABLE-VESTED   (1) *clothed in sables;* (2) *clothed*   S3
in black

> . . . with him Enthron'd
> Sat Sable-vested Night, eldest of things,
> The Consort of his Reign . . .
>   —*Milton.* Paradise Lost. ii, 962.

SACCHARINE (sak/a-rin) *sugary; sweet*   S4

This is an adjective, not to be confused with the small tablets now extensively and necessarily used as a substitute for sugar.

SACKBUT (sak/but) *a trumpet*   S5

SECOND MESSENGER: Good news, good news; the ladies have prevail'd,
The Volscians are dislodged, and Marcius gone:
A merrier day did never yet greet Rome,
No, not the expulsion of the Tarquins.

SICINIUS: Friend,
Art thou certain this is true? is it most certain?

SECOND MESSENGER: As certain as I know the sun is fire:
Where have you lurk'd, that you make doubt of it?
Ne'er through an arch so hurried the blown tide,

As the recomforted through the gates.
Why, hark you!
[*Trumpets; hautboys; drums beat; all
together*]
The trumpets, sackbuts, psalteries and
fifes,
Tabors and cymbals and the shouting
Romans,
Make the sun dance.
—*Shakespeare*. Coriolanus. v, 5.

SACRARIUM (sa-krar/i-um) *a sacred place*   S6

An antique Roman term—a place for keeping sacred things.
May be extended to cover those places which, by some peculiar
association have acquired, for individuals, a sacred or reverential
character.

SAFFRON (saf/ron) *a shade of orange*   S7

There let Hymen oft appear
With saffron robe and taper clear;
And pomp, and feast, and revelry,
With mask, and antique pageantry.
—*Milton*. L'Allegro. 125.

SAGA (sar/ga) *a heroic tale*   S8

It is difficult to decide whether the title " The Forsyte
Saga " is used derisively about rather unheroic people, or whether
the title was considered by the author to be a justifiable and
natural extension of the meaning of the term. Either construction
is possible. All human life and activity can be regarded and
treated as heroic; or it can be regarded and treated as comic.

SALOME (sal/o-mi)   S9

SALONIKA (sa-lo-ne/ka)   S10

SALTATION (sal-tay/shun) *act of leaping*   S11

The locusts being ordained for saltation, their hinder legs do far
exceed the others.—*Sir Thomas Browne*. Vulgar Errors.

SALT MARSH S12

The contraband is conveyed across the salt marsh under a narrow segment of moon to the inn standing lonely amid the few trees bordering the road, not far from the church tower, and the hamlet from where those mysterious dark figures had issued at eleven, singly, to the place that had been whispered to each in turn by the sallow clergyman.

SALUBRIOUS (sa-lu/bri-us) *healthy* S13

The word has a pleasanter connotation than *salutary*. It suggests superabundant health rather than the possession of curative properties. *Salubrious* is health with joy; *salutary* is health by discipline.

SAMITE (sam/ite) *a rich silk* S14

> With him went Hope in rancke, a handsome Mayd,
> Of chearefull looke and lovely to behold:
> In silken samite she was light arayd,
> And her fayre lockes were woven up in gold:
> She alway smyld, and in her hand did hold
> An holy-water-sprinckle, dipt in deowe,
> With which she sprinckled favours manifold
> On whom she list, and did great liking sheowe,
> Great liking unto many, but true love to feowe.
> —*Spenser*. The Faerie Queene. Bk. iii, xii.

SANCTIMONY (sank/ti-mo-ni) *hypocritical piety* S15

The derivative " sanctimonious " is more frequent.

IAGO: If sanctimony, and a frail vow between an errant barbarian and a supersubtle Venetian, be not too hard for my wit and all the tribe of hell, thou shalt enjoy her.
—*Shakespeare*. Othello. i, 3.

SANDEMANISM (san-de-may/ni-an) *a religious sect* S16 *founded by Robert Sandeman (1718-81)*

One of the hardest things to remember is that a man's merit in one sphere is no guarantee of his merit in another. Newton's mathematics don't prove his theology. Faraday was right about electricity, but not about Sandemanism.—*Aldous Huxley*. Point Counter Point. Ch. xxvi. (Chatto & Windus).

SANS SOUCI (sahn soos/ey) *free from care* S17

SAPID†   S18

Thus camels, to make the water sapid, do raise the mud with their feet.—*Sir Thomas Browne.* Vulgar Errors.

The Sevillians, and especially the women of Seville, possess a quality which, like the ancient Romans, the Spaniards call " salt," a sapid and antiseptic quality of bright intelligence which permeates all that they are and all that they do. They do nothing quite in the same way as other people, and are thus placed, perhaps a little consciously, apart from other people.—*Havelock Ellis.* The Soul of Spain. " Seville in Spring." (Constable).

SAPIENT (say/pi-ent) *wise*   S19

. . . where the Sapient King
Held dalliance with his faire *Egyptian* Spouse.
                              —*Milton.* Paradise Lost. ix, 442.

The fact is that . . . we sapient men have practically no human virtues at all.—*Aldous Huxley.* Those Barren Leaves. (Chatto & Windus).

Providence was teaching me yet once more that the unsapient life is a dreary and hopeless business, and that it is, for all practical purposes, the only life—lived everywhere by all but a negligibly few exceptions.—*Aldous Huxley.* Those Barren Leaves. (Chatto & Windus).

SAPPHIRE (saf/ire) *a profound blue*   S20

To-day I saw the dragon-fly
Come from the walls where he did lie.
An inner impulse rent the veil
Of his old husk: from head to tail
Came out clear plates of sapphire mail.
                              —*Tennyson.* The Two Voices.

SAPPHIRINE (saf-ire-ene/) *the colour of sapphire*   S21

She looked at the sky overhead, and saw that the sapphirine hue of the zenith in spring and early summer had been replaced by a metallic violet.—*Thomas Hardy.* The Return of the Native. Bk. iv, (5). (Macmillan).

SARCENET (sars/net) *a thin silk*   S22

QUEEN CAROLINE
She landed at Dover in the afternoon of June 5th [1820] wearing a puce-coloured sarcenet pelisse lined with ermine, and a white willow hat . . .—*Roger Fulford.* George the Fourth. Bk. iii (1). (Duckworth).

SATRAP (say/trap) *the ruler of a province*   S23

While the Roman emperor and the Persian monarch, at the distance of three thousand miles, defended their extreme limits against the barbarians of the Danube and of the Oxus, their intermediate frontier experienced the vicissitudes of a languid war and a precarious truce. Two of the eastern ministers of Constantius, the Praetorian praefect Musonian,. whose abilities were disgraced by the want of truth and integrity, and Cassian duke of Mesopotamia, a hardy and veteran soldier, opened a secret negotiation with the satrap Tamsapor.—*Edward Gibbon.* The Decline and Fall of the Roman Empire. Vol. ii, Ch. xix.

SATURNINE† S24

An environment which would have made a contented woman a poet,. a suffering woman a devotee, a pious woman a psalmist, even a giddy woman thoughtful, made a rebellious woman saturnine.—*Thomas Hardy.* The Return of the Native. Bk. i (7). (Macmillan).

SA'UDI ARABIA (sord/i ar-ay/bia) S25

SAUTÉ (so/tay) *lightly fried* S26

SAVANNAH (sa-van/a) *treeless plain* S27

> To all swift things for swiftness did I sue;
> Clung to the whistling mane of every wind.
> But whether they swept, smoothly fleet,
> The long savannahs of the blue:
> Or whether, thunder-driven,
> They clanged his chariot 'thwart a heaven,
> Flashy with flying lightnings round the spurn o' their feet:
> Fear wist not to evade as Love wist to pursue.
> —*Francis Thompson.* The Hound of Heaven.

SAVOIR FAIRE (sav/wahr fare) *the faculty of doing the right thing at once; tact, address* S28

SCÆVOLA (sev/o-la) S29

SCHERZO (skert/so) *playfully; a light, playful movement in a musical work* S30

SCIOLISM† S31

As to Poe's management of his metres one cannot do better than quote Mr. Saintsbury's criticism again—the same indefinite but intensely poetic effect is produced still more obviously by Poe's management of his metres. Every one who is acquainted with his critical work knows the care (a care that brought on him the ridicule of sciolists and poetasters) which he bestowed on metrical subjects.—*Andrew Lang.* The Poems of Edgar Allan Poe. Preface. xx. (Kegan Paul).

SCION†   S32

> POLIXENES: Sweet maid, we marry
> A gentle scion to the wildest stock;
> And make conceive a bark of baser kind
> By bud of nobler race.
> —*Shakespeare*. The Winter's Tale. iv, 3.

SCONCE (skons) (1) *a hanging candlestick;* (2) *a bulwark;*   S33
(3) *fort;* (4) *headpiece;* (5) *skull;* (6) *piece of ice-floe;*
(7) *a fire;* (8) *a lantern.*

SCOW (skow) *a flat-bottomed boat*   S34

SCRANNEL (skran/l) *slight; slender*   S35

> Blind mouthes! that scarce themselves know how to hold
> A Sheep-hook, or have learn'd ought els the least
> That to the faithfull Herdmans art belongs!
> What recks it them? What need they? They are sped;
> And when they list, their lean and flashy songs
> Grate on their scrannel Pipes of wretched straw,
> The hungry Sheep look up, and are not fed,
> But swoln with wind, and the rank mist they draw,
> Rot inwardly, and foul contagion spread:
> Besides what the grim Woolf with privy paw
> Daily devours apace, and nothing sed,
> But that two-handled engine at the door,
> Stands ready to smite once, and smite no more.
> —*Milton*. Lycidas.

SCREE (skre) *débris of rocks*   S36
See DETRITUS in D.U.W.(A).

SCRIPTORIUM (skrip-tor/i-um) *writing-room*   S37

SCRYMEGEOUR (skrim/jer)   S38

SCUD (skud) *to move swiftly*   S39
The wind was high; the vast white clouds scudded over the blue
heaven; the leaves yet green, and tender branches snapped like glass, were
whirled in eddies from the trees; the grassy sward undulated like the ocean
with a thousand tints and shadows.—*Disraeli*. Coningsby. Bk. iv, Ch. xvi.

SEBACEOUS (se-bay/shus) *fat*   S40

SEMPITERNAL (sem-pi-ter/nal) *everlasting*   S41

. . . the footbridge over the Ancre by Aveluy, where a sad guard of trees dripping with the dankness of autumn had nothing to say but sempiternal syllables, of which we had our own interpretation.—*Edmund Blunden*. Undertones of War. Ch. xi.

SENNIGHT (sen/ite) *week*   S42

ROSALIND: Time trots hard with a young maid between the contract of her marriage and the day it is solemnized: if the interim be but a sennight, time's pace is so hard that it seems the length of seven year.
—*Shakespeare*. As You Like It. iii, 2.

SENTENTIOUS (sen-ten/shus) *terse; brief*   S43

DUKE: . . . he is very swift and sententious.
Shakespeare. As You Like It. v, 4.

SEPULCHRAL (se-pul/kral) *deep; hollow*   S44

Mine eye hath found that sad sepulchral rock,
That was the casket of Heaven's richest store.
—*Milton*. Odes. " The Passion." 43.

SEQUACIOUS (se-kway/shus) (1) *following;* (2) *logical;*   S45
(3) *servile*

Orpheus could lead the savage race,
And trees uprooted left their place,
Sequacious of the lyre;
But bright Cecilia raised the wonder higher:
When to her organ vocal breath was given,
An angel heard, and straight appear'd,
Mistaking earth for heaven.
—*Dryden*. Song for St. Cecilia's day.

" Poor Henry, I cannot understand why he is attempting this Parliamentary career. Even if North-West Middlesex elects him some years hence, which, I may add, is extremely improbable, what good will it do him? He will be merely a sequacious back-bencher."—*Compton Mackenzie*. The Darkening Green.

SEQUELÆ (se-kwee/lee) *results; consequences*   S46

Benham was the son of a schoolmaster. His father was assistant first at Cheltenham, and subsequently at Minchinghampton, and then he became head and later on sole proprietor of Martindale House, a high-class preparatory school at Seagate. He was extremely successful for some years, as success goes in the scholastic profession, and then disaster overtook him in the shape of a divorce. His wife, William Porphyry's mother, made the acquaintance of a rich young man named Nolan, who was recuperating at Seagate from the sequelæ of snake-bite, malaria, and a gun accident in Brazil. She ran away with him, and she was divorced.—*H. G. Wells*. The Research Magnificent. Ch. i. (Collins).

SEQUENTIAL (se-kwen/shal) *succeeding; consecutive*   S47

Three things only have been discovered of that which concerns the inner consciousness since before written history began. Three things only in twelve thousand written or sculptured years, and in the dumb, dim time before then. Three ideas the Cavemen primeval wrested from the unknown, the night which is round us still in daylight—the existence of the soul, immortality, the deity. These things found, prayer followed as a sequential result.—*Richard Jefferies.* The Story of My Heart. Ch. iii.

SERAI (ser-i) *a caravanserai*   S48

My boat on shore, my galley on the sea;
Oh, more than cities and serais to me.
Byron. The Bride of Abydos.

SERBONIAN (ser-bo/ni-an) *inescapable; fatally obstructive*   S49

SEVEN WONDERS OF THE WORLD   S50

The Pyramids.
The Hanging Gardens of Babylon.
The Temple of Diana at Ephesus.
The Tomb of Mausolus of Caria.
The Colossus of Rhodes
The Statue of Zeus by Phedias.
The Pharos of Alexandria.

SFORZANDO (sfort-zan/do) *suddenly; emphatically*   S51

" I am so glad to make your acquaintance, Mr. Meldrum," said Lady Rendle. " I have heard so much of you from my boy. One likes to meet someone who takes an interest in one's belongings, doesn't one?"

Philip, painfully unravelling this sentence, suddenly caught his hostess' eye, and realised that an answer was expected of him. " Yes," he said *sforzando.* "Oh yes! One does."—*Ian Hay.* A Knight on Wheels. Ch. xix (ii). (Hodder & Stoughton).

SHAWM (shawm) *the forerunner of the oboe*   S52

As when a mighty people rejoice
With shawms, and with cymbals, and harps of gold,
And the tumult of their acclaim is roll'd
Thro' the open gates of the city afar,
To the shepherd who watcheth the evening star.
—*Tennyson.* The Dying Swan.

221

SHEET ANCHOR *a large anchor* S53

"Up to the present you don't know what life is. You've got no
Sheet-Anchor . . ." (All Benedicts, when roused to argument, made great
play with this over-apt simile). "After you leave here in the evenings,
what do you do? You fly round on that bloody great bus of yours from
pub to pub, or else you take some little tart to a dance-hall. Where does
it lead you to? Nowhere."

As this point Mr. Billiter was heard to suggest the Lock Hospital as
a probable alternative destination.—*Hugh McGraw.* Rude Society. iv, (2).
(Heinemann).

SHELDRAKE (shel/drake) *a wild duck* S54

Compare MANDRAKE.

Teals, sheldrakes, and peckled fowls, that come hither in winter out
of Scandia, Muscovy, &c.—*Burton.* Anatomy of Melancholy.

SHIPWRIGHT† S55

MARCELLUS: Good now, sit down, and tell me, he that knows,
Why this same strict and most observant watch
So nightly toils the subject of the land,
And why such daily cast of brazen cannon,
And foreign mart for implements of war;
Why such impress of shipwrights, whose sore task
Does not divide the Sunday from the week;
What might be toward, that this sweaty haste
Doth make the night joint-labourer with the day:
Who is't that can inform me?
    —*Shakespeare.* Hamlet. i, 1.

SHIRAZ (shi-raz/) S56

SILLABUB† S57

CORRECTION: "Sillabub" is not a bowl, but a drink,
usually of milk beaten up with sugar.

SIMONY (si/mon-i) *the crime of buying or selling* S58
ecclesiastical preferment

KATHLEEN: So may he rest; his faults lie gently on him!
Yet thus far, Griffith, give me leave to speak him,
And yet with charity. He was a man
Of an unbounded stomach, ever ranking
Himself with princes; one that by suggestion
Tied all the kingdom: simony was fair-play
His own opinion was his law: i' the presence
He would say untruths, and be ever double
Both in his words and meaning: he was never,

But where he meant to ruin, pitiful:
His promises were, as he then was, mighty;
But his performance, as he is now, nothing:
Of his own body he was ill, and gave
The clergy ill example.
                    —*Shakespeare.* Henry VIII. iv, ii.

SIMULACRUM†   S59

. . . when we wander today through the streets of Segovia we feel
ourselves back in a Romanesque city. It is still full of parish churches,
not one of them said to be later than the thirteenth century, and the slow
shrinkage of the population, compensated by no such modern industrial
expansion as we find in Granada and Toledo—for the presence of a
barracks and some associated military avocations alone seem to give
Segovia any simulacrum of life—has left nearly all these churches more
or less untouched, some still in use, some locked up and abandoned, one
or two used as museums or for other secular purposes, and a considerable
number in a more or less advanced state of ruin and decay.—*Havelock
Ellis.* The Soul of Spain. " Segovia." (Constable).

Is it not strange to reflect, that hardly an evening passes in London
or Paris, but one of those cottages is painted for the better amusement of
the fair and idle, and shaded with pasteboard pines by the scene-shifter;
and that good and kind people, poetically minded, delight themselves in
imagining the happy life led by peasants who dwell by Alpine fountains,
and kneel to crosses upon peaks of rock? that nightly we lay down our
gold, to fashion forth simulacra of peasants, in gay ribands to the picturesque crosses; and all the while the veritable peasants are kneeling, song-
lessly, to veritable crosses, in another temper than the kind and fair
audiences deem of, and assuredly with another kind of answer than is got
out of the opera catastrophe; an answer having reference, it may be, in
dim futurity, to those very audiences themselves? If all the gold that has
gone to paint the simulacra of the cottages, and to put new songs in the
mouths of the simulacra of the peasants, had gone to brighten the existent
cottages, it might in the end, perhaps, have turned out better so, not only
for the peasant, but for even the audience.—*John Ruskin.* Modern
Painters. " The Mountain Gloom." Vol. iv (50).

SOLECISM (sol/e-sizm) *impropriety in language*   S60

This confusion of tenses, this grand solecism of *two presents,* is in a
degree common to all postage.—*Charles Lamb.* Essays of Elia. " Distant
Correspondents."

SOMNIFEROUS (som-nif/er-us) *inducing sleep; narcotic*   S61

They ascribe all this redundant melancholy to somniferous potions.—
Burton. Anatomy of Melancholy.

I wish for some somniferous potion that might force me to sleep
away the intermediate time, as it does with men in sorrow.—*Izaac Walton.*
The Compleat Angler.

SOPHISM (sof/izm) *a fallacious argument* S62

The ambiguity of the word "infinite" is the real fallacy in the amusing logical puzzle of Achilles and the Tortoise, a puzzle which has been too hard for the ingenuity or patience of many philosophers, and among others of Dr. Thomas Brown, who considered the sophism as insoluble; as a sound argument, though leading to palpable falsehood; not seeing that such an admission would be a reductio ad absurdum of the reasoning faculty itself. The fallacy, as Hobbes hinted, lies in the tacit assumption that whatever is infinitely divisible is infinite.—*J. S. Mill.* System of Logic. Pt. v, Ch. vii.

SOPHISTRY† S63

What probability was there that any sheriff would pack a jury, that any barrister would employ all the arts of sophistry and rhetoric . . . in order to convict an innocent person of burglary or sheepstealing? But on a trial for high treason a verdict of acquittal must always be considered as a defeat of the government; and there was but too much reason to fear that many sheriffs, barristers, and judges might be impelled . . . to do anything which might save the government from the inconvenience and shame of a defeat.—*Macaulay.* History of England. Ch. xviii.

After we came out of the Church we stood talking for some time together of Bishop Berkeley's ingenious sophistry to prove the non-existence of matter, and that every thing in the universe is merely ideal. I observed, that though we are satisfied his doctrine is not true, it is impossible to refute it. I never shall forget the alacrity with which Johnson answered, striking his foot with mighty force against a large stone, till he rebounded from it,—"I refute it *thus."*—*James Boswell.* Life of Johnson. A.D. 1763. Ætat. 54.

SOPORIFEROUS (sop-or-if/er-us) *causing sleep* S64

Erdaviraph, a young but holy prelate, received from the hands of his brethren three cups of soporiferous wine. He drank them off and instantly fell into a long and profound sleep. As soon as he waked, he related to the king and to the believing multitude his journey to Heaven, and his intimate conferences with the Deity.—*Edward Gibbon.* The Decline and Fall of the Roman Empire. Ch. viii.

SPAGYRIC (spa-jir/ik) *an alchemist; relating to alchemy* S65

It was a huge diligence and care of the divine mercy that discovered to man the secrets of spagyric medicines . . . and the strange effects of accidental mixtures.—*Jeremy Taylor.* Miracles of Divine Mercy.

SPOLIATION (spo-li-ay/shun) *act of plundering* S66

Of all the agents of the foreign government he [Sunderland] was, with the single exception of Jeffreys, the most odious to the nation. Few knew that Sunderland's voice had in secret been given against the spoliation of Magdalene College and the prosecution of the bishops; but all knew . . . he had turned or pretended to turn Papist, that he had, a few days after his apostasy, appeared in Westminster Hall as a witness against the oppressed fathers of the church.—*Macaulay.* History of England. Ch. xx.

SQUIREEN (skwi-reen/) *a country gentleman (a squire) of*   S67
    lesser importance

Not every man was welcomed into the Association. G. J. Harney, a young man who dreamed of pikes and saw himself as the English Marat, was compelled to resign, consoling himself with forming a rival " Democratic Association," and the bar was also up against Feargus O'Conner, a powerful Irish orator and squireen, one-time Irish M.P. and follower of O'Connell, who went North and induced some supporters to help him to start a new paper called *The Northern Star.—Cole & Postgate.* The Common People 1746-1946. Ch. xxiii. (Methuen).

STANZA (stan/za) *a division of verse in accordance*   S68
    with a metrical scheme

    Before his sacred name flies every fault,
And each exalted stanza teems with thought.
               —*Pope.* Essay on Criticism. ii, 422.

STRAMINEOUS (stra-min/i-us) (1) *straw-coloured;*   S69
    (2) *worthless*

Other discourse, dry, barren, stramineous, dull and heavy.—*Burton.* Anatomy of Melancholy.

STRATOPHOBIA (strat-o-fo/bi-a) *hatred of militarism*   S70

He had apologised for his attack on the soldiers by an ingenious fiction. In his youth, he said, he had had an unfortunate experience with some military men, and ever since then he had been liable to sudden and uncontrollable fits of violent stratophobia.—*Eric Linklater.* Juan in China. (Jonathan Cape).

STRIDULOUS (strid/u-lus) *strident; harsh; shrill*   S71

Spaniards, I may remark, are peculiarly fascinated by sound, especially by the loud, stridulous, rhythmic classes of sound which may be said to come midway between mere noise and music. It is an intoxicant which they indulge in more intemperately than they do in wine.—*Havelock Ellis.* The Soul of Spain. " Spanish Dancing." (Constable).

STROPHE (strow/fi)   S72

    Originally, a part of the verse sung by a Greek chorus, which was answered by the antistrophe, and closed with the epode. It may be used nowadays to mean any sound which calls forth or is answered by a corresponding sound. Thus, H. G. Wells speaks of the strophe and antistrophe of frogs.

The measure of verse used in the chorus is of all sorts . . . without regard had to strophe, antistrophe, or epode, which were a kind of stanzas framed only for the musick.—*Milton.* Samson Agonistes. (Preface).

STUPEFACIENT (stu-pe-fay/shent) *making stupid or*   S73
     senseless

For him, there were two great and criminal distractions. First, work, which he regarded as a mere stupefacient, like opium. (Don't exhaust yourself too much; he writes to an industrious friend; it is immoral!) Immoral, because, among other reasons it is too easy, a shirking of man's first duty, which is to live.—*Aldous Huxley.* D. H. Lawrence. (Chatto & Windus).

STUPENT (stu/pent) *amazed*   S74

The klaxon sounds stridently. The colonel draws his revolver and makes a dash for the top of the sandhill, but is outraced by Meek, who gets there first and takes the word of command with irresistible authority, leaving him stupent.—*G. B. Shaw.* Too True to be Good. Act ii. (Constable).

SUBAUDITION (sub-aw-dish/un) *something implied*   S75

" Subaudition " is also a term of grammar, indicating a meaning which is implied although not expressed. Thus, in: " She gave a little laugh," *little* means " short; not loud." This is a subaudition. *Gave* means " uttered." This also is a subaudition.

All authors can do, is to depict men *out* of their business—in their passions, loves, laughters, amusements, hatreds, and what not—and describe these as well as they can, taking the business-part for granted and leaving it as it were for subaudition.—*W. M. Thackeray.* The Virginians. Ch. lix.

SUBLUNAR (sub-lu/ner) *terrestrial; of this world*   S76

Nor, truely, can I peremptorily deny that the Soul, in this her sublunary estate, is wholly and in all acceptions inorganical; but that for the performance of her ordinary actions there is required not only a symmetry and proper disposition of Organs, but a Crasis and temper correspondent to its operations.—*Sir Thomas Browne.* Religio Medici. First Part.

     Night measured, with her shadowy cone,
  Half way up hill this vast sublunar vault.
          —*Milton.* Paradise Lost. iv, 776.

     The moon was hanging low
Over the Asian mountains, and outspread
The plain, the city, and the camp below,
Skirted the midnight ocean's glimmering flow;
The city's moon-lit spires and myriad lamps,
Like stars in a sublunar sky did glow,
Like springs of flame, which burst where'er swift
Earthquake stamps.
          —*Shelley.* The Revolt of Islam. v, i.

There is no doubt that the poorer classes in our country are much more charitably disposed than their superiors in wealth. And I fancy it must arise a great deal from the comparative indistinction of the easy and the not so easy in these ranks. A workman or a pedlar cannot shutter himself off from his less fortunate neighbours. If he treats himself to a luxury, he must do it in the face of a dozen who cannot. And what should more directly lead to charitable thoughts? . . . Thus the poor man, camping out in life, sees it as it is, and knows that every mouthful he puts in his belly has been wrenched out of the fingers of the hungry.

But at a certain stage of prosperity, as in a balloon ascent, the fortunate person passes through a zone of clouds, and sublunary matters are thenceforward hidden from his view. He sees nothing but the heavenly bodies, all in admirable order and positively as good as new. He finds himself surrounded in the most touching manner by the attentions of *Providence*, and compares himself involuntarily with the lilies and the sky-larks. He does not precisely sing, of course; but then he looks so unassuming in his open *Landau!* If all the world dined at one table, this philosophy would meet with some rude knocks.—*R. L. Stevenson.* An Inland Voyage. " Pont-sur-Sambre." (Chatto & Windus).

SUBEQUAL (sub-e/kwal) *nearly equal*   S77
Compare SUBTRIANGULAR.

SUBORN (su-born/) *to bribe a person to commit a crime*   S78

Firm we subsist, yet possible to swerve,
Since Reason not impossibly may meet
Some specious object by the Foe subornd,
And fall into deception unaware,
Not keeping strictest watch, as she was warnd.
Seek not temptation then, which to avoide
Were better, and most likelie if from mee
Thou sever not: Trial will come unsought.
Wouldst thou approve thy constancie, approve
First thy obedience; th' other who can know,
Not seeing thee attempted, who attest?
—*Milton.* Paradise Lost. ix.

SUCCEDANEUM (suk-se-day/ne-um) *substitute*   S79

. . . the jolly and fox-hunting succedaneum of beer.—*Leigh Hunt.* Essays—" Coffee Houses and Smoking."

To all quacks . . . the effect of mystery is well known: here and there some Cagliostro, even in latter days, turns it to notable account: the blockhead also, who is ambitious, and has no talent, finds sometimes in " the talent of silence," a kind of succedaneum.—*Carlyle.* Critical and Miscellaneous Essays. " Characteristics."

SUMPTUARY†   S80

Whether allowable to ruin oneself? The political economist replies that it is! . . . Political economists therefore tell us, that any regulations would be ridiculous which, as Lord Bacon expresses it, should serve for " the repressing of waste and excess by sumptuary laws." Adam Smith is not only indignant at " sumptuary laws," but asserts . . . that " it is the highest impertinence and presumption in kings and ministers to pretend to watch over the economy of private people, and to restrain their expense by sumptuary laws . . . Sumptuary laws, so often enacted, and so often repealed, and always eluded, were the perpetual, but ineffectual attempts of all governments, to restrain what, perhaps, cannot be restrained— criminal folly! And to punish a man for having ruined himself would usually be to punish a most contrite penitent! It is not surprising that before " private vices " were considered as " public benefits," the governors of nations instituted sumptuary laws—for the passion for pageantry, and an incredible prodigality in dress were continually impoverishing great families.—*D'Israeli.* Curiosities of Literature. " Whether allowable to Ruin Oneself?"

To those persons who have seen it, the interior of this church will have given an impression such as is to be had from few other places in Europe, or indeed, in any other land where the art of the baroque age is made credible in its sumptuary magnificence. The gilded ceiling of Santa Clara and its high altar could only be described as a glittering cavern, but seeped and penetrated in its own refulgence.—*Sacheverell Sitwell.* Sacred & Profane Love. Bk. v, Pt. v. (Faber & Faber).

[Here possibly used to mean *sumptuous*]

SUPERABLE (su/per-a-bl) *that which may be overcome*   S81

Antipathies are generally superable by a single effort.—*Dr. Johnson.* Rambler. No. 126.

SUPEREMINENT (su-per-em/i-nent) *eminent in a*   S82
high degree

As humility is in suitors a decent virtue, so the testification thereof by such effectual acknowledgements not only argueth a sound apprehension of his supereminent glory and majesty before whom we stand, but putteth also into his hands a kind of pledge or bond for security against our unthankfulness.—*Hooker.* Ecclesiastical Polity.

SUPERFICIES (su-per-fish/eze) *surface; external part;*   S83
superficial matters

Much of history is necessarily of little value,—the superficies of cir- cumstance, the scum of events.—*Walter Bagehot.* " Lord Macaulay."

SUPERNACULUM (su-per-nak/u-lum) *liquor*   S84

The origin of the word is shown in the first extract.

Drinking super nagulum, a devise of drinking new come out of Fraunce; which is, after a man hath turned up the bottom of the cup, to drop it on his naile, and make a pearl with that that is left; which if it slide, and he cannot make it stand on, by reason there's too much, he must drinke again for his penance.—*Nash.* Piers Pennilesse.

Bacchus, the god of brewed wine and sugar, grand patron of rob-pots, upsy-freesy tipplers, and supernaculum takers . . . headwarden of Vintner's

Hall, ale-conner . . . This boon Bacchanalian skinker did I make legs to.
—*Massinger*. Virgin Martyr. ii, 1.

> But here approaches
> Our sage intendant, with the wine: however,
> For the cup's sake I'll bear the cupbearer.—
> 'Tis here! the supernaculum! twenty years
> Of age, if 'tis a day.—Which epoch makes
> Young women and old wine.
> > —*Byron*. Werner. i, 1.

SUPERNAL (su-per/nal) *celestial*   S85

> That supernal Judge that stirs good thoughts
> In any breast of strong authority,
> To look into the blots and stains of right.
> > —*Shakespeare*. King John. ii, 1.

> He with frequent intercourse
> Thither will send his winged messengers,
> On errands of supernal grace.
> > —*Milton*. Paradise Lost. vii, 571.

. . . we are compelled to serve now under only one economic flag.
We do not know who designed it and ran it up, but there it is, and the
more often we try to desert from it the more brutally we shall be starved
into submission. It is as if a supernal being were determined to make this
planet one whole or depopulate it.—*J. B. Priestley*. English Journey.
Ch. viii (4). (Heinemann & Gollancz).

The best talker who ever lived. He brings a supernal air into life.—
Frank Harris. " Oscar Wilde."

SUPERVENIENT (su-per-ven/i-ent) *supervening*   S86

" I who have no sisters nor brothers, look with some degree of
innocent envy on those who may be said to be born to friends; and cannot
see, without wonder, how rarely that native union is afterwards regarded.
It sometimes, indeed, happens, that some supervenient cause of discord
may overpower the original amity, but it seems to me more frequently
thrown away with levity, or lost by negligence, than destroyed by injury
or violence."—from a letter by Dr. Johnson addressed to Bennet Langton,
Esq., and dated 9th Jan. 1758.—*James Boswell*. Life of Johnson. A.D. 1758.
Ætat. 49.

SUPPURATE (sup/u-rate) *to generate pus; fester*   S87

. . . William, Duke of Cumberland, more familiarly known as " Billy
the Butcher." He weighed nearly twenty stone, was blind in one eye, and
suffered from a suppurating wound in the leg. Although he was in fact a
man of some æsthetic appreciation, as was evidenced by his development
of Windsor Park and his encouragement of the manufacture of Chelsea
china, he was regarded by the public as a monster of brutality.—*Roger
Fulford*. George the Fourth. Bk. i. (Duckworth).

SUPRALAPSARIAN (su-pra-lap-sar/i-an)   S88

. . . strictly interrogated by a synod of lowering Supralapsarians.—
Macaulay.

The supralapsarians think that God does only consider his own glory
in all that he does; and that whatever is done, arises, as from its first
cause, from the decree of God; that, in this decree, God, considering only
the manifestation of his own glory, intended to make the world, to put a
race of men in it, to constitute them under Adam as their fountain and
head; that he decreed Adam's sin, the lapse of his posterity, and Christ's
death, together with the salvation or damnation of such as should be most
for his glory; that to those who were to be saved, he decreed to give such
efficacious assistances, as should certainly put them in the way of salvation;
and to those he rejected, he decreed to give such assistances and means
only, as should render them inexcusable; that all men do continue in a
state of grace or sin, and shall be saved or damned according to that first
decree.—*Burnet.* On the Thirty-nine Articles. Art. xvii.

SURQUEDRY (sur/kwi-dri) *pride; insolence*   S89

Five years later Maximian puffed up with pride and surquedry by
reason of the passing great store of gold and silver that did daily flow in
upon him, fitted out an exceedingly mighty fleet and assembled every
single armed warrior in Britain.—*Geoffrey of Monmouth.* Histories of
the Kings of Britain. Bk. v, Ch. xii.

SURTOUT (sur-too/) *a close-fitting men's overcoat*   S90

There are the office lads in their first surtouts, who feel a befitting
contempt for boys at day-schools: club as they go home at night, for
saveloys and porter: and think there's nothing like "life."—*Dickens.* The
Pickwick Papers. Ch. xxxi.

SWAG-BELLIED†   S91

Your Dane, your German, and your swag-bellied
Hollander are nothing to your English.

                               —*Shakespeare.* Othello. ii, 3.

SWIM* *an abundance*   S92

In the evening, when the milking was finished, and all the things fed,
then we went out to look at the snares. We wandered on across the
stream and up the wild hillside. Our feet rattled through black patches
of devil's-bit scabius; we skirted a swim of thistle-down, which glistened
when the moon touched it.—*D. H. Lawrence.* The White Peacock. Ch. vi.

    [Here, presumably, the word indicates a large patch of
thistle-down.]

SWINK†   S93

> Two such I saw, what time the labour'd ox
> From the loose traces of the furrow came,
> And the swink'd hedger at his supper sate.
>
> —*Milton.* Comus.

SYBARITE†   S94

Then there is Helvetius, the well-fed Farmer-General, enlivening his sybaritic life with metaphysic paradoxes.—*Carlyle.* Critical and Miscellaneous Essays. " Diderot."

SYCOPHANT (sik/o-fant) *an obsequious flatterer, a*   S95
parasite

The multitude was unable to conceive that a man who, even when sober, was more furious and boastful than others when they were drunk, and who seemed utterly incapable of disguising any emotion or keeping any secret, could really be a coldhearted, farsighted scheming sycophant. Yet such a man was Talbot.—*Macaulay.* History of England.

SYLLOGISM (sil/o-jizm)   S96
See Whately's definition *infra.*

Every conclusion is deduced in reality, from two other propositions (thence called premises): for though one of these may be, and commonly is suppressed, it must nevertheless be understood as admitted; as may easily be made evident by supposing the denial of the suppressed premiss, which will at once invalidate the argument; e.g., if any one from perceiving that " the world exhibits marks of design," infers that " it must have had an intelligent author," though he may not be aware in his own mind of the existence of any other premiss, he will readily understand, if it be denied, that " whatever exhibits marks of design must have had an intelligent author "; that the affirmative of that proposition is necessary to the validity of the argument: or, again, if anyone on meeting with " an animal which has horns on the head " infers that " it is a ruminant," he will easily perceive that this would be no argument to anyone who should not be aware of the general fact that " all horned animals ruminate." An argument thus stated regularly, and at full length, is called a syllogism, which therefore is evidently not a peculiar kind of argument, but only a peculiar form of expression, in which every argument may be stated. When one of the premises is suppressed, which for brevity's sake it usually is, the argument is called an enthymeme.—*Whately.* Elements of Logic.

In practical matters, for example, has it not become almost proverbial that the man of logic cannot prosper? . . .Nay, in mere speculation itself, the most ineffectual of all characters, generally speaking, is your dialectic man-at-arms; were he armed cap-à-pie in syllogistic mail of proof, and perfect master of logic-fence, how little does it avail him?—*Carlyle.* Critical and Miscellaneous Essays. " Characteristics."

SYLPH (silf) *an angelic fairy; a graceful woman*   S97

" Ah!" cried Mr. Pecksniff, whose eyes had in the meantime wandered
to the pupil; "certainly. And how do you do my very interesting child?"
—"Quite well, I thank you, sir," replied that frosty innocent. "A sweet
face this, my dears," said Mr. Pecksniff, turning to his daughters. "A
charming manner!"—Both young ladies had been in ecstasies with the
scion of a wealthy house (through whom the nearest road and shortest cut
to her parents might be supposed to lie) from the first. Mrs. Todgers
vowed that anything one quarter so angelic she had never seen. "She
wanted but a pair of wings, a dear," said that good woman, " to be a young
syrup": meaning, possibly, young sylph, or seraph.—*Dickens*. Martin
Chuzzlewit. Ch. ix.

SYMBIOSIS (sim-bi-o/sis) *partnership; union*   S98

In the presence of Johnson, Boswell undoubtedly displayed what was
best, or at any rate what was least undignified, in his nature. It was a
case of moral symbiosis: Johnson received the benefit of Boswell's cheer-
fulness, while Boswell received the greater benefit of Johnson's wisdom
and learning. That is why Boswell tried so frequently to recover his
earlier veneration for Johnson when he felt that it was declining; for he
felt, at the same time, that he was in danger of losing the full value of this
beneficient reciprocity.—*C. E. Vulliamy*. Ursa Major. Ch. xiii. (Michael
Joseph).

SYNDERESIS (sin-de-ree/sis) *logic*   S99

Dinner was served in the Saloon of the Ancestors. In Mrs. Aldwinkle's
enthusiastic imagination what marvellous symposia had been held within
those walls—centuries even before they were built—what intellectual
feasts! Aquinas, here, had confided to an early Malaspina his secret
doubt on the predictability of rollations, had twitted the robber marquess,
over a goblet of wine, with the feebleness of his synderesis.—*Aldous
Huxley*. Those Barren Leaves. (Chatto & Windus).

SYNERGIC (sin-er/gik) *co-operation of human and*   S100
divine energy

This, I think, is what constitutes the real singularity of Boswell: the
union of great abilities with a degree of silliness which is equally rare.
It seems to me that Macaulay was perfectly right in attributing the peculiar
merit of Boswell's performance to the combined operation of these
apparently incompatible ingredients; an odd, though perhaps not excep-
tional, synergic phenomenon. Look at the matter more closely and you
will see Boswell and his book moving slowly towards mutual assimilation
or a common focus.—*C. E. Vulliamy*. Ursa Major. Ch. xiii. (Michael
Joseph).

SYRTIS (ser/tis) *a quicksand*   S101

A boggy syrtis—neither sea
Nor good dry land.
                    —*Milton*. Paradise Lost. ii, 939.

SYSTOLE (sis/to-le) *a beat; an alternate movement*   S102

For three hundred years and more the long, steadily accelerated diastole of Europeanised civilization had been in progress: towns had been multiplying, populations increasing, values rising, new countries developing: thought, literature, knowledge unfolding and spreading . . .

Three hundred years of diastole, and then came the swift and unexpected systole . . .—*H. G. Wells.* The War in the Air. Ch. x (iii). (Collins).

TABID

TABINET

TAFFETA

TAHITI

TALUS

TANG

TANGANYIKA

TAPIS

TAP-ROOM

TAXIMETER

TE DEUM

TEGUMENT

TELEOLOGY

TENEBRIFIC

TERESA

TERMINOLOGY

TERRENE

TER-SANCTUS

TETRALOGY

THEO-

THESMOTHETE

THESPIAN

THRASONICAL

THREE PER CENTS

THUCYDIDES

THULE

TIARA

TICHBORNE

TILBURY

TORCH SINGER

TRADUCTION

TRANSLUCENT

TRANSMOGRIFY

TRANSPONTINE

TRAUMA

TRAVAIL

TRIBRACH

TRINAL

TRITURATE

TUMID

TABID (tab/id) *wasted by disease; consumptive*   **T**

Leprosy awakes not sometimes before Forty, the Gout and Stone often later; but consumptive and tabid Roots sprout more early, and at the fairest make seventeen Years of our Life doubtful before that Age.— *Sir Thomas Browne*. Letter to a Friend.

He that is tabidly inclined, were unwise to pass his days in Portugal.— *Ibid.*

> . . . in the dungeon of a sick room drained
> By some tabescent horror . . .
> > —*John Davidson.* "Testament of John Davidson."

TABINET (tab/i-net) *waved or watered silk, etc.*   **T2**

That is the widow; that stout woman in . . . crimson tabinet.— *Thackeray*. Book of Snobs. Ch. xliii.

TAFFETA (taf/e-ta) *glossy silk material*   **T3**

> BIRON: Taffeta phrases, silken terms precise,
> Three-piled hyperboles, spruce affectation,
> Figures pedantical; these summer-flies
> Have blown me full of maggot ostentation:
> I do forswear them.
> > —*Shakespeare*. Love's Labour Lost. v, ii.

TAHITI (ta/he-ti)   **T4**

TALUS (tay/lus) (1) *a slope;* (2) *detritus*   **T5**

At the foot of the track which ascended the talus of the mountain to his door, the doctor overtook me at a trot.—*R. L. Stevenson*. The Dynamiter. "Story of the Destroying Angel." (Heinemann).

TANG (tang) *the extrusion of a knife-blade, etc.,*   **T6**
connecting the blade with the handle

TANGANYIKA (tan-jan-e/ka)   **T7**

Former German colony on the East coast of Africa taken over by Great Britain as a mandated territory after the war of 1914-1918. The island of Zanzibar lies off its coast. Its port and principal town is Dar es Salaam (dar-ess-se-larm/) pronounced rapidly as one word.

TAPIS (ta-pee/) T8

  Literally, tapestry, which was formerly used as a table-covering. Hence the meaning—"matters coming up for discussion " i.e. laid on the table.

  The work last out is the first that people talk and inquire about. It is the subject on the *tapis*—the cause that is pending. It is the last candidate for success (other claims have been disposed of), and appeals for this success to us, and us alone. Our predecessors can have nothing to say to this question, however they may have anticipated us on others; future ages, in all probability, will not trouble their heads about it; we are the panel.—*William Hazlitt*. Sketches and Essays. " On Reading New Books."

TAP-ROOM T9

  The meaning of the word is obscure, and it is often used as a synonym for " bar." Literally, it means any room in a public-house where beer, etc., is drawn off for consumption.

  " There is a great stir in Hell-house yard," said a miner who entered the tap-room at this moment, much excited.—*Disraeli*. Sybil. Bk. vi, Ch. vi.

TAXIMETER (tak-sim/e-ter) T10

  Incorrectly and frequently pronounced tax/i-meter.

TE DEUM (tee dee/um) T11

  A hymn of thanksgiving, so called from the words of the Latin— *Te Deum laudamus.*

> . . . the choir,
> With all the choicest musick of the kingdom,
> Together sung Te Deum.
>   —*Shakespeare.* Henry VIII. iv, i.

TEGUMENT (teg/u-ment) *clothing; cover; envelope* T12

  Such evidences of his unceasing ardour, both for " divine and human lore," when advanced into his sixty-fifth year, and notwithstanding his many disturbances from disease, must make us at once honour his spirit, and lament that it should be so grievously clogged by its material tegument. —*James Boswell*. Life of Johnson. A.D. 1774. Ætat. 65.

TELEOLOGY† T13

The study or doctrine of final causes, i.e. of causes which are thought to be produced as a part and an indication of a design.

Without attempting in this place to justify my opinion, or even to define the kind of justification which it admits of, I merely declare my conviction that the general principle to which all rules of practice ought to conform, and the test by which they should be tried, is that of conduciveness to the happiness of mankind, or rather, of all sentient beings: in other words, that the promotion of happiness is the ultimate principle of teleology.—*J. S. Mill.* System of Logic. Pt. vi, Bk. ii, s. 7.

TENEBRIFIC (ten-e-brif/ik) *producing darkness* T14

The chief mystics in Germany, it would appear, are the transcendental philosophers, Kant, Fichte, and Schelling! With these is the chosen seat of mysticism, these are its " tenebrific constellations " from which it doth " ray out darkness " over the earth.—*Carlyle.* Critical and Miscellaneous Essays. " State of German Literature."

TERESA (te-ree/za) T15

TERMINOLOGY (ter-min-ol/o-ji) *language* T16

Such . . . are the inquiries which form the subjects of the most important of Plato's Dialogues; as ," What is rhetoric?" the topic of the Gorgias, or " What is justice?" that of the Republic. Such, also, is the question scornfully asked by Pilate, " What is truth?" and the fundamental question with speculative moralists in all ages, " What is virtue?" It would be a mistake to represent these difficult and noble inquiries as having nothing in view beyond ascertaining the conventional meaning of a name. They are inquiries not so much to determine what is, as what should be, the meaning of a name. which, like other practical questions of terminology, requires for its solution that we should enter, and sometimes enter very deeply, into the properties not merely of names but of the things named.—*J. S. Mill.* System of Logic. Pt. i, Bk. ix, s. 7.

TERRENE (ter-ene/) *temporal; pertaining to the earth* T17

Time hath his revolutions. There must be a period and an end to all temporal things, an end of names and dignities and whatsoever is terrene. And why not of de Vere? For where is Bohun? Where is Mowbray? Where is Mortimer? Nay, which is more and most of all, where is Plantagenet? They are buried in the urns and sepulchres of mortality.—*Source unknown.*

> Our terrene moon is now eclipsed,
> And it portends alone the fall of Antony.
> —*Shakespeare.* Antony and Cleopatra. iii, 11.

Who was he . . . to aspire to such a creature made of fire and air, and hallowed and adorned by such incomparable passages of life? What should he do to be more worthy? By what devotion call down the notice of these eyes to so terrene a being as himself?—*R. L. Stevenson.* The Dynamiter. " The Brown Box." (Heinemann).

TER-SANCTUS (ter-sank/tus) *a hymn used in the liturgies*   T18
          of the Greek and Eastern Churches

TETRALOGY (te-tral/o-ji) *a group of four dramatic*   T19
          works, novels, etc.

He thus made up a total of four dramas or a tetralogy, which he got
up and brought forward to contend for the prize at the festival.—*Grote.*
History of Greece. Pt. ii, Ch. lxvii.

THEO-   T20
     A prefix indicative of God or religious thought.

But if theology and theosophy, then why not theography and theometry,
why not theognomy, theotrophy, theotomy, theogamy? Why not theo-
physics and theochemistry? Why not that ingenious toy, the theotrope or
wheel of gods? Why not a monumental theodrome?—*Aldous Huxley.*
Antic Hay. Ch. i. (Chatto & Windus).

THESMOTHETE (thes/mo-thete) *a lawgiver*   T21

THESPIAN (thes/pi-an) *an actor*   T22

Yes, France is free. O glorious France, that has burst out so; into
univeral sound and smoke; and attained—the Phrygian cap of liberty!   In
all towns, trees of liberty also may be planted; with or without advantage.
Said we not, it was the highest stretch attained by the Thespian art on this
planet, or perhaps attainable?—The Thespian art, unfortunately, one must
still call it; for behold there, on this Field of Mars, the national banners,
before there could be any swearing, were to be all blessed.—*Carlyle.*
The French Revolution. Pt. ii, Bk. i, Ch. xii.

THRASONICAL (thra-son/i-kal) *bragging*   T23

HOLOFERNES: . . . his humour is lofty, his discourse per-
                     emptory, his tongue filed, his eye ambitious, his
                     gait majestical, and his general behaviour vain,
                     ridiculous, and thrasonical. He is too picked, too
                     spruce, too affected, too odd, as it were, too
                     peregrinate, as I may call it.
                       —*Shakespeare.* Love's Labour Lost. v, 1.

Is there a trace of depreciation in the gait of a croquet-player as he
walks across the ground after his ball, when it has been helped by a daisy
to roll within six inches of where he wanted it? On the contrary, insolent
pride, hybristic confidence, thrasonical vain-glory and utter self-absorption
possess him.—*Compton Mackenzie.* The Darkening Green.

THREE PER CENTS T24
TIMOTHY FORSYTE
. . . a publisher by profession he had some years before, when business was at full tide, scented out the stagnation which, indeed, had not yet come, but which ultimately, as all agreed, was bound to set in, and, selling his share in a firm engaged mainly in the production of religious books, had invested the quite conspicuous proceeds in three per cent. consols. By this act he had at once assumed an isolated position, no other Forsyte being content with less than four per cent. for his money.—*John Galsworthy.* "The Man of Property." Pt. i, Ch. i. (Heinemann).

THUCYDIDES (thu-sid/i-deze) T25

THULE (thu/le) *far distant place* T26
It is a question if the exclusive reign of orthodox beauty is not approaching its last quarter. The new Vale of Tempe may be a gaunt waste in Thule: human souls may find themselves in closer and closer harmony with external things wearing a sombreness distasteful to our race when it was young.—*Thomas Hardy.* The Return of the Native. Bk. i (i). (Macmillan).

TIARA† T27
Thrones, altars, judgment-seats, and prisons, wherein,
And beside which, by wretched men were borne
Sceptres, tiaras, swords, and chains, and tomes
Of reasoned wrong, glozed on by ignorance,
Were like those monstrous and barbaric shapes,
The ghosts of a no-more-remembered fame,
Which, from their unworn obelisks, look forth
In triumph o'er the palaces and tombs
Of those who were their conquerors.
     —*Shelley.* Prometheus Unbound.

TICHBORNE (tich/burn) T28

TILBURY (til/bur-i) *light two-wheeled carriage* T29
KING GEORGE IV.
After he gave up riding he used to drive out in the Park in a tilbury, a light two-wheeled carriage, with his groom sitting by his side. Greville said that "grave men are shocked at this undignified practice." In the afternoon he would drive up in his yellow Berlin to Manchester House to pay a call on Lady Hertford . . .—*Roger Fulford.* George the Fourth. Bk. ii (v). (Duckworth).

TORCH SINGER T30
One who sings in the beam of a spot-light and thereby relies on some adventitious assistance in his or her performance.

TRADUCTION (tra-duk/shun) *derivation; transition;*   T31
   transmission

The similitude and derivation of languages afford the most indubitable proof of the traduction of nations, and the genealogy of mankind.—From a letter by Dr. Johnson to Mr. William Drummond dated August 13th, 1766.—*James Boswell.* Life of Johnson. A.D. 1766. Ætat. 57.

TRANSLUCENT (tranz-lu/sent) *semi-transparent*   T32

Wherever fountain or fresh current flow'd
Against the eastern ray, translucent, pure,
With touch ethereal of heaven's fiery rod,
I drank.
                                   —*Milton.* Samson Agonistes. 547.

   . . . Raising me on ethereal wing
Lighter than the lark can spring
When drunk with dewlight, which the Morn
Pours from her translucent horn
To steep his sweet throat in the corn . . .
                                   —*Darley.* "Nepenthe." Ch. i.

The translucent waters poured towards her ceaselessly, and parted at the ship's iron nose.—*H. M. Tomlinson.* "All Hands!" Ch. 33. (Heinemann).

There was a calmness in those translucent leagues and the undulation amid a vast implacable light until she drifted, like a feather fallen from an unguessed star, into a place which was extraordinarily like the noonday world, so green and warm was its valley.—*A. E. Coppard.* Clorinda Walks in Heaven. Ch. ii. (Jonathan Cape).

Compton Mackenzie prefers TRALUCENT, e.g.,
   . . . innumerable juvenile bugs, partially tralucent creatures as bright as rubies . . .—*Compton Mackenzie.* Gallipoli Memories. Ch. xv.

The smoke of the shells, which at dawn had been ethereal, almost tralucent, was now in the sunset turbid and sinister.—*Compton Mackenzie.* Gallipoli Memories.

TRANSMOGRIFY (tranz-mog/ri-fi) *to change; transform*   T33

TRANSPONTINE (trans-pon/tine)   T34

(1) That part of London which lies *across the river,* i.e. in Surrey; (2) melodrama from the theatres which were formerly situated there and which favoured this variety of Thespian art.

Surrey has seen some changes in the past year or two. Vauxhall is now a Mecca for milk-churns, a sort of Atlactic Ocean having submerged the pleasant gardens where Lady Kitty walked abroad. Some of the strongholds of transpontine drama have vanished, but the Old Vic and the Battersea Dogs' Home still stand.—*Reginald Arkell.* A Cottage in the Country.

TRAUMA (trau/ma) *a wound*   T35

   . . . a pink-fouled cigarette dangling from the traumatic crimson slash that may once have resembled a mouth.—*Sir Ronald Storr*s. " I Was About To Say." Strand Magazine. January, 1942.

TRAVAIL (trav/ale) *to toil; to labour*   T36

TRIBRACH (trib/rak) *constellation of three short syllables*   T37

   Never take an iambus as a christian name. Trochees and tribrachs do very fairly.—*Coleridge*. Table Talk.

TRINAL (trine/al) *threefold*   T38

       That far-beaming blaze of majesty
    To sit the midst of trinal unity,
    He laid aside.
    —*Milton*. Ode on the Morning of Christ's Nativity. ix.

TRITURATE (trit/ure-ate) *to grind to powder*   T39

   Here it rushes and pushes, the atoms triturate and grind, and eagerly thrusting by, pursue their separate ends. Here it appears in its unconcealed personality, indifferent to all else but itself, absorbed and rapt in eager self, devoid and stripped of conventional gloss and politeness, yielding only to get its own way; driving, pushing, carried on in a stress of feverish force like a bullet, dynamic force apart from reason or will, like the force that lifts the tides and sends the clouds onwards.—*Richard Jefferies*. The Story of My Heart. Ch. vi.

TUMID (tu/mid) *swelled; inflated*   T40

    So high as heaved the tumid hills, so low ·
  Down sunk a hollow bottom broad and deep,
  Capacious bed of waters.
               Milton. Paradise Lost. vii, 288.

UBIQUITOUS

ULIGINOSE

ULTRAMONTANE

ULULATION

ULYSSES

UNBED

UNCIAL

UNCOFFIN

UNCOMEATABLE

UNDEPRESSED

UNEXAMPLED

UNICORN

UNTOWARD

URQUHART

UTILITARIANISM

UBIQUITOUS (u-bik/wit-us) *everywhere*   U

At this moment the empty air suddenly became full of whispers. I walked on, wondering what they were. The whispers turned to attenuated Æolian whinnyings, a haunting half-melodious sound rising and falling . . . . Could this actually be the noise of shells? . . . I tried to determine from which direction the whinnying came; but it was circumambient, ubiquitous, inestimable.—*Compton Mackenzie*. Gallipoli Memories.

ULIGINOSE†   U2

He had a narrow forehead, and, in general, a narrow, flattened look, which suggested that as a child he had been pressed between the pages of some gigantic ledger. There was nothing uliginose in his stature or countenance, and his voice altogether lacked the succulence of the paternal tones, grating painfully and rising angrily even when at peace, while his lisp was arid and arrogant.—*Osbert Sitwell*. Miracle on Sinai. Bk. i, Ch. iii. (Duckworth).

ULTRAMONTANE (ul-tra-mon/tane) *beyond the mountains*   U3

Hence, South of the mountains, i.e. the Alps; hence, Roman Catholic; hence, favourable to Romish doctrine.

Compare TRANSPONTINE.

Is every person a Papist who is willing to concede to the Bishop of Rome a primacy among Christian prelates? If so, James the First, Charles the First, Laud, Heylin, were Papists. Or is the appellation to be confined to persons who hold the ultramontane doctrines touching the authority of the Holy See? If so, neither Bossuet nor Pascal was a Papist. —*Macaulay*. History of England. Ch. xiv.

How admirable, for example, is his denunciation of all pagan art on the ground that it is not Christian! While all the rest of the world grovel before the Greeks and Romans, Veuillot, the logical ultramontanist, condemns them and all their works, on principle, contemptuously.—*Aldous Huxley*. " Guide Books." (Chatto & Windus).

ULULATION†   U4

George looked around the curved Long Bar, with its appetizing colour scheme of lobsters, hams and salads, its bottles of wine and flasks of liqueur. The ripe, spirituous aroma of the place, its masculine uproar, exerted a curiously nostalgic attraction that made the mere thought of the cafés, with their grease-laden atmosphere and irritating feminine ululation, impossibly repugnant.—*Hugh McGraw*. The Unwary. Ch. i. (Michael Joseph).

ULYSSES (u/lis-ez)   U5

The title of a book in which James Joyce exhibited a new and subtle technique.

UNBED* (un-bed/) *to rouse from bed*   U6

Eels unbed themselves, and stir at the noise of thunder.—*Izaak Walton.* The Compleat Angler.

UNCIAL (un/shal) *a form of script used in ancient manuscripts*   U7

. . . anon getting to con
The fair uncial comment that science hath penn'd
Glossing the mazy hieroglyph of Nature's book;
   —*Robert Bridges.* The Testament of Beauty. Bk. ii.
                                        (Clarendon Press).

It is the portrait of someone who through concentration of thought is no longer solely and entirely his physical self. He has fallen into a trance. His eyes have been focussed for so long a time upon the uncial letters in the manuscript before him that the texture of their sacred words has become the spell by which he has escaped from his body.—*Sacheverell Sitwell.* Sacred & Profane Love. Bk. viii   (Faber & Faber).

UNCOFFIN (un-kof/in) *to unpack*   U8

Fan-shaped, blond, mounted on gauze and guaranteed undetectable, it arrived from the wig-maker, preciously packed in a stout cardboard box six times too large for it and accompanied by a quarter of a pint of the choicest spirit gum. In the privacy of his bedroom Gumbril uncoffined it, held it out for his own admiration, caressed its silkiness and finally tried it on, holding it provisionally to his chin, in front of the looking-glass. The effect, he decided immediately, was stunning, was grandiose. From melancholy and all too mild he saw himself transformed on the instant into a sort of jovial Henry the Eighth, into a massive Rabelaisian man, broad and powerful and exuberant with vitality and hair.—*Aldous Huxley.* Antic Hay. Ch. ix. (Chatto & Windus).

UNCOMEATABLE (un-kum-at/abl) *unobtainable*   U9

UNDEPRESSED (un-de-prest/)   U10

UNEXAMPLED (un-eg-zampld/) *unprecedented*   U11

UNICORN (u/ni-corn) *a fabulous creature*   U12

DECIUS: . . . if he be so resolved,
         I can o'ersway him; for he loves to hear
         That unicorns may be betray'd with trees
         And bears with glasses, elephants with holes,
         Lions with toils and men with flatterers:
         But when I tell him he hates flatterers,
         He says he does, being then most flattered.
                  —*Shakespeare.* Julius Cæsar. ii, i.

UNTOWARD†   U13

> HORTENSIO: Have to my widow; and if she be froward,
> Then hast thou taught Hortensio to be untoward.
> —*Shakespeare*. The Taming of the Shrew. iv, 5.

URQUHART (er/kart)   U14

UTILITARIANISM (u-til-i-tare/i-an-izm)   U15

The doctrine of " the greatest good of the greatest number."

. . . there is still a minority with a good deal of life in it which is not content with what is called utilitarianism, which, being interpreted, means the reckless waste of life in the pursuit of the means of life.— *William Morris*. Arts and Crafts Essays. (Preface).

VAGARY	VIATICUM
VANILLA	VICEGERENT
VANSITTART	VICINAL
VARIEGATE	VICISSITUDE
VATICIDE	VILIFY
VATICINATE	*VINCI*
VEGETAL	VIOLACEOUS
VEHEMENT	VIRAGO
VEILLEUSE	VIRELAY
VERDIGRIS	VIRTU
VERISIMILITUDE	VITREOUS
VERMICULATION	VOCIFERATE
VERNAL	VOLANT
VERONESE	VOLUMIST
VERS LIBRE	VOLUPTUARY
VERTIGINOUS	VOLUTE
VERVAIN	VOX ET PRAETEREA NIHIL
VESPER	VULPINE

VAGARY (va-gar/i) *unaccountable behaviour*   V

> They changed their minds,
> Flew off, and into strange vagaries fell,
> As they would dance.
> > —*Milton.* Paradise Lost. vi, 613.

. . . it was the explanation and excuse of most of Basil's vagaries that he had never had any money of his own.—*Evelyn Waugh.* Put Out More Flags. Ch. i (6). (Chapman & Hall).

. . . it was one of the vagaries of her character to cover acres of silk yearly, with exquisite embroidery.—*Evelyn Waugh.* Put Out More Flags. Ch. i (5). (Chapman & Hall).

VANILLA (va-nil/a) *a tropical plant of the orchid family*   V2
from which a flavouring essence is extracted

I saw that island first when it was neither night nor morning. The moon was to the west, setting, but still broad and bright. To the east, and right amidships of the dawn, which was all pink, the daystar sparkled like a diamond. The land breeze blew in our faces, and smelt strong of wild lime and vanilla; other things besides, but these were the most plain; and the chill of it set me sneezing.—*R. L. Stevenson.* Island Nights' Entertainments. " The Beach of Falesá."

VANSITTART (van-sit/art)   V3

VARIEGATE (vare/i-gate) *to diversify*   V4

> Ladies like variegated tulips show;
> 'Tis to the changes half the charms we owe;
> Such happy spots the nice admirers take,
> Fine by defect, and delicately weak.
> > —*Pope.* Moral Essays. ii, 41.

VATICIDE (vat/i-cide) *the murder or murderer of a*   V5
prophet or poet

> The caitiff vaticide conceived a prayer.
> > —*Pope.* The Dunciad. ii, 78.

VATICINATE (va-tis/in-ate) *to prophesy; foretell*   V6

The phenomena of nature are alike visible to all: but all have not alike learned the connexion of natural things, or understand what they signify, or know how to vaticinate by them.—*Bishop Berkeley.* Siris. s. 258.

It is no very good symptom either of nations or individuals, that they deal much in vaticination. Happy men are full of the present, for its bounty suffices them; and wise men also, for its duties engage them.—*Carlyle.* Critical and Miscellaneous Essays. " Signs of the Times."

VEGETAL* (vej/e-tal) *a vegetable*   V7

> Your minerals, vegetals, and animals.
> > —*Ben Jonson.*   The Alchemist.

VEHEMENT†   V8

> Thus I have told thee all my State, and brought
> My storie to the sum of earthly bliss
> Which I enjoy, and must confess to find
> In all things else delight indeed, but such
> As us'd or not, works in the mind no change,
> Nor vehement desire, these delicacies
> I mean of Taste, Sight, Smell, Herbs, Fruits, and Flours,
> Walks, and the melodie of Birds; but here
> Farr otherwise, transported I behold,
> Transported touch; here passion first I felt,
> Commotion strange, in all enjoyments else
> Superiour and unmov'd, here onely weake
> Against the charm of Beauties powerful glance.
> Or Nature faild in mee, and left some part.
> > —*Milton.* Paradise Lost. viii.

VEILLEUSE†   V9

A French politician I know has put what he calls a "veilleuse" on his bedside table—a tiny electric night-lamp showing a faint blue light. And although he is not an extravagant man or prone to seeing things in the dark, he keeps that lamp on all night.

"That way," he says, "I know what is happening as soon as I open my eyes. If the light is on, I can go to sleep again. But if it is out, I shall get dressed at once and leave the house.

"For if the light goes out that means that the Communists have called out the power station, and that means the Government will have to put soldiers in to work the power station.

"The Communists are bound to resist that, and voila, we have open civil war. If there is civil war I do not want to be caught at home in my bed."—*Sefton Delmer.* "Newsmap." Daily Express. 1st December, 1947.

VERDIGRIS (ver/di-gris) *a green rust*   V10

On the left there is a high church tower of red and yellow stucco. An archway connects this with San Gregorio Armeno, upon which stands a copper statue of a saint, green with verdigris. The nimbus round his head has wild snapdragons sprouting from it.—*Sacheverell Sitwell.* Sacred & Profane Love. Bk. v, Pt. vi. (Faber & Faber).

VERISIMILITUDE (ver-i-sim-il/i-tude) *resemblance to*   V11
truth

He was no doubt looking at the shaded face of the Sea Lady, framed in a frame of sunlit yellow-green lawn and black-green ilex leaves—at least so my impulse for verisimilitude conceives it—and she at first was pensive and downcast that afternoon, and afterwards she was interested and looked into his eyes.—*H. G. Wells.* The Sea Lady. Ch. vi. (Collins).

. . . I had always imagined that the scenes that embellished Havana cigar-boxes dealt in fantasy, and not in verisimilitude, but I found that, in spite of the improbability of the scenes they depict, they are, in the finest sense, true.—*Osbert Sitwell.* Sing High! Sing Low! " Still Life." (ii). (Macmillan).

VERMICULATION (ver-mik-u-lay/shun) (1) *a worm-hole;* V12 (2) *motion like a worm*

. . . the floors above were found to have a very irregular surface, rising to ridges, sinking into valleys; and being just then uncarpeted, the face of the boards was seen to be eaten into innumerable vermiculations.— *Thomas Hardy.* Far From the Madding Crowd. Ch. ix. (Macmillan).

VERNAL† V13

> With the year
> Seasons return; but not to me returns
> Or sight of vernal bloom or summer's rose.
> —*Milton.* Paradise Lost.

VERONESE (var-o-nay/sa) V14

VERS LIBRE (vahr lebr/) *free verse; verse without metre* V15

VERTIGINOUS (ver-tij/in-us) *giddy; turning round; dizzy* V16

Inconstant they are in all their actions, vertiginous, restless, unapt to resolve of any business.—*Burton.* Anatomy of Melancholy.

OF " MAN AND SUPERMAN "
Being then at the height of my inventive and comedic talent I decorated it too brilliantly and lavishly. The effect was so virtiginous apparently, that nobody noticed the new religion in the centre of the intellectual whirlpool.—*G. B. Shaw.* Preface to " Back to Methuselah." (Constable).

VERVAIN (ver/vane) *a plant supposed to possess magical* V17 *properties*

> She night-shade strows to work him ill,
> Therewith the vervain, and the dill,
> That hindreth witches of their will.
> —*Drayton.* Nymphidia.

VESPER (ves/per) *the evening star; evening; Venus*   V18

        The night-wind's lonely vesper-hymn.
                                 —*Emily Brontë.* Poems.

ANTONY: Sometime we see a cloud that's dragonish,
                A vapour sometime like a bear or lion,
                A tower'd citadel, a pendent rock,
                A forked mountain, or blue promontory
                With trees upon't, that nod unto the world
                And mock our eyes with air: thou hast seen these signs;
                They are black vesper's pageants.
                 , —*Shakespeare.* Antony and Cleopatra. iv, xiv.

VIATICUM (vi-at/i-kum) *provision for a journey*   V19

    I found myself just out of Faido on this blessed date of God with eight francs and forty centimes for my viaticum and temporal provision. —*Hilaire Belloc.* The Path to Rome. (Allen & Unwin).

VICEGERENT (vice-je/rent) *an officer acting in place*   V20
                of another

        Whom send I to judge? Whom but thee,
    Vicegerent son! To thee I have transferr'd
    All judgement, whether in heaven, or earth, or hell.
                    —*Milton.* Paradise Lost. x, 55.

VICINAL (vis/in-al) *near; bordering*   V21

    The above-mentioned highway traversed the lower levels of the heath from one horizon to another. In many portions of its course it overlaid an old vicinal way, which branched from the great Western road of the Romans, the Via Iceniana or Ikenild Street, hard by.—*Thomas Hardy.* The Return of the Native. Bk. i (i). (Macmillan).

VICISSITUDE (vi-sis/i-tude) *a change of fortune*   V22
        All night the dreadless Angel unpursu'd
    Through Heavn's wide Champain held his way, till Morn
    Wak't by the circling Hours, with rosie hand
    Unbarr'd the gates of Light. There is a Cave
    Within the Mount of God, fast by his Throne,
    Where light and darkness in perpetual round
    Lodge and dislodge by turns, which makes through Heav'n
    Grateful vicissitude, like Day and Night;
    Light issues forth, and at the other dore
    Obsequious darkness enters, till her houre
    To veile the Heav'n, though darkness there might well
    Seem twilight here; and now went forth the Morn
    Such as in highest Heav'n, arrayed in Gold
    Empyreal, from before her vanisht Night,
    Shot through with orient Beams: when all the Plain
    Covrd with thick embattld Squadrons bright,
    Chariots and flaming Armes, and fierie Steeds
    Reflecting blaze on blaze, first met his view.
                    —*Milton.* Paradise Lost. vi.

VILIFY (vil/i-fi) *to slander or to defame*   V23

     . . . their Maker's image
    Forsook them, when themselves they vilified
    To serve ungovern'd appetite, and took
    His image whom they served.
            —*Milton.* Paradise Lost. xi, 515.

VINCI (vin/che)   V24

VIOLACEOUS (vi-o-lay/shus) *violet colour*   V25

VIRAGO (vi-ray/go) *a masculine woman; a termagant*   V26

    To arms! to arms! the fierce virago cries,
  And swift as lightning to the combat flies.
            —*Pope.* The Rape of the Lock. Canto v.

VIRELAY (vir/e-lay) *an ancient form of poem consisting*   V27
      of short verses with two rhymes

    The mournful mirth in muse now list ne mask,
  As she was wont in youngth and summer days;
  But if thou algate lust light virelays,
  And looser songs of love to undersong.
            —*Spenser.* Shepherd's Calendar.

VIRTU†   V28

    I had thoughts in my chamber to place it in view,
  To be shown to my friends as a piece of virtu.
            —*Oliver Goldsmith.* The Haunch of Venison.

VITREOUS (vit/re-us) *glassy; like glass*   V29

    . . . So far we are forcing our Michael Angelos to carve in snow.
The first duty of the economist in art is, to see that no intellect shall thus
glitter merely in the manner of hoar-frost; but that it shall be well vitri-
fied, like a painted window, and shall be set so between shafts of stone
and bands of iron, that it shall bear the sunshine upon it, and send the
sunshine through it, from generation to generation.—*John Ruskin.* The
Political Economy of Art. Lecture delivered at Manchester, July 10th,
1857.

VOCIFERATE (vo-sif/er-ate) *to call out; to talk loudly*   V30

    The mention of the wolf had led Johnson to think of other wild
beasts; and while Sir Joshua Reynolds and Mr. Langton were carrying on
a dialogue about something which engaged them earnestly, he, in the
midst of it, broke out, " Pennant tells of Bears—" [what he added I have
forgotten]. They went on, which he being dull of hearing, did not perceive, or, if he did, was not willing to break off his talk; so he continued
to vociferate his remarks, and *Bear* (" like a word in a catch " as Beau-
clerk said) was repeatedly heard at intervals, which coming from him
who, by those who did not know him, had been so often assimilated to
that ferocious animal, while we who were sitting around could hardly
stifle laughter, produced a very ludicrous effect. Silence having ensued,

he proceeded: "We are told, that the black bear is innocent; but I should not like to trust myself with him." Mr. Gibbon muttered, in a low tone of voice, "I should not like to trust myself with *you*."—*James Boswell*. Life of Johnson. A.D. 1775. Ætat. 66.

VOLANT (vol/ant) *flying*   V31

> His volant touch
> Instinct through all proportions, low and high,
> Fled, and pursued transverse the resonant fugue
> > —*Milton*. Paradise Lost. xi, 561.

I have considered the structure of all volant animals and find the folding continuity of the bat's wings most easily accommodated to the human form. Upon this model I shall begin my task tomorrow, and in a year expect to tower into the air beyond the malice and pursuit of man. *Dr. Johnson*. Rasselas.

VOLUMIST†   V32

Ye write them [volumes] in your closets, and unwrite them in your courts; hot volumists, and cold bishops!—*Milton*. Animadversions upon a Defence of the Humble Remonstrance.

VOLUPTUARY (vo-lupt/u-ar-i) *a devotee of sensual*   V33
pleasure

. . . fired with jealousy and whisky in about equal proportions, was denouncing Mr. Hammond in no uncertain terms as a lecher and voluptuary of the worst order.—*Hugh McGraw*. Rude Society. Ch. x. (Heinemann).

VOLUTE†   V34

I have no ear.—

Mistake me not, dear reader,—nor imagine that I am by nature destitute of those exterior twin appendages, hanging oranments, and (architecturally speaking) handsome volutes to the human capital. Better my mother had never borne me.—I am, I think, rather delicately than copiously provided with those conduits; and I feel no disposition to envy the mule for his plenty, or the mole for her exactness, in those ingenious labyrinthine inlets—those indispensable side-intelligencers.—*Charles Lamb*. Essays of Elia. "A Chapter on Ears."

VOX ET PRAETEREA NIHIL (vox et pri-tere/e-a ni/hil)   V35
mere verbosity

VULPINE (vul/pine) *like a fox*   V36

In any other circumstances, Stephen might well have believed that he was having his leg mildly pulled, but there was something in the vulpine eye of Mr. Gallagher, the tersely cynical phraseology of Mr. Cuffings, that dispelled this comforting thesis.—*Hugh McGraw*. The Boon Companions. Ch. xii. (Heinemann).

WAIN

WAINSCOT

WALCHEREN

WAREHOUSE

WEAPON-SALVE

WEDNESBURY

WELKIN

WENCESLAUS

WHIT

WHITSUN

WIMPLE

WINDLE STRAW

WINTON

WITHERS

WITWATERSRAND

WOLD

WORMS

WUTHER

WYKEHAMIST

WAIN (wane) *a waggon* W

> There auncient Night arriving did alight
> From her high weary wayne, and in her armes
> To Æsculapius brought the wounded knight:
> Whome having softly disaraid of armes,
> Tho gan to him discover all his harmes,
> Beseeching him with prayer and with praise,
> If either salves, or oyles, or herbes, or charmes,
> A fordonne wight from dore of death mote raise,
> He would at her request prolong her nephews daies.
> —*Spenser*. The Faerie Queene. i, v, 41.

WAINSCOT (wane/skot) *panelling or lining of walls* W2 *of rooms*

DR. JOHNSON IN FRANCE

Oct. 14. Saturday. We went to the house of Mr. Argenson, which was almost wainscotted with looking-glasses and covered with gold.—The ladies closet wainscotted with large squares of glass over painted paper. They always place mirrours to reflect their rooms.—*James Boswell.* Life of Johnson—from Johnson's Memoranda of his journey. A.D. 1775. Ætat. 66.

WALCHEREN (varl/cher-en) W3

WAREHOUSE (ware/hous) W4

One of the most pleasant sounds in the English language.

I looked out at the great arc of the Mississipi, walled in with wharves and warehouses, overhung with a huge dense canopy of lustrous mist.— *Eric Linklater.* God Likes Them Plain. "The Wrong Story." (Jonathan Cape).

WEAPON-SALVE (wep/on salv) W5

A salve applied to the instrument causing a wound instead of to the wound itself.

In June, 1902, a local English weekly reported that a woman called Matilde Henry of Norwich accidentally ran an iron nail into the sole of her foot. Without having the wound examined or even taking off her stocking, she bade her daughter to oil the nail thoroughly in the expectation that then nothing could happen to her. She died a few days later of tetanus in consequence of postponed antisepsis.—*Sigmund Freud.* Totem and Taboo. Ch. iii.

WEDNESBURY (wenz/bu-ri) W6

WELKIN† W7

> Spur your proud horses hard, and ride in blood:
> Amaze the welkin with your broken staves.
> > —*Shakespeare*.   Richard III.   v, 3.

> . . . with feats of arms
> From either end of heaven the welkin burns.
> > —*Milton*.   Paradise Lost.   ii, 337.

WENCESLAUS (ven/ses-lous) W8

Some names are sacred. It is, to say the least, doubtful whether the traditional *wen/ses-lass* or *wence/lass* will, or should, be abandoned.

WHIT (whit) *a point; a jot* W9

> If every just man that now pines with want
> Had but a moderate and beseeming share
> Of that which lewdly-pamper'd Luxury
> Now heaps upon som few with vast excess,
> Natures full blessings would be well dispenc't
> In unsuperfluous eeven proportion,
> And she no whit encomber'd with her store,
> And then the giver would be better thank't,
> His praise due paid, for swinish gluttony
> Ne're looks to Heav'n amidst his gorgeous feast,
> But with besotted base ingratitude
> Cramms, and blasphemes his feeder.
> > —*Milton*.   Comus.

WHITSUN (wit/sun) W10

Whit-Sunday is the seventh after Easter.

> . . . busied with a Whitsun morrice-dance.
> > —*Shakespeare*.   Henry V.   ii, 4.

WIMPLE (wim/ple) *a nun's linen head-dress* W11

> So faire and fresh, as freshest flowre in May;
> For she had layd her mournefull stole aside,
> And widow-like sad wimple throwne away,
> Wherewith her heavenly beautie she did hide,
> Whiles on her wearie journey she did ride;
> And on her now a garment she did weare
> All lilly white, withoutten spot or pride,
> That seemd like silke and silver woven neare:
> But neither silke nor silver therein did appeare.
> > —*Spenser*.   The Faerie Queene.   i, xii, 42.

WINDLE STRAW (windl/ stror) *old, dead grass-stalks*   W12

>Tall spires of windlestraw
>Threw their thin shadows down the rugged slope.
>>—*Shelley*. Alastor.

WINTON (*Lat.* Wintoniensis) *signature of the Bishop of*   W13
    Winchester

WITHERS (with/erz) *the joint that unites the neck and*   W14
    shoulders of a horse

>Let the gall'd beast winch;
>Our withers are unwrung.
>>—*Shakespeare*. Hamlet. iii, 2.

"Witherwrung," to use the old expression, means that a horse has been chafed on the withers by an ill-fitting saddle, or that the withers have been bruised or made sore by some other means. Applied to persons the phrase means worried or affected in some way. It is, however, most frequently used in the negative —"our withers are unwrung."

WITWATERSRAND (vit/va-terz-rant)   W15

Stockbrokers should note that "West Wits" are to be pronounced "Vest Vits."

WOLD (wold) *open uncultivated tract of country*   W16

>St. Withold footed thrice the wold.
>>—*Shakespeare*. King Lear. iii, 4.

Who sees not a great difference betwixt the wolds in Lincolnshire and the fens?—*Burton*. Anatomy of Melancholy.

>The wind that beats the mountain, blows
>More softly round the open wold,
>And gently comes the world to those
>That are cast in gentle mould.
>>—*Tennyson*.

WORMS (vorm)   W17

An ancient German city on the Rhine.

WUTHER (wuth/er) *to moan*   **W18**

    . . . happily for the investor, forgery is an affair of practice. And as Morris sat surrounded by examples of his uncle's signature and of his own incompetence, insidious depression stole upon his spirits. From time to time the wind wuthered in the chimney at his back; from time to time there swept over Bloomsbury a squall so dark that he must rise and light the gas; about him was the chill and the mean disorder of a house out of commission—the floor bare, the sofa heaped with books and accounts enveloped in a dirty table-cloth, the pens rusted, the paper glazed with a thick film of dust; and yet these were but adminicles of misery, and the true root of his depression lay round him on the table in the shape of misbegotten forgeries.—*R. L. Stevenson and Lloyd Osbourne. The Wrong Box. Ch. vi.* (Heinemann).

WYKEHAMIST (wik/a-mist) *a person belonging to*   **W19**
                    Winchester

XANADU

XANTHOCHROI

XANTHOMELANOUS

XANTHOPHYLL

XENELASIA

XENODOCHY

XENOPHANES

XENOPHOBIA

XEROSTOMIA

XANADU (zan/a-doo)   X

XANTHOCHROI (zan-thok/ro-i) *blond or fair-skinned*   X2
persons, with blue eyes

XANTHOMELANOUS (zan-tho-mel/a-nus) *brunettes;*   X3
with dark hair and skin

XANTHOPHYLL (zan/tho-fil) *the yellow colouring-matter*   X4
in dead leaves

XENELASIA (zen-e-lay/zi-a) *restriction of immigration;*   X5
exclusion of foreigners

XENODOCHY (ze-nod/o-ki) *hospitality*   X6

XENOPHANES (ze-nof/a-nez)   X7

XENOPHOBIA (zen-o-fo/bia) *hatred of foreigners*   X8

THOMAS ROWLANDSON

He resided for two years in Paris, where he learnt to speak French perfectly, and he must have greatly enjoyed his stay, for he often returned, although, while he was there, as an obituarist declares in a fit of popular xenophobia, he " occasionally indulged that satirical talent, in portraying the characteristics of that fantastic people, whose outré habits, perhaps, scarcely demanded the exaggeration of caricature."—*Osbert Sitwell*. Sing High! Sing Low! (Macmillan).

Moreover we live in an age of unparalleled because organized xenophobia. For some time past I have done my best to support the foreign policy of Mr. Bevin, but since last Thursday I find myself in disagreement with him on one point. I would like to see advantage taken of the resumption of negotiations for re-modelling the Anglo-Russian Treaty and to try at least to abate the flow of venom. That seems to be the test of sincerity in any treaty.—*Lord Vansittart*. Speech in the House of Lords, 5th March, 1947.

XEROSTOMIA (zer-o-sto/mi-a) *thirst*   X9

YAHOO

YARE

YEAR-LONG

YEMEN

YOSEMITE

YPSILANTI

YAHOO (ya-hoo/) *a coarse, vicious person*   Y

YARE (yare) *ready; quick*   Y2
 Yare, yare, good Iras, quick:—methinks I hear Antony call.
   —*Shakespeare*. Antony and Cleopatra. v, 2.

YEAR-LONG (yere/long) *lasting a year*   Y3

YEMEN (yem/en)   Y4

YOSEMITE (yo-sem/i-te)   Y5

YPSILANTI (ip-si-lan/ti)   Y6

ZAMBO

ZANY

ZEITGEIST

ZEUS

ZOANTHROPHY

ZODIAC

ZOIC

ZOLAËSQUE

ZOLLVEREIN

ZOOGEOGRAPHY

ZOOGONY

ZOOMORPHIC

ZOOPHAGOUS

ZOROASTER

ZAMBO (zam/bo) *species of coloured man*   **Z**

There is nothing Dutch about this scene, languid and voluptuous yet fiery, for here is the mulatto world of octoroon, griffo, zambo and creole, and the music is a rumba played on the skulls of animals to a shuffling in the dust.—*Osbert Sitwell.* Sing High! Sing Low! "Still Life." (ii). (Macmillan).

ZANY†   **Z2**

Some slight zany . . .
Told our intents before.
　　　—*Shakespeare.* Love's Labour Lost. v, 2.
Preacher at once, and zany of thy age.
　　　—*Pope.* The Dunciad. iii, 205.

Well, well, well, his lordship may have reflected stroking his Disraeli-like profile and sipping his China tea by the fire. Johnson's zany in trouble at last, and not to be wondered at, indeed, considering his habits! Perhaps this accident will increase the sales of his absurd and tedious book—who knows? The public is so *saugrenu!*—*D. B. Wyndham Lewis.* The Hooded Hawk. Ch. vii. (Eyre & Spottiswoode).

ZEITGEIST (tsite/gy-st) *moral or intellectual tendency*   **Z3**
　　　　　　of a period

ZEUS (zoos)   **Z4**

ZOANTHROPHY (zo-an/thro-pi)   **Z5**

A mental disease of delirium in which a person imagines himself to be an animal.

ZODIAC (zo/di-ak) *the apparent path of the sun in*   **Z6**
　　　　　　heaven

The golden sun . . .
Gallops the zodiak in his glist'ring coach.
　　　—*Shakespeare.* Titus Andronicus. ii, 1.

ZOIC (zoo/ik) *relating to animal life*   **Z7**

ZOLAËSQUE (zo-la-esk/) *like a character of Zola's novels;*   Z8
   degraded

   Few of Boswell's leading critics, apparently, have ever been drunk.
This disability no doubt makes them tend, when they assume the pince-nez
of the *juge d'instruction* and open Dossier D, to lean more towards drama
than reality. For example, the shambling Zolaësque wretch we are invited
to contemplate slithering down the slope to boozy dissolution from 1777
onwards is actually the Boswell to whom Johnson says contentedly at this
very period, "Sir, I don't care though I sit all night with you," and the
Boswell who two years later is charming the Bishop of Chester and the
prim tea-tables of Lichfield with his agreeable presence. How does this
chime with the prosecution's case? And what of the trip to Cornwall in
1792? And the dinner at Lambeth Palace in 1794?—*D. B. Wyndham
Lewis.* The Hooded Hawk. (Eyre & Spottiswoode).

ZOLLVEREIN (tsol/fe-rine) *a customs union*   Z9

ZOOGEOGRAPHY (zoo-o-je-og/ra-fi) *geography, in*   Z10
   relation to the distribution of animals

ZOOGONY (zoo-og/o-ni) *doctrine of the origin of life*   Z11

ZOOMORPHIC (zoo-o-mor/fik) *in the form of an animal*   Z12

   But psychology had no more right to be anthropomorphic, or even
exclusively zoomorphic, than any other science. Besides a reason and an
animal, man was also a collection of particles subject to the laws of
chance.—*Aldous Huxley.* Eyeless In Gaza. Ch. iii. (Chatto & Windus).

ZOOPHAGOUS (zoo-off/a-gus) *carnivorous*   Z13

ZOROASTER (zo-ro-as/ter)   Z14

LIST OF WORDS

ABACUS

ABBÉ

ABDOMINOUS

ABDUCE

ABEAM

ABERCROMBIE

ABERRANT

ABJURE

ABNORMOUS

ABSTERSIVE

ACCABLÉ

ACCIACATURA

ACCIDENCE

ACCLIVITY

ACHERON

ACHROMATIC

ACUITY

ACULEATE

ACUMINATE

ADAGIO

ADIAPHORISM

ADOBE

AERATE

AERIAL

AESCHYLUS

AGAR

AGIO

AGNAIL

AGNUS CASTUS

AGNUS DEI

AIGRETTE

AIGUILLE

AIT

ALBEIT

ALCAIC

ALCHYMY

ALEXANDRINE

ALEXIPHARMIC

ALHAMBRA

ALLEYN

ALL OVERISH

ALL SAINTS' DAY

ALL SOULS' DAY

ALMA TADEMA

ALTO-RELIEVO

AMARACUS

AMARANTH

AMARANTHINE

AMARI ALIQUID

AMARYLLIS

AMBERGRIS

AMBIENT

AMBIVALENT

AMETHYST

AMPHIBOLOGY

AMPHITHEATRE

AMUSIVE

ANACREONTIC

ANADEM

ANALOGUE

ANAPEST

ANASTROPHE

ANATHEMA

ANFRACTUOUS

ANIMALCULE

ANIMISM

ANNUNCIATE

ANNUNZIO

ANODYNE

ANTELUCAN

ANTEMUNDANE

ANTHROPOMORPHOUS

ANTHROPOPHAGI

APHASIAC

APLOMB

APOCALYPSE

APPETENCE

APPLAUSIVE

APPOSITE

A PRIORI

APSE

AQUILON

ARBUTUS

ARCHANGEL

ARCH-FLAMEN

ARCHIDIACONAL

ARCHITECTONIC

ARCHIVES

ARCUATE

AREA

ARGAL

ARGENTINE

ARIETTA

ARMAGEDDON

ARMOZEEN

ARRAS

ASCETIC

ASHLAR

ASSEMBLY ROOM

ASSEVERATE

ASYNDETON

ATOLL

ATRAMENTAL

ATROPOS

ATTIC

AUREOLE

AUTONOMY

AVATAR

BACCHANTE

BAEDEKER

BAGGAGE-SMASHER

BALCARRES

BALEFUL

BALLAD

BALSAMOUS

BARBECUE

BARBICAN

BARTON

BASHI-BAZOUK

BASILISK

BAVIN

BEACONSFIELD

BEAD-ROLL

BEATIFY

BEAUCHAMP

BEAULIEU

BEAUNE

BÉCASSE

BEDEL

BEDIZEN

BED-PRESSER	BOHEA
BEEROCRACY	BOSCAGE
BELAMOUR	BOSKY
BELLEROPHON	BOTRYOIDAL
BENTHAM	BOUGAINVILLÆA
BERKELEY	BOUILLABAISSE
BERKSHIRE	BOUILLON
BERSERK	BOURBON
BERYL	BOURDON
BESTEAD	BOURG
BHAGAVAD-GITA	BOURGEON
BIBLIOPHILE	*BOVARY*
BIBLIOPOLE	BRAGGADOCIO
BICAMERAL	BRASSARD
BICESTER	BRASSERIE
BISTRE	BRAVURA
BLACKAMOOR	BREAKDOWN
BLACK MASS	BROCADE
BLACK MONDAY	BUCKRAM
BLAZE	BUGLOSS
BLOWZE	BUHL
BODEGA	BULIMY
BŒOTIAN	BY-END

CABARET

CABBALISTIC

CABOCHON

CACHEXIA

CACODEMON

CACOPHONY

CADILLAC

CAIN-COLOURED

CALAMITOUS

CALEFACTORY

CALUMNIATE

CAMOMILE

CANAKIN

CANDENT

CANOROUS

CAPRICCIO

CARAPACE

CARAT

CARAVANSARY

CARBUNCLE

CARIOUS

CASEMENT

CASTE

CATAFALQUE

CATAMARAN

CATENERY

CAUDAL

CENOBITE

CENTRIFUGAL

CEPHALALGIC

CERULEAN

CHALICING

CHAMELEON

CHAMPERTY

CHANDOS

CHARYBDIS

CHEVRON

CHICANERY

CHILDE

CHOPINE

CHRYSOLITE

CHRYSOPRASE

CICERONE

CINNABAR

CINQUE-SPOTTED

CIRCUMAMBIENT

CIRCUMVALLATION

CITRINE

CLANRICARDE

CLEMENT

CLERISY

CLOTTED NONSENSE

CLOUD-ECLIPSED

CODDAM

COEVAL

COIFFEUR

COLLYRIUM

COLORATURA

COMMINUTE

COMMONALTY

COMPLIN

CONCATENATION

CONCUPISCENCE

CONDIGN

CONGENER

CONGERIES

CONGLOBULATE

CONJURATION

CONNOTATIVE

CONSTELLATED

CONSUMMATE

CONSUMMATE

CONTUMACY

CONURBATION

CORBEL

CORNUCOPIA

CORVINE

COSMOGONY

COSMOGRAPHY

CREEPING JESUS

CREPUSCULAR

CUBAN HEEL

CULMEN

CURACAO

CYNOSURE

DAEDAL

DAGUERREOTYPE

DALMATIC

DALZIEL

DÉBUT

DECADE

DECADENT

DECAHEDRON

DE CRESPIGNY

DEFERVESCENCE

DELIQUESCE

DELIQUIUM

DÉMENTI

DEMONIAC

DEMOTIC

DENIGRATE

DÉNOUEMENT

DERACINATE

DESCARTES

DESCENSION

DÉTENTE

DEVOIR

DEWBESPRENT

DEWFALL

DIABLERIE

DIABOLISM

DIÆRESIS

DIAGNOSTIC

DIALECTIC

DIALYSIS

DIAPASON

DIAPEPHRADIZING

DIDACTIC

DIES IRÆ

DIFFLUENT

DIGAMMA

DIONYSIAC

DIORAMA

DIOSCURI

DISANCHOR

DISCANDY

DISEMBOGUE

DISHABILLE

DISPITEOUS

DISSONANT

DITHYRAMB

DIURNAL

DON JUAN

DONNE

DON QUIXOTE

DORP

DOVE-EYED

DOWN PLATFORM

DUBIETY

DUDINE

DÜRERESQUE

EAR-WITNESS

EAU DE NIL

EBBW

EBRIETY

ECARTÉ

ÉCLAT

ECLECTIC

ECLIPTIC

ECLOGUE

EDENTATE

EFFLORESCENCE

EFFULGENCE

ELECTRO-BIOLOGY

ELLIPSIS

EMBATHE

EMBEZZLE

EMBRASURE

EMBRYO

EMIR

EMPIRIC

ENCAUSTIC

ENDEMIC

ENSAFFRONED

EPHYDRIAD

EPICENE

EPITOME

EQUIVOCAL

EREMITE

EROTOMANIA

ESCULENT

ESTHER

ESURIENT

ETERNIZE

ETIOLATION

EULENSPIEGEL

EUNICE

EUPEPSIA

EVANESCENCE

EXANIMATE

EXEGESIS

EXEQUIES

EXIGIBLE

EXILITY

EXORDIAL

EXOTERIC

EXPATIATE

EXSUCCOUS

EXTOL

EX-VOTO

FABULIST

FACILE

FAIENCE

FAMILY GROCER

FAMULUS

FARTHINGALE

FASCINE

FAUN

FEAST-WON

FECULENT

FENCIBLE

FEU DE JOIE

FEUILLETON

FIDELIO

FIELD-NIGHT

FIESOLE

FIGURINE

FINALE

FINICAL

FLAGITIOUS

FLAMEN

FLASH HOUSE

FLEXILE

FLOCCULENT

FLORET

FLOWERET

FORECASTLE

FORENSIC

FREMESCENCE

FRENTIC

FRÖBEL

FRORE

FUGACIOUS

FULGOROUS

FUNAMBULIST

GALA

GALACTIC

GALACTOPHAGIST

GALANTINE

GALBANUM

GALILEO

GALLIPOT

GARNITURE

GAZEBO

GELID

GENERIC

GEODESIC

GEOGHEGAN

GEORGIC

GERMINAL

GIAOUR

GIGLOT

GIGOT

GIOTTO

GIOVANNI

GITANO

GLAUCOUS

GLOZE

GODAVARI

GOETHE

GOLUPTIOUS

GRACIOSITY

GRAVAMEN

GRAVID

GRAVIGRADE

GREEN-SICKNESS

GREGARIOUS

GRINGO

GROTESQUE

GUADELOUPE

GUERDON

GULES

GULOSITY

GYMNOSOPHIST

GYNÆOSYNCRASY

HARUN-AL-RASCHID

HAWARDEN

HAY

HEAVY-BELLY

HEBDOMADAL

HEBE

HEBETUDE

HECATE

HECATOMB

HEINOUS

HELICAL

HELIOLATRY

HELOÏSE

HEMICYCLE

HERMENEUTIC

HERVEY

HETEROCLITE

HETEROGENEOUS

HETEROPATHIC

HEXAMETER

HIERARCHY

HIEROGLYPH

HIEROPHANT

HIGH TEA

HIPPOGRIFF

HIRSUTE

HISTORIETTE

HISTORIOGRAPHER

HISTORY, ANCIENT

HISTORY, MEDIÆVAL

HISTORY, MODERN

HOBART

HOLOCAUST

HOLOGRAPH

HONG

HORRENT

HOURI

HOY

HUSBANDRY

HYALINE

HYDROCEPHALIC

HYPERBATON

HYPERBOLE

HYPERBOREAN

HYPODERMIC

HYPOSTASIS

IAGO

ICHTHYOLOGY

IMBRICATE

IMBROGLIO

IMMEDICABLE

IMMINENT

IMMITIGABLE

IMMOLATE

IMPARADISE

IMPLEX

IMPRESARIO

IMPRIMATUR

INCONDITE   INGURGITATE

INCRASSATE   INSOUCIANT

INCULCATE   INTEGUMENT

INCURVATE   INTERREGNUM

INDICT   INTROIT

INDICTION   INURBANE

INDURATE   *IQUIQUE*

INEFFABLE   IRASCIBLE

INELUCTABLE   *IRENE*

INENARRABLE   IRREFRAGABLE

INEXIGENT   ITALIAN WAREHOUSEMAN

INGRESS

JACINTH   JONQUIL

JACK TOWEL   JOUST

JINN   *JOWETT*

JOCUND   JUBILEE

KALEIDOSCOPE   KEENING

KAVANAGH   KINGCUP

KEDLESTON   *KNOLLYS*

LABYRINTHIAN

LACHRYMA CHRISTI

LACKADAISICAL

LACONISM

LACUSTRINE

LADY DAY

LAMBENT

LAMMAS

LAOCOÖN

LAO-TSZE

LAPIDARY

LARBOARD

LA ROCHEFOUCAULD

LASCAR

LATITUDINARIAN

LAVEROCK

LAZZARONE

LEE

LEFEBVRE

LE FEUVRE

LEIBNITZ

LEMAN

LEMMA

LENITIVE

LEOMINSTER

LEONCAVALLO

LE QUEX

LEVIATHAN

LEVIN

LIBERTICIDE

LIGHT-YEAR

LITERATI

LITTORAL

LORIMER

LUCULENT

LUSH

LUSKISH

LUSTRATION

LUSTRUM

LYCEUM

LYDIAN

LYSAGHT

MACERATE	MENISCUS
MADREPORIC	*MENZIES*
MAGENTA	MEPHISTOPHELIAN
MAGGIORE	MEPHITIC
MAGIC	MERIDIONAL
MAGNIFIC	METATHESIS
MAHON	METEMPSYCHOSIS
MAHONEY	METONYMY
MAINWARING	MEZZO-RILIEVO
MALEFIC	MIASMA
MALKIN	MILLENNIUM
MALTWORM	MIRIFIC
MANCIPLE	MITHRIDATE
MANDARIN	MIZZLE
MANDRAKE	MNEMONIC
MANSARD FLOOR	*MNEMOSYNE*
MARL	MOLLUSC
MARPLOT	MONEGASQUE
MASQUERADE	MORDANT
MATHESIS	MOUJIK
MAUGRE	MOUNTEBANK
MAZARINE	MUNGE
MEGALOMANIAC	MYRRH
MEIOSIS	MYSTAGOGUE
MELHUISH	

NADIR

NAIAD

NARD

NARGHILE

NEOLOGY

NEOPHYTE

NEPENTHE

NEPHRITIC

NEREID

NEUMANN

NEXUS

NIMBUS

NONAGE

NONPAREIL

NORNS

NOSOLOGY

NOSTALGIA

NUGATORY

OBER-AMMERGAU

OBFUSCATE

OBLIQUITY

OBLOQUY

OBSIDIAN

OFFICINAL

OLIGARCHY

OLIO

ONEIROCRITIC

ONTOLOGY

OPHICLEIDE

ORDER

OREAD

ORISON

ORTHOGRAPHER

OSTLER

OUIDA

OUTRÉ

OUZEL

OVERT

PACHYDERM

PAGURIAN

PALADIN

PALIMPSEST

PALINDROME

PALINGENESIA

PALINODE

PALMER

PANACEA

PAN-AMERICAN

PANDICULATION

PANEGYRIC

PANURGIC

PAOLI

PARABOLICAL

PAPERASSERIE

PARGET

PARIAN

PARONOMASIA

PARONYM

PARTHENOGENESIS

PARVENU

PARVIS

PASQUINADE

PATINA

PAVANE

PAVONINE

PEA-JACKET

PEASECOD

PEJORATIVE

PELLUCID

PENMAENMAWR

PENTASTICH

PENTHOUSE

PEPYS

PERIAPT

PERIPHERY

PERIPHRASIS

PERISTYLE

PERNOCTATION

PERPEND

PERSPICUITY

PHAETON

PHILOSOPHE

PHYLACTERY

PINFOLD

PISHOGUE

PLEDGET

PLENARY

PLENILUNE

PLETHORIC

PLURIPRESENCE

POETASTER

POLEMIC

POLITIC

POLYGRAPHY

POMACE

POMEGRANATE

PONDERABLE

PONTIFICAL

PORTICO

POSSET

POTABLE

PRAGMATIC

PRECATORY

PREDATORY

PREFIGURE

PRELAPSARIAN

PRELIBATION

PRELUSIVE

PRESAGE

PRESBYOPIA

PRESCIENT

PRESCIND

PRETERNATURAL

PREVENIENT

PROCELEUSMATIC

PROLATE

PROLEGOMENON

PROLIFERATION

PROPHYLACTIC

PROSCENIUM

PROSCRIBE

PROTAGONIST

PROTEAN

PROTOTYPE

PRURIENT

PSEUDONYM

PSYCHE

PUDENCY

PUISSANT

PURBLIND

PURLIEUS

PURULENT

PUSILLANIMOUS

PYROMANCY

PYRRHONISM.

QUADRATURE

QUADRILLE

QUAG

QUALM

QUALMISH

QUARTO

QUATERNION

QUEASY

QUIDNUNC

QUIETUS

QUILLER-COUCH

QUINCUNX

QUITO

QUIXOTIC

QUOIN

RABELAISIAN

RACONTEUR

RADDLE

RAILWAY NOVEL

RAKE-HELL

RAMADAN

RAMPANT

RATHE

RATIOCINATION

RATIONALE

REAVE

REBECK

RÉCHERCHÉ

RECUSANT

REDDITION

REDINTEGRATE

REDOLENT

RE-EDIFY

REGIMEN

REMBRANDTESQUE

REQUIEM

RESTAURATEUR

RESUSCITATE

RETICULAR

RHABDOMANCY

RHETORICIAN

RHOMB

RHOMBOID

RIANT

RIO GRANDE

ROAN

ROC

ROCHET

RODOMONTADE

ROMFORD

ROMOLA

ROSICRUCIAN

ROTUNDA

ROULADE

ROULEAU

ROUNDEL

ROUNDELAY

ROUTINEER

ROWTON

RUG-HEADED

RUM BLOSSOM

RUTHVEN

RUY BLAS

SABBATIC YEAR

SABLE

SABLE-VESTED

SACCHARINE

SACKBUT

SACRARIUM

SAFFRON

SAGA

SALOME

SALONIKA

SALTATION

SALT MARSH

SALUBRIOUS

SAMITE

SANCTIMONY

SANDEMANISM

SANS SOUCI

SAPID

SAPIENT

SAPPHIRE

SAPPHIRINE

SARCENET

SATRAP

SATURNINE

SA'UDI ARABIA

SAUTÉ

SAVANNAH

SAVOIR FAIRE

SCÆVOLA	SHELDRAKE
SCHERZO	SHIPWRIGHT
SCIOLISM	*SHIRAZ*
SCION	SILLABUB
SCONCE	SIMONY
SCOW	SIMULACRUM
SCRANNEL	SOLECISM
SCREE	SOMNIFEROUS
SCRIPTORIUM	SOPHISM
SCRYMGEOUR	SOPHISTRY
SCUD	SOPORIFEROUS
SEBACEOUS	SPAGYRIC
SEMPITERNAL	SPOLIATION
SENNIGHT	SQUIREEN
SENTENTIOUS	STANZA
SEPULCHRAL	STRAMINEOUS
SEQUACIOUS	STRATOPHOBIA
SEQUELÆ	STRIDULOUS
SEQUENTIAL	STROPHE
SERAI	STUPEFACIENT
SERBONIAN	STUPENT
SEVEN WONDERS OF THE WORLD	SUBAUDITION
SFORZANDO	SUBLUNAR
SHAWM	SUBEQUAL
SHEET ANCHOR	SUBORN

SUCCEDANEUM	SWAG-BELLIED
SUMPTUARY	SWIM
SUPERABLE	SWINK
SUPEREMINENT	SYBARITE
SUPERFICIES	SYCOPHANT
SUPERNACULUM	SYLLOGISM
SUPERNAL	SYLPH
SUPERVENIENT	SYMBIOSIS
SUPPURATE	SYNDERESIS
SUPRALAPSARIAN	SYNERGIC
SURQUEDRY	SYRTIS
SURTOUT	SYSTOLE

TABID	TELEOLOGY
TABINET	TENEBRIFIC
TAFFETA	*TERESA*
TAHITI	TERMINOLOGY
TALUS	TERRENE
TANGANYIKA	TER-SANCTUS
TAPIS	TETRALOGY
TAP-ROOM	THEO-
TAXIMETER	THESMOTHETE
TE DEUM	THESPIAN
TEGUMENT	THRASONICAL

THREE PER CENTS

THUCYDIDES

THULE

TIARA

TICHBORNE

TILBURY

TORCH SINGER

TRADUCTION

TRANSLUCENT

TRANSMOGRIFY

TRANSPONTINE

TRAUMA

TRAVAIL

TRIBRACH

TRINAL

TRITURATE

TUMID

UBIQUITOUS

ULIGINOSE

ULTRAMONTANE

ULULATION

ULYSSES

UNBED

UNCIAL

UNCOFFIN

UNCOMEATABLE

UNDEPRESSED

UNEXAMPLED

UNICORN

UNTOWARD

URQUHART

UTILITARIANISM

VAGARY

VANILLA

VANSITTART

VARIEGATE

VATICIDE

VATICINATE

VEGETAL

VEHEMENT

VEILLEUSE

VERDIGRIS

VERISIMILITUDE

VERMICULATION

VERNAL

VERONESE

VERS LIBRE

VERTIGINOUS

VERVAIN

VESPER

VIATICUM

VICEGERANT

VICINAL

VICISSITUDE

VILIFY

VINCI

VIOLACEOUS

VIRAGO

VIRELAY

VIRTU

VITREOUS

VOCIFERATE

VOLANT

VOLUMIST

VOLUPTUARY

VOLUTE

VOX ET PRAETEREA NIHIL

VULPINE

WAIN

WAINSCOT

WALCHEREN

WAREHOUSE

WEAPON-SALVE

WEDNESBURY

WELKIN

WENCESLAUS

WHIT

WHITSUN

WIMPLE

WINDLE STRAW

WINTON

WITHERS

WITWATERSRAND

WOLD

WORMS

WUTHER

WYKEHAMIST

XANADU

XANTHOCHROI

XANTHOMELANOUS

XANTHOPHYLL

XENELASIA

XENODOCHY

XENOPHANES

XENOPHOBIA

XEROSTOMIA

YAHOO

YARE

YEAR-LONG

YEMEN

YOSEMITE

YPSILANTI

ZAMBO

ZANY

ZEITGEIST

ZEUS

ZOANTHROPHY

ZODIAC

ZOIC

ZOLAËSQUE

ZOLLVEREIN

ZOOGEOGRAPHY

ZOOGONY

ZOOMORPHIC

ZOOPHAGOUS

ZOROASTER

D. U. W. (A)

DICTIONARY OF UNUSUAL WORDS PART "A"

Press Opinion

A first instalment of what will be a progressive attack on our ignorance of the language we speak.
—*Continental Daily Mail.*

There is much that is useful and interesting in D.U.W. (A).
—Ivor Brown in *The Observer.*

A fascinating compilation of educational value.
—*National Newsagent.*

An interesting and instructive book.
—*The Bookshelf.*

D.U.W. (A) is a fascinating book.
—*Overseas Daily Mail.*

Price 8/6 net
9/- post free from the publishers

THE THAMES BANK PUBLISHING COMPANY LIMITED
1773 LONDON ROAD, LEIGH-ON-SEA, ESSEX